DAVID WOOD
DESSERT · BOOK

DAVID WOOD
DESSERT · BOOK

DAVID WOOD with Karen Barnaby,
Daphna Rabinovitch, and Darlene MacDavid

WHITECAP BOOKS LTD.
Vancouver & Toronto

ON THE COVER Fresh Strawberry Tart

Copyright © 1989 David Wood

First published in 1989 by Whitecap Books (Toronto) Ltd.
77 Mowat Avenue, Suite 403, Toronto M6K 3E3

Photography © Derik Murray
Creative: Derik Murray
Stylist/Co-ordinator: Joanne Facchin
Front and Back Cover Design: Orest Kinasevych
Shoot Co-ordinator: Frank Vena
Photography Assistants: Grant Waddell, Giles Hancock

Edited by Beverley Beetham Endersby
Typesetting by Type a Grafik
Printed and bound in Canada by D.W. Friesen & Sons Ltd.
   Altona, Manitoba

ISBN 0-921396-18-X

Canadian Cataloguing in Publication Data

   Wood, David, 1944 May 7-
      David Wood dessert book

   ISBN 0-921396-18-X

   1. Desserts.   I. Title

TX773.W66 1989   641.8'6   C89-094815-1

To my mother and father, who started me on the road; and to Nancy, my companion along the way—
David Wood

To my mother and father, who taught me the art of laughter and of good food —
Daphna Rabinovitch

To my mother, and Big Steve —
Karen Barnaby

To my parents, Walt and Alice MacDavid —
Darlene MacDavid

CONTENTS

INTRODUCTION

There are some cultures in the world where dessert is not a particularly important part of the meal, but ours is certainly not one of them. In Canada, an appreciation of dessert is a national past-time, right up there with making money and keeping up with the sports results (even above supporting the Conservative party). By and large, apart from some minor damage to the waistline, dessert is a perfectly harmless obsession, and one that is nothing to be ashamed of. We should be thankful that the time and energy we put into making desserts (not much, but may be more after you have finished reading this book), consuming them (quite a lot), or thinking about them (more than we care to admit) are not being devoted to anything more destructive.

Desserts are an important part of our diet for no more profound reason than people like them. A taste for sweetness seems to be present at a very early age, and it is one that we do not grow out of. There is a time in early and middle adulthood when we go off desserts, but as we get older (I am, of course, speaking from observation, not experience) the liking returns. We learn at an early age that desserts are the reward for eating everything on our plate and, for some, eating desserts remains the only good reason for eating the rest of dinner. Nothing stirs the pleasant memories of childhood more readily than our sense of smell, and the aromas of good things baking in the oven are particularly evocative. But, for everyone, hosts or parents as well as guests or members of the family, desserts have a special importance. There are two reasons for this: dessert is the last course eaten, and so is the one that lingers longest in the memory; and the visual appeal of desserts is very strong, because the palette of colours, shapes, and textures available is enormous. If you want to leave a lasting impression, the best opportunity lies in desserts.

When you are entertaining, it is always much easier to choose a dessert that all your guests will like than to find a main course that they all can eat. In fact, it is much easier to choose a dessert — period. I am sure that is a good part of the reason why, when we go out to dinner, we generally choose the main course first, then find a starter and dessert to fit with it. The sweet tooth is accommodating and will usually be content with a dessert chosen to fit in with the rest of dinner.

There is another aspect of dessert behaviour that is becoming deeply ingrained in Canadians, and that is buying rather than making them. Fortunately for us at the David Wood Food Shop and for thousands of other pastry shops across the country, no one today expects a host or hostess to serve a dessert prepared at home. In all but a few remote, and, frankly, rather old-fashioned, communities, people are amazed if you actually make a dessert yourself; those who do are believed to have unearthed the philosophers' stone and to be able to turn base metal into gold. One of our objectives in this book is to convince you that making desserts is considerably easier than alchemy, although perhaps not quite so profitable!

The habit of buying desserts is presumably born of the belief that they are difficult to make. It is not just the Canadian housewife (or househusband) who seems to subscribe to this notion; there are not that many restaurants in Canada that make all their own desserts (at least in the cities, where they have a choice). It's hard to believe, I know, but there are still places in this country where you cannot buy a dessert to take out, even for cash.

LEARNING TO COOK DESSERTS

Even if you are a confirmed buyer of desserts (and we hope that you are and will continue to be one — at least some of the time), we would like to introduce you to the enjoyment there is to be had in making them yourself. I am a firm believer that anyone who can read, and who really wants to do it, can learn to cook well, and that includes making good desserts. If you have read this far, you are over the first hurdle; to clear the second, all you need is motivation. A liking for eating desserts is a very good starting-point — it has been the beginning of many a cook (including me) — and there is a further inducement in the fact that, most of the time, the dessert you make yourself will be better than the one you buy — fresher, made in smaller quantity using only top-quality ingredients, by someone (you!) who really cares about what he or she is doing; 99 times out of 100 these factors are more than enough to offset the fact that purchased desserts are made by an experienced professional cook.

To be fair, there are a couple of ways in which making good desserts is more demanding than preparing items from other realms of cooking, and desserts do intimidate some people. For a start, there is the question of precision; it is a source of pride to some cooks that they never measure, adding a handful of this ingredient, a scoop of that one, a pinch of the next; there is a sense that their creativity will be diminished by the use of a measuring spoon. They trust to their intuition, which is often excellent; and to the forgiving nature of their guests' palates — a forgiving palate might notice that the combination does not taste the same as it did last time, but will not judge it a failure on that basis. In fact, it probably does not matter that the taste is not the same; most dishes have the potential of an infinite number of tastes, each as correct as the others.

This cavalier approach to preparation does not work with desserts; although the taste may vary from one occasion to the next, the texture and composition should not. There is a very real difference between a crème caramel made with a random number of eggs (with one more thrown in "just for luck"), and one made with the number of eggs that testing and experience have shown to be necessary if the custard is to be firm enough to hold its shape, and soft enough to maintain the silky creaminess that is the essential character of the dish. Even those rustic cousins of dessert – sweet breads, muffins, and cookies — require you to be just as careful when you measure the ingredients. Perhaps what is really needed in making desserts is not only a certain degree of precision, but consistency — the discipline to do the same thing the same way every time you do it, unless you deliberately choose to change.

Presentation is a very important aspect of any food preparation, but it is particularly so with desserts (the subject is discussed later in this introduction). It is an advantage for any cook to have an artist's eye when it comes to arranging a plate; and it is no harder to arrange a dessert plate than one featuring meat or fish (in fact, it is easier, because the array of colours at your disposal when working with desserts is far greater). Where a sense of design becomes important is in making cakes and pastries. At the beginning of the nineteenth century, Marie-Antoine Carême, perhaps the greatest chef of all time, argued that architecture was a suitable area of study for a pastry chef. Today a penchant for elaborate structures of sugar, pastry, and whipped cream is much less common; but we still expect a cake, or a *croquembouche,* to be neat and well-finished; and, if it is beautiful as well, so much the better. Practice will make any cook more proficient at anything; but we probably have to accept that the patience and attention to detail required to be really good at pastries are traits that not everyone has. If you firmly believe that you lack this commitment, you may be wise to steer clear of pastries and more formal cakes, at least until experience in making other desserts gives you the confidence to want to try them.

MATCHING DESSERT TO DINNER

You can serve any dessert you like at a party — as long as it is chocolate! Chocolate goes with just about everything, and you know in advance that everyone will like it: it is not surprising that it is served so often.

But there are many occasions when chocolate is not the right choice, or at least when there is a better choice. The goal in putting together a menu is to achieve a balance — between rich food and lighter dishes; saucy dishes and ones without sauce; creamy food and sharper, more acidic types; crispness and smooth textures; bright colours and pastels; highly seasoned and less-fiery dishes. The contrasts are endless, and you cannot hope to cover them all in one meal. What you can do is offer your guests enough variety, course to course and within each of them, that the food does not blur into a monotone of tastes and textures.

When planning a menu it does not really matter which course you select first; traditionally, most people start by choosing a main course, but you can have just as much success building from a different base. In fact, many people do not start with the food at all, but build their menu around the wines. (The introduction to the *David Wood Food Book* has more suggestions on how to plan a menu.) In matching a dessert to a chosen menu, the rules (if they can be called that) are really very simple. Often, the occasion dictates the dessert: for an anniversary, birthday, or special celebration, there has to be a cake — but something dramatic, such as a Gâteau Saint-Honoré, would be an excellent and unusual choice. You can either choose a cake that does not conflict with the main course, or choose the main course to suit the cake you want to make.

A few of the other general tenets are: don't serve a dessert that includes pastry (for example, a pie, tart, or French pastry) if you are serving a savoury pie as the main course; don't offer a creamy dessert (for example, crème brulée or floating island) after a main course with a cream sauce (chicken, or veal, for example with wild mushrooms and cream). A cool and soothing dessert is what you want after a hot curry (Coconut Crème Brulée with Water Chestnuts (p. 19) would be wonderful after a spicy Thai dinner). After a heavy main course, such as duck or Beef Wellington, a fruity dessert is what is called for; Pears Poached in Red Wine (p. 6) would provide the right note of acidity to cleanse the palate and still be in keeping with the rich and classic tone of the dinner.

The recipes that follow are organized under descriptive headings (Rich and Creamy, Fruit-Based, Pies and Tarts, and so on) to enable you to review all your choices together once you have decided on the type of dessert you want to serve. Remember, too, that there are many more dessert recipes in our *David Wood Food Book* (not to mention some wonderful first-course and main-course ideas).

Rules, of course, are made to be broken, and there is nothing to stop you from serving exactly what you like for dessert, regardless of how it fits with the rest of the menu. What matters most is that you like the combination; if your guests look surprised when you give them Blackberry and Apple Pie (p. 119) after steak and kidney pudding, tell them it is done in England all the time (it is; but that doesn't make it right) and that we said you could serve whatever you liked!

SOME IDEAS FOR DESSERT PRESENTATION

When a dessert is set down in front of you, or when you see a dessert selection arranged on a buffet, the promise of good tastes should be conveyed to the eye. Of course the dessert itself must make good on that promise, but the promise itself, made through visual presentaion, is what concerns us here.

Presentation is what transforms something as mundane as a slice of pie into DESSERT. A piece of pie on a plate is a piece of pie on a plate; but a slice of pie on a pool of fruit purée, with more fruit tumbling out of the filling or arranged around the edge, a sprig of mint on top, and some whipped cream floating on the purée — that is dessert. Even if only one or two of the decorations are used, the transformation can be achieved, and the pie made into a dessert for any occasion. Of course, it is a little extra trouble; but when you consider what effort you have already put into the pie (even if it was only the time to go out and buy it) and the difference in the impact that is created, the extra trouble does not seem like very much. Here, then, for those who agree with us that you eat first with your eyes, and only afterwards with your tastebuds, are some ideas for dressing up your dessert plates and platters.

FRUIT PURÉES

Fruit Purées, particularly the deep colours of raspberry and blackcurrant (or the two mixed together), add an element of drama to almost any dessert. Both raspberry and blackcurrant go well with: anything lemon — lemon mousse, lemon tart (even lemon meringue pie), lemon carousel cake, are enhanced by sitting on a deep-purple purée. Raspberry and chocolate are a natural combination; just about any chocolate cake will look and taste much better with the complement of raspberry sauce. Fruit purées also go well with fresh-fruit tarts; the purée can be made either with the same type of fruit used as a filling for the tart, or with one that provides a contrast in colour or taste.

A more elaborate presentation of fruit purée can be made by swirling another purée, or crème fraîche, on top of the first. A raspberry purée swirled over a mango or apricot purée looks very good, as does crème fraîche (or very lightly whipped cream — just to the thickness where it still pours) over a dark red purée (any combination of blackcurrant, strawberry, and raspberry); this can be done by drizzling the second purée over the first in a spiral pattern (many professional cooks put the second purée in a hotdog stand–style squeezable ketchup container to get more control); or the second purée can be dropped on in dabs, and then drawn out in whatever pattern you like with a fork or the end of a knife.

FRUIT DECORATIONS

Fruit Decorations, such as a few berries nestled beside a slice of chocolate cake, will dress a dessert up no end, and work well with almost any dessert based on fruit or chocolate, but not with nut tarts, or such things as pumpkin and sweet potato pecan pie.

Sometimes, when you have a perfect slice from a fresh-fruit tart, you want nothing to spoil the precision of the slice (although a fruit sauce could only make it even more perfect); at other times, a cascade of the same fruit flowing over onto the plate can give an already good-looking tart extra charisma. However, when the fruit filling has been baked, as in a pie, the contrast of fresh and cooked fruit may not be pleasing and you might want to stick to other decorative ideas.

Remember that you are not restricted to using berries for fruit decorations. Although berries are the simplest and, for many dishes, the most attractive choice, caramelized orange slices, or sautéed apples, can work very well too. You may also use fruit that is purely decorative and not designed to be eaten (although they may be); Cape or Chinese gooseberries are very attractive little lanterns with a round orange fruit; pomegranate seeds can provide a very dramatic accent; star fruit, persimmon, and the familiar kiwi can also provide the contrast in colour or texture that you need.

CREATING SHADOWS AND REVERSE IMAGES

By sifting icing sugar or cocoa powder over shapes placed on the plates (or the top of cakes), you can create some very interesting effects. There is one technique, which we have used several times, that always draws favourable comments: set the dessert slightly to one side of centre on a white plate; on the other side of the plate, towards the rim, set a crossed spoon and fork with the handles hanging over the edge. Sieve some cocoa powder over the plate (over the whole plate if you want cocoa on the dessert, or just over the spoon and fork), then carefully remove the spoon and fork, leaving their reverse image on the side of the plate. You can do the same thing with icing sugar on a dark plate.

Other patterns that are easy to do and effective include diagonal lines, an effect achieved by laying several strips of paper, about 1" wide, 1" apart across the plate (or the top of the cake); a constellation, using either star fruit or cut-out stars of different sizes; at Christmas time, you can do the same with bells or holly shapes; you could use a menorah cut-out for Hanukkah. Ground nuts or praline (crushed, caramelized almonds) sprinkled onto the plate can produce a very attractive effect, either an abstract or a pattern, and is particularly successful with a nut dessert or a meringue cake.

FLOWERS, HERBS, AND SPICE DECORATIONS

There is a heated debate in professional plate-garnishing circles about whether it is playing fair to use non-edible flowers to decorate plates of food. Some people claim that it is not cricket (rather like dropping a nuclear bomb on Crusaders defending a castle with bows and arrows); but the majority (we among them) regard it as a perfectly reasonable thing to do. Not only do they look good on the side of a plate, but on top of a cake, they can give an air of refinement that is hard to achieve by other means. (They are particularly effective on wedding and other anniversary-celebration cakes.)

Most herbs are savoury in nature and are not used in dessert making, and therefore can look somewhat incongruous as part of the decoration on a dessert plate. The exception is mint, which is a wonderful decoration for any fruity dessert; a sprig of mint sticking out of a mound of cream beside a lemon tart, or on top of a heap of strawberries, adds the touch of contrasting colour that makes the plate.

A few other herbs can be used cautiously to create a mood: fresh basil can be used in much the same way as mint; the larger, brighter green leaves can be very effective on large dessert plates. The fresh, summer feeling produced by a feathery sprig of tarragon is hard to create in any other way; it looks very good alongside a dessert that is also light and fresh, such as a lemon mousse or a coeur à la crème with fresh berries.

Spices are more widely used to flavour desserts, and they can offer some interesting decorating possibilities; pears poached in red wine look very good with a stick of cinnamon on the side of the plate, or stuck into the dollop of whipped cream beside the pear. You could also use cinnamon with a pie made of dried fruit; and ground cinnamon or nutmeg could be sifted (sparingly) to create an image on the plate for any dessert where they are used in the recipe.

CARAMELIZED SUGAR AND CANDIED PEEL

Caramelized sugar can be used to create the most elaborate of decorations, such as the sugar cages for caramelized oranges (see photograph facing page 14); and it is an essential part of the decoration of a *croquembouche*. Although it must be done close to serving time because it has a tendency to melt, caramelized sugar spun around almost any dessert will give it a magical look, and make it very special indeed. Even liquid caramelized sugar drizzled over the plate or the whole dessert (usually in an abstract pattern, as it is hard to create a regular pattern with it) can be very attractive; we often use it on Snow Eggs (and on other desserts with a crème anglaise sauce).

Candied citrus peel is a traditional but none the less good-looking (and good-tasting!) alternative (see page 32 for instructions on how to make it). It is a natural on desserts during the holiday season, but can add a touch of elegance at any time of the year.

COOKIES AND WAFERS

Finally, do not overlook how much a home-made cookie or wafer can add to a plate. Ice cream tastes good (particularly if you made it yourself) but it looks ordinary — until you place an almond tuile on the plate and transform it into an elegant dessert. Small sugar cookies create a wonderful synergy with fresh or poached fruit: the whole is so much more than the sum of the parts. The same is true of ladyfingers, or java sticks; they are a small addition, but the effect they produce is substantial.

These are some of the little things that great food presentation are based on; by themselves they do not seem like much, but used judiciously they produce an effect out of proportion to their size. Treasure them when you find them; they will make your reputation as the good cook you deserve to be.

THE FACES BEHIND THE GREEN-BAIZE DOOR

When I was very young, before my father came back from the war, my mother and I lived in my grandfather's house. In one corner of the hall there was a door, covered in green baize, that led to the kitchen and the servants' quarters. Behind this door were the people who did all the work, but got none of the credit.

There are no green baize doors in our stores or catering business; but there are a lot of people who do all the work and get very little of the credit. I do a small proportion of the former, and get the lion's share of the latter. In a way this is inevitable: people address themselves to the tip of the iceberg because it is the most visible part.

What makes our business work is not the recipes or the food, or the design of the stores, or the products from around the world, but the people who do the work. Most of our people, most of the time, are exceptional. We provide a level of service that is all but unheard of in Canada; we treat our customers like human beings and respond to their needs and complaints responsibly. It is a sad-but-true fact of modern Canadian retailing that anyone prepared to treat the customer as a person, and to provide the best service possible, will find that there is very little competition: such a retailer can have as much of the market share as he or she wants.

We get a lot of compliments on our staff. Most of the time I simply say, that we are lucky to have good people applying to work with us. This is true; but it is only half the story. Good people apply, and it is our responsibility to learn how to keep them. We treat our employees as human beings, mostly because we think that is the way people should be treated. One cannot expect staff to treat customers well if they are not well-treated themselves. We give our staff members responsibility and all the freedom they want, and the people who love it stay. I am proud of having started something that allows me to work with such a good and decent group of people. Many of them are talented, too, and that is a bonus; but hard work and decency will beat talent any day — and, most especially, it will beat it every day, day in and day out, from five o'clock in the morning, when the bakers come in, until the small hours of the next morning, when the catering staff are cleaning up after a party, which is what the food business is all about.

So, when people compliment me — on the store, on the food at a party, or on the recipes in a cookbook — I accept it, not because I think I did it all myself, but because I know that, in our work, we are not separate, but part of something that is much more than each of us could be separately. The compliments belong to us all.

I want to acknowledge and thank all of the people who make my life easier and more enjoyable, and who make going to work in the morning worthwhile. The list includes everyone with whom I work, each in his or her own way. I particularly want to thank Alanna Lefcovitch and Marc Sullivan because their recipes are included, along with the people who get the credit on the cover of this book. Alanna is the pastry chef at our Rosedale store, and Marc is the assistant pastry chef at the North Yonge store; without their work this book would not taste nearly so good.

HERBS AND SPICES

Some people use these terms interchangeably, and many more use "spice" to describe both. In fact, there is a very clear difference; a herb is the leaf of a plant; a spice is its fruit or seed. For example, cilantro (or fresh coriander) is a herb; but coriander seed is a spice. Once you understand this difference, it is easy to tell what something is, even if you have never seen it before. If it is green, or was when it was fresh, 99 to 1 it is a herb (green peppercorns are a spice!); and if it is fruit or seed-like, it is almost certainly a spice. A few items, such as cinnamon, are none of the above (it is the bark of the cinnamon tree — and it is a spice).

FRUIT-BASED DESSERTS

There are times at the end of a meal when only something fruity will do. Most of the time this means (at least, in my house) some fresh fruit; and many times there is nothing that could be better. When the muscat grapes are in the shops, or you have found a perfectly ripe peach or mango, there are very few things that can compare. However, there are other times when the bananas are brown, the grapes wrinkled, and the choice limited, and there are some occasions that simply demand a dessert that has been thought about and slaved over. When, for any number of good reasons (e.g., to balance your menu or to limit cholesterol), that dessert has to be fruity, those in this section will provide, in varying degrees, the clean acid tang of fruit that makes such a good ending to a rich meal — and an essential part of a rich diet.

Most of the recipes here will allow you to enjoy dessert without feeling like a traitor to your cardio-vascular system. It could be the most important chapter in this book.

BANANAS CREOLE

Very simple and quick to make. A good emergency dessert — provided, of course, that you have some bananas in the house, and some vanilla ice cream.

Serves 4.

¹/₄ cup	**water**
1 cup	**granulated sugar**
2 oz	**unsalted butter** (¹/₄ cup)
¹/₄ cup	**water**
2 large	**bananas**
¹/₄ cup	**rum** or **bourbon**

FOR SERVING

4 scoops	**vanilla ice cream** (see page 132 or bought)

1. Make a caramel: Combine ¹/₄ cup of water and the sugar in a heavy-bottom saucepan, and cook over medium heat until the sugar is dissolved, then increase the heat to high, and cook to a medium-brown caramel (see page 11). Immediately remove the pan from the heat and add the butter, swirling it gently until it melts. Add the water, and return the pan to a low heat.

2. Peel the bananas, cut them in half across, and put them into the sauce. Pour in the rum or bourbon, and cook gently, turning the bananas once, for 10 to 15 minutes, until they are quite soft.

3. Place a scoop of ice cream in each serving plate, lay the banana alongside, and spoon the sauce over the top. Serve immediately.

PINEAPPLE WITH SALT

In Southeast Asia, fruit that is deemed sour (this would include almost all of our fruits) is served with salt, or salt mixed with dry hot peppers, as a midday or late-night eye-opener. The contrast of the salt with the pineapple makes its flesh taste sweeter.

Serves 6 to 10, depending on the size of the pineapple.

1 ripe	**pineapple** quartered (see page 3)
fine	**sea salt**

1. Cut the pineapple quarters across, into ¹/₃" slices, and arrange attractively on a platter. Pour the salt into small dishes and serve along with the pineapple. Dip the corner of a pineapple piece lightly into the salt and eat. You may become a convert. Try it with plums, peaches, apples, or grapes!

TESTING PINEAPPLES FOR RIPENESS
The most reliable way to determine if a pineapple is ripe is to pull out the centre leaves of the crown. If they come out fairly easily, it is ready to eat. If you wait for the skin to turn yellow, you will probably find that you have waited too long, and there will be over-ripe soft spots in the flesh.

HOW TO PEEL A PINEAPPLE
Peeling a pineapple is easy, once you know how. A sharp knife is an asset.
1. Lay the pineapple on its side and cut off the crown and the base.
2. Set the pineapple on one end. Cut straight down into quarters (one cut along the 12 o'clock–6 o'clock line; then along the 3 o'clock–9 o'clock line).
3. With the quarter standing up (i.e., as it was in Step 2), cut off the core, using one cut straight down on the inside edge.
4. Lay the quarters skin-side down. Cut just above the skin all the way round the perimeter (as if you were separating melon flesh from its rind), almost all the way through; give the flesh a final twist to release it from the skin.
5. Cut the quarters lengthwise into spears (2 or 3 per quarter). Store in a covered container in the fridge. The pineapple will keep for several days like this, much longer than it would if you had not peeled it.

CANDIED KUMQUATS

1 lb	**kumquats**, fresh
2 cups	**granulated sugar**
1 cup	**water**

1. Cut the kumquats in half through their equator. Pick out any seeds with the point of a small knife.
2. Stir the sugar and water together in a heavy saucepan. Bring to a boil and add the kumquats. Turn the heat down to medium and simmer for about $\frac{1}{2}$ hour, or until the kumquats turn darker and become translucent. Pour the kumquats and their syrup into a bowl to cool. Candied kumquats will keep indefinitely refrigerated.

Dried Figs Poached in Red Wine with Black Pepper, Fennel, and Orange

If you like cheese to end a meal, try a wedge of creamy Gorgonzola accompanied by these figs. The pronounced flavour of the one perfectly complements the other.

24	**dried figs** (choose figs that have been individually dried and are still soft and fresh)
3½ cups	**red wine**
1 tsp	**whole black peppercorns**
½ tsp	**whole fennel seeds**
4 strips	**orange peel**
2 Tbs	**grappa** or **cognac**

1. Choose a non-corrodable pan (see page 5) that will hold the figs upright in a single layer. Stand the figs in the pan.

2. Pour the red wine, pepper, and fennel over the figs. Tuck the orange peel in between the figs. Bring to a boil over medium-high heat, then turn the heat down to a simmer.

3. Cover the figs tightly; place a pot lid or heat-proof plate that will just fit inside the pot over the figs, or use a piece of parchment paper pressed down onto the figs. Poach for 1½ hours until the figs are set and the wine is reduced and syrupy.

4. Transfer the figs and sauce to a shallow bowl to cool. Serve at room temperature, sprinkled with the grappa or cognac. The figs will keep for two months in a tightly closed container.

Raspberry and Fig Gratin

This quick dessert can be done in a variety of containers — in a French gratin dish, individual ramekins, or in a boat made from banana leaves, as was done recently at one of our special seasonal dinners. A light but rich end for a great meal.

Serves 6.

1½ cups	**fresh raspberries**
¾ cup	**sour cream**
3 Tbs	**milk**
2 Tbs	**granulated sugar**
½ tsp	**vanilla extract**
1½ cups	**fresh figs**, thickly sliced
7 Tbs	**brown sugar**

1. Preheat the oven to 350° F. Select the container you plan to use.

2. Place the raspberries in the chosen container. Mix the sour cream with the milk, sugar, and cinnamon. Pour over the raspberries. Top with the sliced figs. *(May be made 3 or 4 hours ahead to this point.)*

3. Fifteen minutes before serving: Place the gratin in the preheated oven and bake for 10 minutes (15 minutes if straight out of the fridge). Remove from the oven and turn the broiler up to high.

4. Sprinkle the brown sugar over the top of the gratin; pass it quickly under the preheated broiler, until the sugar has melted and slightly caramelized.

5. Serve warm.

Rasberry Gratin with Fresh Cream

This version is a bit sweeter and richer (for some, the sour cream is a bit tart), but it does take a little longer.

Serves 6.

1½ cups	**fresh raspberries**
1 cup	**whipping cream** (35%)
4	**egg yolks**
¼ cup	**granulated sugar**
½ tsp	**vanilla extract**
6	**fresh figs**, thickly sliced

1. Preheat the oven to 350° F. Select the container you plan to use, and spread the raspberries over the bottom.

2. In a bowl that can go over hot water, or in the top of a double boiler, beat the sugar and egg yolks until quite thick and pale yellow.

3. Add the cream, set the bowl over simmering water, and whisk the mixture until it becomes very hot (hotter than your finger can stand for more than an instant) and quite thick (you are actually making a slightly whipped custard). Now, remove from the heat and transfer to the bowl of an electric mixer (can be done by hand but it is a lot more work); whisk on medium-high speed until quite cool and increased in volume (about 15 minutes). *(May be done 4 hours ahead to this point; if more than 2 hours, refrigerate the cream.)*

4. Preheat the oven to 375° F.

5. Pour ½ the cream over the raspberries; top with the sliced figs, then pour on the rest of the cream. Bake in the preheated oven for 6 minutes (10 minutes if the cream has been refrigerated).

6. Remove from the oven; turn on the broiler and allow to get very hot. Pass the gratin under the broiler, until the custard has browned lightly – it will not take long.

NON-CORRODABLE COOKWARE

When cooking an acidic ingredient, such as tomatoes or wine, it is important to choose a pan whose material will not react with the acid and spoil the dish. In general, this means avoiding uncoated aluminum, which will turn acid sauces black. Pans made from aluminum that has been coated with a special finish (such as Calphalon) are fine. Uncoated copper should not be used for cooking anything; its only use is for beating egg whites, where the acid reaction helps to develop the volume that you want.

PEARS POACHED IN RED WINE

One of the great fruit desserts; the spiciness of the red-wine syrup goes very well with the tender pear and cool, lightly whipped cream. (See photograph opposite p. 14)

Serves 6.

2 cups	**dry red wine**
1½ cups	**granulated sugar**
1 stick	**cinnamon**
3	**cloves** or
1 bag	**mulling mix**
peel of 1	**lemon**
6	**pears** (Bartlett, Bosc, or a well-shaped Anjou, since an elegant presentation is important. Choose pears that are not fully ripe — but not brick-hard — with long stems.)
	water to cover the pears
½ cup	**whipping cream** (35%)

1. Pour the wine into a non-aluminum saucepan large enough to hold all the pears lying down. Add the sugar, the cinnamon and cloves (or mulling mix), and the lemon peel, and bring to a boil over medium heat, stirring frequently until the sugar has dissolved.

2. Peel and core the pears: With a vegetable peeler or sharp knife, carefully peel the pears from stem to base. Starting at the stem, take off a long strip straight down to the base; continue with parallel strips all the way around the pear. Do it carefully; appearance is important. Then, with the point of a knife (I find the point of the vegetable peeler works well) and working from the base, dig out the core of the pear, being careful not to make a hole in the outside. As each pear is done, drop it in the red-wine syrup.

3. When all the pears are done, add water until the pears are just afloat. Bring back to a simmer and cook at a gentle bubble until the pears are tender (the time will vary greatly, depending on the ripeness of the pears). The only hints we can give are: that it will take longer than you think, and that the pears should be quite tender, since they will have to cut easily with a spoon. When ready, remove to a plate or shallow bowl and allow to cool — they will still be quite pale but do not worry. Leave the syrup in the pan.

4. Increase the heat to high and boil the syrup until almost all the water has evaporated, and the syrup becomes thick and sticky. When the surface of the syrup is completely covered with bubbles (so that the only way you can see the syrup is to take the pan off the heat and let the bubbles subside), it is almost ready. Lift some syrup in a spoon and let it fall back: it should fall in sticky drops, not in a thin watery stream. There will not be a large amount of it remaining.

5. Remove the syrup from the heat and pour it over the pears. Spoon the syrup over the pears whenever you think about it, until it is time to serve. As you baste, the pears will pick up the deep rich red of the syrup. You will find that there is something very soothing about watching the syrup slide down the side over the curves of the pear as you baste.

6. Whip the cream to soft peaks (see page 31); do not sweeten it. Serve the pears on white plates, with the syrup around them and a glob of whipped cream cascading down the side.

PEARS FOR POACHING

The same qualities that make a pear worth eating make it good for cooking – good flavour and a smooth, not gritty, texture. Pears are not good keepers, and are at the height of perfection for a very short time. When buying pears, feel for a little give at the stem end, but avoid softness at the blossom end, as this may indicate a core that has gone bad. Pears for cooking need not be in such a perfect state of ripeness, but avoid any that are rock-hard as they will not have had a chance to develop any flavour, even if, by extended cooking, you can render them soft enough to eat. Over-ripe pears should not be used.

Bosc, Bartletts, and Anjous are all good eaters, and will cook well. Make your decision based on shape and ripeness.

POACHED PEARS WITH RASPBERRY CASSIS

A traditional dish: pears poached in white wine, with a blackcurrant sauce and whipped cream — an absolutely great combination.

Serves 8 people (4, if you serve a whole pear each).

1½ cups	**white wine**
1 cup	**granulated sugar**
1	**cinnamon stick**
peel of 1	**lemon** (yellow part only)
4	**pears**, almost ripe (Anjou, Comice, or Bartlett)
2 cups	**Raspberry Purée** (see page 211)
¼ cup	**blackcurrant jam**
1 cup	**whipping cream** (35%)

OPTIONAL:

2 Tbs	**cassis liqueur**
	fresh raspberries

1. Pour the wine into a non-aluminum saucepan in which all the pears will fit when cut in half; add the sugar, cinnamon, and lemon peel, and bring to a boil over medium heat, stirring frequently until the sugar has dissolved.

2. Peel, halve, and core the pears: With a vegetable peeler or sharp knife, carefully peel the pears from stem to base. Starting at the stem, take off a long strip straight down to the base; continue with parallel strips all the way around the pear. Cut each pear in half lengthwise. Then, with a spoon (the point of the vegetable peeler works well), scoop out the core of the pear, being careful not to make a hole in the outside. As each pear half is done, drop it in the wine syrup.

3. When all the pears are prepared, add water until they float, bring to a simmer, and poach gently for about 30 minutes — a little less if the pears are ripe; quite a bit longer (up to 1 hour) if they are not. They should be tender enough to be cut with a spoon (but not so soft that they loose their shape). Add more water as necessary to keep the pears afloat. When they are ready, remove the pan from the heat and allow the pears to cool in the syrup.

4. Make the raspberry purée following the recipe on page 211.

5. In a small saucepan, heat the blackcurrant jam until liquid, then stir into the raspberry purée. Add the cassis if you are using it.

6. Whip the cream to soft peaks (see page 31), adding the sugar when almost ready.

7. To serve: Surround a half-pear with the raspberry-cassis sauce and top it with whipped cream and a sprinkling of a few raspberries. This dessert also looks very good on a round platter: lay the pears, cut-side down, in a circle, stem ends pointing inward. Surround them with the raspberry sauce, and pile the whipped cream in the middle. Decorate with fresh raspberries.

POACHED PEACHES WITH RASPBERRY PURÉE

The combination of raspberries with peaches, although not so traditional as raspberries with pears, is even more successful. Good, tree-ripened peaches are important, so save this dessert for summer menus.

For 8 people (or 4, if you serve a whole peach per person).

1½ cups	**white wine**
1 cup	**granulated sugar**
peel of 1	**lemon** (yellow part only)
1	**vanilla bean**
4	**large peaches**
1½ cups	**Raspberry Purée** (see page 211)

1. Pour the wine into a non-aluminum saucepan in which all the peaches will fit when cut in half; add the sugar, lemon peel, and vanilla bean, and bring to a boil over medium heat, stirring frequently until the sugar has dissolved.

2. Bring a separate saucepan of water to a boil. Drop in the peaches (not necessarily all at once) and leave for 20 to 40 seconds, depending on how ripe they are. Remove from the water with a slotted spoon, then carefully remove the skins. If they won't come off, give them a bit longer in the water.

3. Cut the peeled peaches in half and remove the stone. Drop the peeled and pitted halves into the sugar syrup. Poach for 15 to 30 minutes, depending on the ripeness of the peaches - they should be quite tender (but not at all mushy). Remove the peaches from the heat and allow them to cool in the syrup. Then chill, still in the syrup: they will keep in the fridge for several days.

4. Make the raspberry purée following the recipe (on page 211); it should be quite tart, to offset the sweetness of the peaches, so add some lemon juice if you think it needs it.

5. Serve the chilled peaches with room-temperature raspberry purée.

GREEN FRUIT SALAD

A very charming customer asked us to make this for a buffet where all the other desserts were red. It looked very cool and elegant — and tasted good too.

Serves 10 to 12 as part of a dessert buffet.

1 recipe	**Light Sugar Syrup** (see page 227)
3	**Granny Smith apples**
1	**green melon**
12	**kiwi fruit**
1 lb	**seedless green grapes**

1. Make the sugar syrup following the recipe on page 227; when the sugar is dissolved, remove from the heat and allow to cool.

2. Peel, quarter, core, and slice the apples; add immediately to the syrup (it doesn't matter if it is still warm) to prevent discoloration.

3. Cut the melon in half, remove the seeds, and scoop out the flesh with a melon baller (or cut each half into 4 or 6 slices lengthwise, run a knife between the skin and the flesh, and cut each long strip of melon into cubes). Add the melon to the cool syrup.

4. Peel the kiwi, cut lengthwise into quarters, then into chunks; add to the syrup.

5. Cut the grapes in half (don't, if you can't be bothered, but it does look better); add to the syrup. *(May be made 6 hours ahead to this point.)*

6. Refrigerate the fruit salad until ready to serve.

CARAMELIZED ORANGES

A quick and elegant dessert; very good as a light but classy end to a rich dinner. Serve it with Zabaglione (see page 26) to really dress it up. (See photograph opposite page 14.)

Serves 6.

6	**large oranges**
3 Tbs	**water**
1½ cups	**granulated sugar**
OPTIONAL:	
	candied orange zest (see page 32)

1. With a very sharp knife, peel the oranges as you would an apple, in a spiral from top to bottom. Take off all the pith as you cut, so that just the flesh is left: it takes a bit of practice, but is not difficult. Then cut the peeled orange into 1/4" slices across (each slice will be a circle). Arrange in a shallow serving dish.

2. Combine the water and sugar in a heavy-bottom saucepan. Cook over medium heat until the sugar dissolves, then increase the heat to high and cook until the sugar caramelizes and turns a very dark golden brown (see page 11). While the sugar is cooking, fill a sink or roasting pan with cold water. As soon as the syrup reaches the colour you want (darker is better for this dessert, almost to the point of burning), remove the pan from the heat and sit its base in the pan of cold water to prevent the syrup from cooking any more. When the pan stops sizzling, pour the syrup over the oranges. The caramel will form a hard coating as it cools, but this will quite quickly be dissolved by the juice from the oranges.

3. The oranges can be served just as they are, in slices, sprinkled if you wish with candied orange zest. Or they can be re-formed (with a little patience) into the shape of oranges and served on plates, surrounded by the dark caramel. As a final touch, you can top each orange with a sugar cage (see below).

COOKING SUGAR SYRUP

When a sugar syrup boils, it will hold its temperature at 212° F (the boiling point of water) until almost all the water has evaporated; this can take a few minutes. (This is a good point at which to calibrate your thermometer; by noting the temperature it reads when the syrup first boils, you can check its accuracy; it should read 212° F.) Then the temperature will start to rise, and eventually the syrup will turn colour and form a caramel, which is very hard and brittle when cooled. Along the way, it will pass through three major stages that are important to pastry chefs — the soft ball (235° F), the hard ball (252° F), and the hard crack (295° F). To test what stage you are at, take a bit of the syrup and drop it in a glass of cold water then take it out once it has cooled; at the soft-ball stage the ball will flatten slightly under its own weight; at the hard-ball stage it will hold its shape, but will yield a bit when squeezed; at the hard-crack stage it will not form a ball at all but a long brittle thread.

SUGAR CAGES

You can see how impressive these look in the photograph facing page 14; but they are not hard to make, just a bit fiddly.

Choose one or two small oranges; wrap them in aluminum foil, but leave one end open so that the orange can be taken out with disturbing the other end. Spear the open end of the orange with a fork.

Make a caramel with 2 Tbs **water** and 1 cup **sugar** (see Step 2, above); cook it to a medium-brown only, then remove from the heat and allow to cool a little. Stir and lift the caramel with a fork; when it has cooled to the point where it falls in thickish strands from the fork, you are ready to start. Lift some caramel out of the pan and let it fall over the foil-covered orange in a lattice pattern (in fact just about any pattern will do) so that it forms a hemisphere, as in the photograph.

The caramel will harden as it cools. When quite hard, carefully remove the orange, then ease out the aluminum foil. Make all the cages and store them in a cool dry place; it they get damp, they start to melt. They will keep for 4 hours or so at room temperature.

LEMON MOUSSE

A wonderful mousse; tart, light and with the right amount of creaminess. Serve with Raspberry Purée (see page 211) and fresh raspberries, decorated with fresh mint leaves, for a very elegant dessert.

Serves 6.

½ cup	**water**
4 tsp	**gelatine**
¾ cup	**fresh lemon juice**
½ cup	**granulated sugar**
3	**egg yolks**
3	**egg whites**
½ cup	**granulated sugar**
1 cup	**whipping cream** (35%)

1. Pour the water into a small bowl: sprinkle the gelatine over the surface and allow it to dissolve (about 5 minutes).

2. Combine the lemon juice, sugar, and egg yolks in a medium-sized bowl that can go over hot water and whisk together. Set over simmering, but not boiling, water and heat until warm, but not really hot (about 115° F — quite hot to your finger). Remove from the heat and set aside.

3. Set the bowl with the gelatine over the hot water and heat until melted. Whisk the gelatine into the lemon-and-egg-yolk mixture. Refrigerate until the mixture is cool, but not yet beginning to set.

4. When the lemon mixture is cool, beat the egg whites to soft peaks (see page 24); then start adding the sugar 2 Tbs at a time and beat the whites to stiff peaks. Gently fold into the lemon-and-egg mixture. Make sure you incorporate all the lemon juice that has sunk to the bottom. Refrigerate for 15 to 20 minutes longer, until it just starts to set around the edges.

5. Whip the cream to soft peaks (see page 31). Gently fold the cream into the lemon mixture, again making sure to incorporate all the juice. The mousse should be a uniform pale yellow, with no white streaks. Pour into a medium glass bowl or into 6 wine goblets. Refrigerate until ready to serve.

6. The mousse may be garnished with whipped cream, candied lemon zest (see page 32), or fresh fruit.

BAKED APPLES

Although they can be ready in less than an hour, they make a delicious end to a meal and should not just be saved for emergencies. Serve with lightly whipped cream.

For each person

1 large	**apple**
1½ Tbs	**mincemeat**
or	
1 Tbs	**raisins** or **sultanas**
1 Tbs	**granulated sugar**
1 Tbs	**unsalted butter**
2 Tbs	**water**
¼ cup	**whipping cream** (35%)

1. Preheat the oven to 350° F. Find a baking dish in which all the apples will fit.
2. Core the apples (this can be done with the tip of a vegetable peeler if you don't have a corer). Score a line with a sharp knife around the waist of the apple (this allows it to puff while baking without bursting).
3. Fill the centre of each apple with the mincemeat, or with the raisins, sugar, and butter. Pour water into the baking dish, then put in the apples, and bake in the centre of the preheated oven for 45 minutes, until the apples are puffed and quite tender.
4. Beat the cream to soft peaks (see page 31), adding the sugar towards the end. Serve the warm apples with cold whipped cream.

RHUBARB COMPOTE

With whipped cream and Ginger Cake (page 55), this is a real treat.

Serves 6 to 8.

2 lbs	**fresh young rhubarb** (pink stems will give the best colour)
1½ cups	**granulated sugar**
¼ cup	**water**

1. Trim the leaves from the rhubarb, wash the stems, and cut into 1" chunks. Put into a heavy, non-aluminum saucepan with the sugar and water, cover, and set over a low heat. Stew gently for at least 1 hour — the slower it cooks the better, as the rhubarb will retain its shape rather than becoming a mush; my mother used to cook it overnight in the warming oven of the Aga (which is about 175° F).
2. For a purée, drain off the juice and whisk the rhubarb to a smooth pulp. It will be soft enough to do it by hand, and English cooks believe that pressing rhubarb through a sieve diminishes its flavour.

RHUBARB FOOL

A fool is a very old and very simple English summer dessert; it can be made with almost any fruit, although rhubarb, strawberries, and raspberries are the most usual. Serve it with homemade Ladyfingers (page 226).

Serves 8.

1 recipe	**Rhubarb Compote** (see page 13)
1¾ cups	**whipping cream** (35%)

1. Make the rhubarb compote following the recipe (on page 13); the colour of the raw rhubarb is particularly important — it should be pink. Allow to cool, then drain off the syrup and whisk the rhubarb to a smooth pulp (it should not be too loose).
2. In a cold bowl, whisk the cream to quite firm peaks (see page 31); you need to beat the cream a little stiffer than usual as the rhubarb will thin it out. Gently fold most of the cream into the rhubarb pulp (reserve some to decorate). Pour into tall wine glasses to make individual servings, or into a larger glass serving dish. Pipe or spoon the reserved cream on top. Refrigerate until ready to serve — with Ladyfingers (page 226), Almond Tuiles (page 152), or MacDavid's Shortbreads (page 154).

STRAWBERRY AND RASPBERRY FOOL

A more luxurious fool — but not necessarily better.

Serves 8.

1 pint	**strawberries**
1 pint	**raspberries**
1 cup	**fruit sugar** (icing or granulated sugar will do)
1¾ cups	**whipping cream** (35%)

FOR DECORATION
8 or 12 good-looking
    strawberries

1. *EITHER*: Combine the strawberries and raspberries in the workbowl of your food processor; pulse only until reduced to a pulp — do not liquify. Transfer to a sieve and push the pulp through the sieve. Or: Push the fruit through a food mill (Mouli or similar).
2. Mix the sieved pulp with the sugar in a bowl; stir until dissolved.
3. In a cold bowl, whisk the cream to quite firm peaks (page 31); you need to beat the cream a little stiffer than usual as the fruit will thin it out. Gently fold most of the cream into the pulp, reserving some for the decoration. For individual servings, pour into tall wine glasses, or into a large glass serving dish. Pipe or spoon the reserved cream on top, and arrange the good-looking strawberries as decoration. Refrigerate until ready to serve — with Ladyfingers (page 226), Almond Tuiles (page 152), or MacDavid's Shortbreads (page 154).

Opposite: *A Pear Poached in Red Wine (see recipe on page 6) and a Caramelized Orange in a Caramel Cage (see recipe on page 10).*

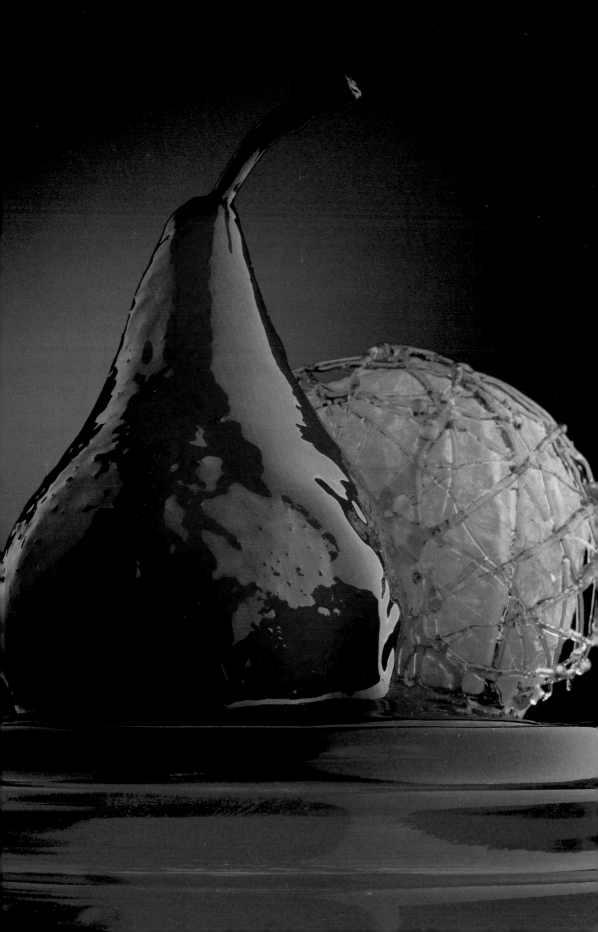

SUMMER PUDDING

One of the greatest treats of the dessert year, which can only be made for a few weeks at the height of summer, when raspberries and red currants are both in season. Very definitely worth waiting for.

Serves 8.

1 loaf	**white bread**, one or two days old
2 cups	**red currants**, stems removed
1 cup	**granulated sugar**
3 Tbs	**water**
2½ pints	**raspberries**

1. Select a bowl of about 2-quart capacity as the mould in which to make the pudding. Line it with plastic wrap.

2. Cut the bread into medium slices and cut off the crusts. Cut each slice diagonally in half. Line the plastic-lined bowl with the bread, so that there are no gaps. Set aside.

3. Combine the red currants, sugar, and water in a medium non-aluminum saucepan , and set over medium heat. Heat, stirring very gently from time to time to prevent the sugar burning, until the juice of the red currants just starts to run out. Now, add the raspberries. Continue to stir, very gently, until the raspberry juice begins to run out, then remove from the heat and pour into the bread-lined bowl. Smooth out the top.

4. Cover the top with a layer of bread, then bring the ends of the plastic wrap over the bread (if it doesn't completely cover it, don't worry).

5. Place a flat plate (I use a removable bottom from a tart pan covered with plastic wrap) inside the bowl on top of the pudding. Place some weights (beer cans or bottles work well) on top and refrigerate for at least 24 hours. *(May be made up to 48 hours ahead.)*

6. To serve: Invert the bowl on a serving platter, and ease the pudding out, using the plastic wrap. Remove the wrap and cut into slices with a sharp knife. Serve with lightly whipped cream if you wish; but it is the only fruit dessert I know that may just be better without it.

FRUIT TERRINE

An elegant dessert — and easy to do if you use store-bought ladyfingers. You may use any combination of fruits, but this one works well. Needs to be refrigerated for 6 hours or more, and may be made the day before.

Serves 8 to 10.

1 recipe	**Ladyfingers** (page 226), or use packaged
4	**kiwi fruit**
3	**oranges**
1 pint	**small strawberries**
½ pint	**raspberries**
8 oz	**unsalted butter**, soft (1 cup)
1 cup	**icing sugar**
1 tsp	**vanilla extract**
¼ cup	**rum**
1⅓ cups	**ground almonds**
2 cups	**whipping cream** (35%)

1. Make the ladyfingers following the recipe on page 226, and allow to cool (or buy good-quality ones from a store).

2. Line a 9" x 5" loaf pan with plastic wrap, leaving enough to cover the top, then line it with the ladyfingers, their ends sticking up out of the top of the pan (it is not necessary to line the ends).

3. Prepare the fruit: Peel the kiwis and cut them lengthwise into 6. Peel the oranges as you would an apple, taking off all the white pith (see the recipe for Caramelized Oranges, page 10), then cut into segments, leaving behind the membrane. Hull the strawberries, and cut them in half if they are a bit big. Set aside all the fruit.

4. With an electric mixer (or by hand), cream the butter with the sugar until light and fluffy; then beat in the vanilla, rum, and ground almonds and mix until smooth.

5. Beat the cream to very soft peaks (page 31), then fold it into the almond mixture (see page 128 on folding).

6. Pour ⅕ of the almond cream into the lined loaf pan; gently lay a layer of kiwi (or any other of the fruits) on top of the cream, pour another ⅕ on top, and smooth gently with a spatula. Add the strawberries, another ⅕ of the cream, the orange segments, more cream, then the raspberries and end with the last of the almond cream.

7. Trim the ends of the ladyfingers that stick up above the edge of the tin, and press them gently into the almond cream; then fold the plastic wrap over the top to cover the pan. Place another pan or flat piece of cardboard over the top and weight it lightly. Refrigerate for 6 hours or overnight.

8. To serve: Remove weights, unwrap the plastic from the top, and invert onto the serving plate. Lift of the pan, then peel off the plastic. Cut into slices with a sharp knife, and serve with extra fruit, if you wish.

RICH AND CREAMY DESSERTS

I am like a moth around a candle flame when it comes to creamy desserts: I cannot resist them. I can appreciate the good points of almost any dessert, but, when it comes time to make a decision, I find myself drawn irresistibly back to the soft, silky textures of creams and custards.

These are what are called, in Britain at least, nursery puddings. Not that I can remember ever having crème brulée in the nursery, or anything else very much worth re-creating. In fact, the only creamy dessert that I actively dislike is rice pudding, which was a frequent visitor to the school dining-room, if not actually in the nursery. The nursery designation has more to do with their smooth textures, and, I suspect, with the element of fantasy that surrounds nursery memories for any number of grown-up Britons — best left unspecified.

Whatever the origins of my liking for these desserts, it is one that is shared by a lot of other people, many of whom are not neurotic at all. There is something immensely satisfying and soothing about the smooth silkiness of cream set against the crunch of burnt sugar or the airy lightness of meringue, or balanced by the tartness of fresh berries. They are an excellent way to end a dinner — provided, of course, that cream has not featured prominently in the other courses. As in all things, a balance is what you want, so marry a creamy dessert with an unsauced main course, or one that features a tart sauce.

When making creams, remember that texture is important: they require a certain care in cooking to make sure that there are no lumps, or that the cream is not so firm (too many eggs spoil the cream, to paraphrase an old adage) that the wonderful softness is lost. If you follow the recipes, you will not have any trouble. The proportions provided have been tested and they work; do not be in too much of a hurry and you will be fine.

CRÈME BRULÉE

Crème Brûlée is one of the truly great desserts, but it is not often made well. The traditional recipe produces a custard that is too runny for my taste; it probably depends on a much-thicker cream than is regularly available in Canada. The bain-marie method is much more reliable; the trick is to get the number of egg yolks right — too few and the custard is still too runny; too many and you can bounce it around the dining-room. This recipe has just the right balance.

Serves 6.

2¹/₂ cups	**whipping cream** (35%)
3	**egg yolks**
¹/₂ cup	**granulated sugar**

FOR THE BURNT CARAMEL
¹/₂ cup **granulated sugar**

THE ORIGINS OF CRÈME BRULÉE
Although it has a French name, crème brûlée is much better known in England than in the rest of Europe. Writing in 1909, Eleanor Jenkinson, sister of the Cambridge University librarian, noted that, in the 1860s, the recipe "was offered to the kitchens of Trinity College by an undergraduate, and rejected with contempt. When the undergraduate became a Fellow (in 1879), he presented it again; this time it was accepted as a matter of course. It speedily became one of the favourite dishes of May week." This version is known in England as "Trinity Cream."

The recipe is very simple, but not always succesful for me:

2¹/₂ cups	**whipping cream**
4	**egg yolks**
	granulated sugar

1. Bring the cream to a boil. Beat the egg yolks in a bowl. Pour the cream into the yolks and whisk together. Pour into a fireproof serving dish and allow to become quite cold (may be refrigerated).
2. When cold, the custard should be set, but not hard (this is the part that does not always work: it often refuses to set); sprinkle the top very liberally with sugar. Heat the broiler until very hot, then brown the sugar until melted, bubbling, and burnt.

1. Preheat the oven to 325° F. Set the oven rack in the middle of the oven. Select a shallow oven-to-table dish with a 4-cup capacity, or a little more; find a roasting pan into which the dish will fit. Bring a kettle of water to a boil.
2. Rinse out a saucepan with water but do not dry; pour in the cream and bring almost to a boil over medium heat. Remove from the heat and set aside.
3. Beat the egg yolks with ¹/₂ cup of sugar until pale yellow and quite thick.
4. Pour the hot cream into the yolks in a thin stream, whisking all the time. Set the baking dish in the roasting pan. Strain the custard through a sieve into the baking dish.
5. Transfer the roasting pan to the oven (or set it on the oven door) and pour in the boiling water (it should come at least half-way up the side of the baking dish). Place in the oven, cover loosely with foil, and bake for 1 to 1¹/₂ hours, until nearly set. It will not — and should not — set completely; a tester inserted into the custard will always come out quite creamy. When you shake the dish it should wobble like a very loose jelly. It will firm up as it cools.
6. Remove from the oven and set aside to cool. *(May be done a day ahead to this point.)*

7. Two hours or more before serving: Preheat the broiler until very hot. Sprinkle ¹/₂ cup of sugar evenly over the top of the cream. Place the dish on a baking sheet (it is easier to move around) and set under the broiler, about 3" from it, and broil until the sugar melts, bubbles, and turns brown (it will burn a bit, but this is fine). Turn the dish to get the browning as even as possible. Set aside at room temperature until ready to serve. Serve on its own, or with fresh raspberries or strawberries.

COCONUT CREME BRULÉE WITH WATER CHESTNUTS

In Thailand, street vendors sell a delicious sweet that is made in tiny banana-leaf cups just a bit larger than a quarter. Smooth and silky rice cream on the bottom, covered with a few pieces of fresh water chestnut for textural interest, with fresh coconut cream on the top. These morsels literally slip down your throat. Although our dessert is not made with the same ingredients, it evokes the same cool creaminess and flavour. It goes wonderfully after any Oriental dinner you may be serving.

Makes 6 servings.

8	**water chestnuts**, fresh or canned
5	**egg yolks**
⅔ cup	**granulated sugar**
⅔ cup	**whipping cream** (35%)
14 oz can	**coconut milk**
¾ cup	**light brown sugar**
½ tsp	**salt**

1. Preheat the oven to 325° F. Set a 6-cup gratin dish in a roasting pan, and bring some water to a boil for the water bath. Finely dice the water chestnuts.

2. Whisk the egg yolks and sugar together until pale yellow and thick.

3. Rinse out a heavy saucepan with water but do not dry; pour in the coconut milk and cream, and heat over medium heat to almost boiling.

4. Slowly pour the hot cream into the egg yolks, and whisk well together. Strain the custard through a sieve into the gratin dish. Pour enough hot water into the roasting pan to come half-way up the sides of the gratin dish. Gently sprinkle the water chestnuts over the custard. Place in the roasting pan in the preheated oven and bake for 1 hour and 20 minutes, until the custard is firm around the edges — it will still be quite loose in the centre, but will firm up as it cools.

5. Remove the dish from the water and and allow to cool completely. Then cover and refrigerate until very cold – about 4 hours. *(The custard may be prepared up to 2 days ahead to this point.)*

6. One or 2 hours before serving: Heat the broiler until very hot. Place the custard dish on a baking sheet (it makes it easier to manoeuvre). Blot off any condensation on the custard with paper towels. Mix the brown sugar and salt together. Gently spread the sugar over the custard, keeping it as even as possible. Broil close to the heat until the sugar caramelizes; if it burns in parts do not worry – that's what the name means. Allow to cool but do not refrigerate before serving.

PEACH AND BLUEBERRY TRIFLE

Trifle is originally a product of Scottish frugality; slices of left-over cake were transformed, by the addition of some jam, a little whipped cream, a good quantity of custard (which had the virtue of being cheap), and a glass of sherry, into a pudding that was considerably more decadent than what most people were used to day-to-day. This recipe is considerably more decadent than the original, but you can still use left-over sponge, if you have it. Trifle always looks good in a glass bowl.

Serves 6.

1 recipe	**Sponge Cake** (see page 224)
2 recipes	**Pastry Cream** (see page 222)
1 recipe	**Sugar Syrup** (see page 227)
10 ripe	**peaches**
2 cups	**water**
dash of	**vanilla extract**
1 cup	**granulated sugar**
3 pints	**fresh blueberries**
1 cup	**whipping cream** (35%)

1. Make the sponge cake following the recipe on page 224; but, if you have any left-over cake, use it.
2. Make the double recipe of pastry cream following the recipe on page 222. Set aside, covered with plastic, to cool.
3. Make the sugar syrup following the recipe on page 227. Allow to cool.
4. Bring a large pot of water to a boil. Blanch the peaches by immersing them in the boiling water for 20 seconds; rinse under cold water, drain, and peel.
5. Combine the water, sugar, and vanilla in a medium saucepan and bring to a boil; allow to boil for 5 minutes. Reduce the heat to low, add the peaches with a slotted spoon, and simmer, covered, until a skewer or toothpick easily pierces the flesh (be careful not to overcook the peaches: they should not be mushy). Remove the peaches with a slotted spoon. Discard the poaching liquid. Refrigerate 6 of the peaches. Coarsely chop or process the remaining 4 peaches, then fold them into the prepared pastry cream.
6. Slice the sponge horizontally into 4 layers: they will be pretty thin, and it does not matter if they are a bit broken (once they are inside the trifle, no one will know).
7. Pit and slice the chilled peaches. Reserve about 12 good-looking slices for garnish, and set the rest aside.
8. Assemble the trifle in a large glass bowl: Place a layer of sponge on the bottom of the bowl: brush it with sugar syrup. Spread ½ cup of the peach pastry cream on top. Arrange half of the peach slices in one layer on top of the cream, with some slices pressed right against the glass. Lay a second layer of

sponge on top and brush with the syrup. Spread on ½ cup of pastry cream, then cover with half the blueberries — again some should sit right against the side of the bowl. Cover with a third layer of sponge. Top with more pastry cream and the rest of the regular peach slices (still reserve the good-lookers). If your bowl is tall enough, add a final sponge layer on top of the peaches, then the last of the pastry cream. If not, proceed to Step 9.

9. Whip the cream to soft peaks (see page 31) and spread this over the top of the trifle.

10. Garnish with the hero peach slices and more blueberries. Chill until ready to serve.

COEUR A LA CREME

Not a common dessert at all. The combination of the smooth cream, the crunch of the sugar and the tart and luscious fruit is a simple but perfect pleasure. If you do not have the porcelain heart-shaped moulds with draining holes in the bottom, you can use small plastic tubs and pierce some holes in the bottom. (Note: A 250 mL /8 oz tub is too much for one person; you could even use large-size paper coffee cups cut down to 2" high, with holes pierced in the base.) You will also need some cheesecloth or muslin. Start the cream cheese at least 1 day before you plan to serve.

Serves 4.

FOR THE CHEESE

1 cup	**fromage blanc, cream cheese,** or **Quark** (see page 72)
1 cup	**whipping cream** (35%)
3	**egg whites**
2 Tbs	**sugar**

FOR THE DECORATION

½ cup	**whipping cream raspberries** or **strawberries** (or **homemade jam**) **granulated sugar**

1. Prepare your moulds: Cut squares of cheesecloth or muslin for each mould; the squares should be large enough to fold over the top of the cheese and completely enclose it.

2. With an electric mixer (or by hand), cream the cheese until soft and smooth.

3. In a separate bowl, beat the cream to medium peaks; fold gently into the cheese.

4. In yet another bowl, whisk the egg whites until foamy, add 2 Tbs sugar, then beat to fairly firm peaks (see page 24). Fold these into the cheese.

5. Spoon the cheese into the moulds, cover with the muslin, and set all the moulds on a cookie sheet or baking dish that will go in the fridge (this is to catch the whey that drains out). Cover the whole tray or dish with plastic wrap to prevent the cheese picking up a fridge taste. *(May be prepared up to 2 days ahead to this point.)*

6. To serve: Invert the moulds on serving plates and turn out the cheese. Whip the cream to soft peaks. Spoon the fruit around the cheese, top with some fresh cream, and sprinkle generously with sugar.

OEUFS A LA NEIGE (SNOW EGGS)

I have often referred to these as Floating Islands, but it seems that I am wrong. Floating Islands (it turns out) are meringues baked in a mould, then turned out and surrounded by a vanilla custard; they are usually large. Oeufs à la Neige are individual scoops of meringue poached in water (or milk), then floated on the custard. The ingredients are the same, but the presentation is different; they are both a very big hit, particularly with children.
It's a good idea to make the custard the day before.

Serves 6.

FOR THE CUSTARD
1 recipe **Crème Anglaise**
(page 208)

FOR THE MERINGUE
6 **egg whites**
³/₄ cup **granulated sugar**

FOR THE OPTIONAL CARAMEL
2 Tbs **water**
¹/₂ cup **granulated sugar**

1. Make the Crème Anglaise, following the recipe on page 208; set aside to cool. *(May be made 1 day ahead.)*

2. Bring a large, wide pan (such as a frying pan) of water to a boil, then reduce the heat and hold at a gentle simmer. If you are using a pastry bag (see Step 3), lay a large sheet of waxed paper (or parchment) on a counter near the pan, and dampen it with a wet cloth.

3. Beat the egg whites to soft peaks, then gradually add the sugar and beat until very thick and glossy. *EITHER* scoop the whites into a pastry bag fitted with a large star tip and pipe 3" diameter mounds onto the wet waxed paper, then transfer with an egg lifter into the water; or with two wet spoons scoop out large egg shapes of meringue directly into the water. Do not crowd the "eggs".

4. Poach for about 7 minutes on one side, then turn them over (this is easier said than done!) and poach another 3 minutes. Transfer to paper towel or a clean cloth to drain.

5. Set the drained eggs on top of the cold custard; refrigerate until almost ready to serve.

6. Shortly before serving, make the optional caramel: Combine the sugar and water in a small heavy saucepan; bring to the boil over medium heat, then increase the heat to high and cook to a medium-brown caramel (see Cooking Sugar Syrup on page 11). Remove from the heat, cool the bottom of the pan in cold water, allow the caramel to cool for a couple of minutes, then with a fork drizzle it in thin threads over the eggs and custard. The caramel will melt in the custard, but stick to the eggs and make an attractive pattern.

Floating Island

Frequently confused (by me) with the recipe on page 22. Floating Islands may be made in a large mould, or in small ones such as ramekins or muffins cups.

Serves 6.

1 recipe **Crème Anglaise**
(page 208)

FOR THE MERINGUE
6 **egg whites**
³/₄ cup **granulated sugar**

1. Preheat the oven to 350° F. Generously butter and sugar (i.e, butter, then sprinkle with sugar) a soufflé mould, or individual moulds. Find a roasting pan into which the mould will fit; bring a kettle of water to a boil. Cut a piece of aluminum foil to fit loosely over the mould, and butter it.

2. Make the Crème Anglaise following the recipe on page 208; set aside to cool. *(May be made 1 day ahead.)*

---

3. Beat the egg whites to firm peaks (page 24), then add the sugar in three batches and beat lightly between each. Scoop the meringue into the prepared mould(s) and smooth the top. Place the mould in the roasting pan and pour in the boiling water so that it comes half-way up the side of the mould. Cover lightly with the foil (butter side down, like a Zook*), and bake in the preheated oven for 30 minutes.

4. Remove from the oven and allow to cool in the mould. When ready to serve, invert onto the serving platter (or individual plates) and surround with the custard sauce.

*Then my grandfather said
"It's high time that you knew
of the terribly horrible thing that Zooks do.
In every Zook house and in every Zook town
every Zook eats his bread
with the butter side down!"
(The Butter Battle Book by Dr. Seuss)

VARIATION: HEDGEHOG

A floating island stuck with toasted slivered almonds, to look like Mrs. Tiggy Winkle.

1 recipe	**Floating Island** (see page 23)
1 cup	**Toasted Slivered Almonds** (sliced are OK but slivered are best — see page 39).

1. Make the floating island following the recipe on page 23. Remove from the oven, allow to cool, then invert onto the serving plate.

2. Stick the toasted almonds all over the meringue, till it is covered with little spines. Pour the custard sauce around and serve.

SYLLABUB

Very old and very English. A useful emergency dessert as it can be made in less than 15 minutes and will not disappoint your guests. If you can, serve with Ladyfingers (page 226) or Almond Tuiles (page 152): they dress it up even more.
Made the day before and left in the fridge overnight syllabub will separate into a thick cream and a clear liquid underneath. It's very good this way — if you can plan far enough ahead.

Serves 4.

zest of 1	**lemon** (see page 210)
juice of 1	**lemon**
3 Tbs	**granulated sugar**
³/₄ cup	**sweet white wine**
1¹/₂ cups	**whipping cream** (35%)

1. Chop the lemon zest very finely; put it with the lemon juice in your mixing bowl (or bowl of the electric mixer). Add the sugar, white wine, and cream.

2. Whisk on high speed until soft peaks form (see box); do not beat it much beyond this stage or it may separate.

3. Pour into 4 tall glasses; refrigerate until ready to serve.

BEATING EGG WHITES
Recipes generally call for egg whites to be beaten to "soft" or "stiff" peaks. Cooks use 4 stages to describe how eggs are to be beaten:
Stage 1: Does not apply to whites, only to whole eggs. Whole eggs at this stage are called "well-beaten eggs"; they are used for omelettes, scrambled eggs etc.
Stage 2: Whites have coarse bubbles, a more or less even consistency, and begin to look white. The recipes call this stage "frothy". Add cream of tartar at this stage; and start to add the sugar, if it is used.
Stage 3: Dip your whisk into the beaten whites and pull it out with some of the whites on it. Turn it so that the peaks of the whites point up. At the lower end of this stage the peaks will bend over, and be very soft – it is called "soft peaks". Keep beating, testing the peaks frequently; soon they will stand straight up — this is "stiff peaks".
Stage 4: If you keep beating, the whites will become very dry, stiff, and brittle. They have gone past the point where they are of any use.
If you add sugar at Stage 2, the beaten whites will become smooth and glossy as you continue to beat. It will take longer to reach stiff peaks, and it will be very hard to overbeat them to Stage 4.

BREAD PUDDING

Not everyone's idea of a good time, but this is a particularly rich and delicious verion.

Serves 8.

1 loaf	**whole-wheat** or **raisin bread**, about 10" long
1 cup	**coffee cream** (18%)
4	**eggs**
1 cup	**granulated sugar**
1¾ cups	**icing sugar**
1½ cups	**raisins**
½ cup	**brandy**
2 tsp	**vanilla extract**
½ tsp	**ground cinnamon**
½ tsp	**ground ginger**
4 oz	**unsalted butter** (½ cup)

1. Cut the bread into 1" slices, remove the crusts, then cut the slices into 1" cubes. Spread them out on a baking sheet, and set in a warm place to dry.
2. In a large bowl, mix together the cream, eggs, the two sugars, raisins, brandy, and vanilla. Mix well together. Set both the bread and the custard aside for 2 hours, or longer.

3. Preheat the oven to 375° F. Butter generously a large oven-proof baking dish.
4. When the bread is dry, stir it into the custard and allow it to become completely soaked. Sprinkle the ground cinnamon and ginger on top.
5. Transfer the soaked bread to the prepared baking dish. Dot the butter on top, and bake in the preheated oven for 35 to 40 minutes, until the pudding has risen, and is nice and brown on top.
6. Serve warm, with Date Crème Anglaise (see below), and a few berries for colour.

DATE CREME ANGLAISE

1 recipe	**Crème Anglaise — Method 1** (see page 208)
½ cup	**dried dates**, the more succulent the better

1. Prepare the crème anglaise, following the recipe on page 208. Proceed to the end of Step 4, where you have completely cooked the custard, but it is still very hot. Remove from the heat, and set aside.
2. Chop the dates well, then scoop them into the hot crème anglaise. Return the saucepan to a low heat, and warm gently, stirring frequently, for 10 to 15 minutes, until the dates have become quite soft. Be careful that the heat is not high enough to cook the custard any more.
3. Pour the mixture into the workbowl of your food processor, and process until reduced to a purée. Strain the custard through a fine sieve into a clean bowl, cover with plastic wrap, and set aside to cool completely. May be refrigerated for 2 days.

THE CREAMIEST RICE PUDDING

I may never be able to like rice pudding; boarding-school has scarred me permanently in that department (and who knows where else). However, there are a few twisted people who actually liked school rice pudding; I am glad to say that this recipe is nothing like it — it doesn't even have a skin. This recipe is Karen's; she swears that, if you like good rice pudding, you will love this one. I will never know.

Serves 6 to 8.

4 cups	**milk**
1½ cups	**Arborio rice**
½ cup	**sugar**
¼ cup	**raisins**, optional
¼ tsp	**salt**
1½ cups	**whipping cream** (35%)

1. Preheat the oven to 300° F. Find a pot with a lid that can go both on top of the stove and in the oven.
2. Rinse out the pot with water but do not dry; pour in the milk, and add the sugar, raisins, and salt. Bring to a boil over medium heat, stirring occasionally.
3. Add the rice and bring to a boil again, stirring steadily. Place the lid on the pot and put it in the preheated oven. Bake for 15 minutes.
4. Remove the lid and stir the pudding well. Replace the lid, turn the heat down to 250° F and bake for 15 minutes longer.
5. Remove the pudding from the oven and uncover. Stir well, then let it rest for 5 minutes.
6. Slowly stir in the whipping cream. Cool the pudding to room temperature before refrigerating it.
7. The pudding can be served warm; some people think it's the best way.

ZABAGLIONE

A quick, absolutely delicious treat that can easily lead to a second helping. It can be served over fresh berries, and is even good with caramelized oranges (page 10). But it may be even better just as it is, eaten out of a tall glass with a small spoon.

For each person (just multiply by the number of guests):

1	**egg yolk**
1 Tbs	**granulated sugar**
1½ Tbs	**Marsala** (or very sweet white wine)

1. Combine the egg yolks, sugar, and Marsala in a large bowl that can go over hot water. Set it over a pan of simmering, but not boiling, water and whisk steadily until the zabaglione is pale yellow, very thick, and warm to the touch. It should not get hot; if becomes uncomfortably warm to your finger, remove from the heat and keep whisking until it has cooled a little. Then return to the heat and whisk until done (the test of doneness is how thick it is).
2. Spoon into tall glasses and serve; you could serve ladyfingers (see page 226) or Amaretti cookies alongside.

MASCARPONE CANNOLI

A new twist on an old theme. Instead of the deep-fried cannoli batter, a lighter, crunchier langue-de-chat batter is used. And the traditional ricotta filling has been replaced by a sweetened mascarpone centre, flavoured with either cinnamon or chocolate. Fill the cannoli at the last minute, as the shells soften once they are filled. However, both the cannoli shells and the filling can be made hours in advance and held until final assembly.

1 recipe **Tulipe Batter** (see page 150)

FOR FILLING NO. 1 (Cinnamon)
500 grams **mascarpone**, preferably imported
$^1/_2$ cup **granulated sugar**
2 Tbs **ground cinnamon**
$^1/_2$ tsp **ground nutmeg**
2 tsp **Grated Lemon Zest** (see page 210)

FOR FILLING NO. 2 (Chocolate)
6 oz **semi-sweet chocolate**
500 grams **mascarpone**, preferably imported
$^1/_2$ cup **granulated sugar**

1. Make the Tulipe batter following the recipe on page 150. Decide on the size of cannoli you want, and make the circles accordingly. When shaping the wafers, remove the circle from the cookie sheet and quickly and carefully fit it around either a cannoli mould or the handle of a wooden spoon to make a cylinder shape. Allow to cool completely.
2. To make filling No. 1: With an electric mixer fitted with the paddle (or by hand) cream the mascarpone; gradually add the sugar and beat until smooth. Add the cinnamon, nutmeg, and lemon, and beat just until incorporated, stopping once to scrape down the sides and the bottom.
3. To make filling No. 2: Place the chopped chocolate in a bowl that can go over hot water; set it over simmering water and melt the chocolate, stirring from time to time. With an electric mixer fitted with the paddle (or by hand), cream the mascarpone; add the sugar and beat until smooth. Pour in the melted chocolate and stir.
4. Spoon the mixture into a pastry bag fitted with a star tip or a $^1/_2$" plain tip. Gently pipe the filling into both ends of the cannoli, so that it meets at the centre. For the cinnamon cannoli, dust lightly with icing sugar. For the chocolate, drizzle melted semi-sweet chocolate over the surface.
5. Serve immediately.

Tiramisu

This dessert has become something of a hallmark for our pastry kitchens. Daphna brought the recipe back from Italy with her; she had been shown it by a lady who spoke no English, but Daphna's incipient Italian and well-developed intuition came to the rescue, and the recipe survived in all its glory. As you can see in the photograph (facing page 142) it looks very good in a straight-sided glass bowl.
Make it a day ahead: it should stay in the fridge overnight.

Serves 8 to 10.

1 recipe	**Ladyfingers** (page 226)
5	**egg yolks**
5 Tbs	**granulated sugar**
1 tub	**mascarpone,** (500 gr) preferably imported
5 Tbs	**dark rum**
5	**egg whites**
1 cup	**strong black coffee**
1 cup	**unsweetened cocoa powder**

1. Prepare the ladyfingers according to recipe on page 226. Allow them to cool completely.
2. With an electric mixer (or by hand), whisk the egg yolks and sugar together until pale yellow and very thick.
3. Fold the mascarpone into the yolk mixture. Stir in the rum. Transfer to a clean bowl (only if you are using the mixer to beat the egg whites — Stage 4).
4. Whisk the egg whites to stiff but not dry peaks (see page 24). Stir ⅓ of the whites into the yolk-and-mascarpone mixture, then gently fold in the rest.
5. With a pastry brush, brush the coffee onto enough ladyfingers to line the bottom of the serving bowl. Gently pour a layer about 1" thick of mascarpone mixture over the ladyfingers. Spread it evenly with a spatula. Place ¼ of the cocoa powder in a fine mesh sieve and sift over the mascarpone. This completes one layer.
6. Repeat the process 2-3 times, so that you have 3 or 4 layers altogether. Its probably best to brush the ladyfingers with coffee on a separate plate and then transfer them to the bowl, so that you don't have coffee everywhere. Finish with a layer of cocoa powder. Cover with plastic wrap and refrigerate overnight.

7. For a more elaborate presentation, decorate the edge with a border of grated semi-sweet chocolate or fresh raspberries.

CHOCOLATE DESSERTS

Chocolate was well-known to the Aztecs and peoples of Central America and the Caribbean islands, before the arrival of the Spanish; and so were its mildly narcotic effects. Chocolate contains caffeine and a smaller amount of theobromine, and the Aztecs frowned severely on all forms of intoxication, whether from alcohol or chocolate.

Chocolate without the addition of sugar is just about inedible. The Mexicans added much less sugar than we do to their chocolate; they made a watery drink with it, which seems to have had a much thicker froth that could be scooped off and cut up, and then, as now, was given to soldiers on long marches. They also made a sauce that was frequently married with savoury dishes, which was probably the ancestor of what is still one of the great chocolate dishes of the world — chicken or turkey with "mole" sauce, a speciality of Puebla. For a long time after its introduction to Europe, chocolate was regarded as a dangerous and barbaric product. For a while it was controlled as a monopoly by the Spanish, shared later by the Portuguese. When Jews expelled from Spain brought chocolate to the French town of Bayonne, the town forbade its production within the city limits. Prohibitions, and heavy import duties, were unsuccessful in suppressing the growing taste for chocolate, and people paid wildly inflated prices to enjoy the new discovery. Towards the end of the seventeenth century, in London, chocolate cost more than half its weight in gold. All of this is not very different from the way we regard the dangerous drugs of today.

It was the Europeans who added the large amount of sugar that is in most of our chocolate today, and, not surprisingly, the Swiss who added the milk! For cooking, unsweetened chocolate is sometimes the best way to go, because it has the most intense chocolate flavour: brownies, for example, are almost always made with unsweetened chocolate — but quite a lot of sugar must be added to the recipe. Most of our recipes require bitter-sweet (the sweetened chocolate with the least amount of sugar) or semi-sweet chocolate: the difference in their sugar contents is not great. For recipes where the appearanceof the chocolate is important — where a good, shiny finish is required — it is a good idea to use semi-sweet chocolate, as it will melt more smoothly, and dry to a glossier sheen. Some recipes in American books (but none in this one) call for German chocolate: this is a sweet, dark chocolate, with more sugar than semi-sweet, but not readily available in Canada.

Chocolate is a wonderful addition to a menu, and unfailingly popular with guests. Used with respect and in moderation, it will do neither you nor them any harm, like most other mild narcotics. Most people's tendency these days is, in any case, to eat and drink less, but to buy better quality: if you take the same approach with chocolate, you will be able to appreciate it for the treat that it is. In addition to the recipes in this section, there are a number of chocolate-based recipes in other sections, which might fit the bill when you are looking for something chocolatey:

The Best Chocolate Fudge Layer Cake	page 37
Chocolate Almond Cheesecake	page 71
Chocolate Cake with Chocolate Icing	page 38
Chocolate Caramel Chewies	page 164
Chocolate Chip Cookies	page 149
Chocolate Cup Cakes	page 176
Chocolate Cluster Ice Cream	page 138
Chocolate Devil's Food Cake	page 49
Chocolate Glazed Caramel Pecan Bars	page 165
Chocolate Mousse Ice Cream	page 142
Chocolate Orange Cake	page 44
Chocolate Reversal Cookies	page 150
Chocolate Walnut Caramel Tart	page 114
Crunchie Bar Cheesecake	page 74
Double Chocolate Cheesecake	page 76
Double Fudge Cookies	page 160
Fudge Truffle Tart	page 116
Gypsy John Cake	page 40
Low-Cholesterol Chocolate Cake	page 65
Macadamia Brownies	page 155
Marc's Chocolate Bourbon Pecan Pie	page 122
Marjolaines	page 50
Skor Bar Cookie Brittle	page 166
White Chocolate Carousel	page 48

White Chocolate Mousse

White chocolate is a bit temperamental, and requires extra care when melting. This is a rich mousse, but it makes a good accompaniment to a dessert made with dark chocolate.

9 oz	**white chocolate**, cut into pieces
2 Tbs	**water**
3 Tbs	**Kirsch**
1½ cups	**whipping cream** (35%)

1. If you are moulding the mousse, lightly oil your mould. Otherwise have ready the serving dish (either one large or individual glasses).

2. Combine the white chocolate, water, and kirsch in a medium-sized bowl that can go over hot water. Set over a pot of simmering, but not boiling, water and stir frequently until melted and smooth. Do not leave the white chocolate unattended; it is extremely temperamental and will burn easily. Once melted, it should look creamy and be very smooth. Remove from the heat and allow to cool to room temperature.

3. Whip the cream to soft peaks (see below). Fold into the white chocolate mixture. Pour into the prepared mould or the serving dishes immediately and chill until 15 minutes before serving.

WHIPPING CREAM

In order to whip, cream must have a high butterfat content — or some additive, such as guar gum, to do the job. It is fat molecules that trap the air and form the walls for the thousands of little air bubbles that give whipped cream its volume and structure. Clearly, cream without additives is better than cream with; check the ingredients on the carton when you buy. But, be prepared for the fact that additive-free cream takes a little longer to whip: it is the price of purity. As with all fats, the butterfat molecules in cream are strongest when cold; this is why the cream (and if possible the bowl and the whisk) should be as cold as possible before you start.

There are three stages to which cream can be whipped:

Soft peaks: When you start to whip, there is a long time when nothing seems to be happening. Then gradually the beaters will start to leave a trail in the cream and the volume will increase. When the cream will hold a soft shape, but before it will adhere to the beaters in a mass, you have reached the soft-peak stage. When serving cream with a dessert, this is the stage you want.

Stiff peaks: It takes very little additional whipping beyond soft peaks to reach the stiff-peak stage; this stage occurs when the cream holds firm, sharp-edged peaks, and can be lifted by the beaters in a mass. Some recipes call for cream to be whipped to this stage.

The useless stage: If you continue to beat cream beyond stiff peaks the cell walls will collapse, and the fats and liquids will separate. You will have a curdled and watery mass that is not good for anything.

A word of caution: North Americans (at least in the opinion of Europeans) tend to overwhip cream; cream is more luscious, and blends in better with whatever it accompanies, when beaten to the soft-peak stage. Try it and see how you like it.

CHOCOLATE FONDANT WITH CANDIED BLOOD ORANGES

A spectacular-looking dessert — whole oranges surrounded by a chocolate pâté. Make it the day before you plan to serve.

Serves 8.

FOR THE ORANGES

1 quart	**water**
4 small	**blood oranges**
1 quart	**water**
3¹/₂ cups	**granulated sugar**

FOR THE CHOCOLATE FONDANT

1³/₄ cups	**whipping cream**, (35%)
1 lb	**bittersweet chocolate**, chopped

FOR THE DECORATION

candied orange zest (see box)

CANDIED ORANGE ZEST

To make candied orange zest:

1	**orange**
¹/₄ cup	**sugar**
3 Tbs	**water**

Bring some water to a boil in a small saucepan over high heat. With a lemon zester (or with a vegetable peeler) remove thin strips of orange peel, taking off only the orange part and not the white pith. If using a vegetable peeler, cut the peel into very narrow strips with a sharp knife. Put the zest into the boiling water for 1 minute, then drain and refresh under cold water. Discard the water.

Rinse out the saucepan and put in the sugar and 3 Tbs water, bring to a boil over medium heat. When the sugar has dissolved, add the orange zest and cook over medium heat for about 10 minutes. Remove from the heat and allow to cool in the syrup. May be used to decorate the top of most orange desserts.

---

1. Bring 1 quart of water to a boil in a large saucepan. Add the oranges, and blanch (cook at a good simmer) for 5 minutes. Drain, discard the water, and set aside the oranges.

2. Combine the second quart of water with the sugar in a clean saucepan. Bring to a boil over medium heat, stirring to dissolve the sugar. Pierce the skin of the oranges all over with a thin skewer. With a slotted spoon, gently lower them into the sugar syrup. Simmer uncovered for 3 hours, turning the oranges occasionally and adding more water to cover as necessary. Remove the oranges gently with the slotted spoon and transfer to a rack to drain and cool completely.

3. While the oranges are cooling, prepare the fondant: Rinse out a saucepan with water but do not dry; pour in the cream and bring to a boil over medium heat.

4. Place the chocolate in a bowl and pour on the hot cream; whisk until completely melted and smooth. If the chocolate does not melt completely, set the bowl over a pan of gently simmering water and stir until it does.

5. Lightly oil a 10¹/₄" x 2³/₄" loaf pan or mould. Line it lengthwise with a piece of parchment paper or plastic wrap that extends 4" beyond the ends; this will make removing the fondant a lot easier. Pour in about 1¹/₃ cups of the chocolate mixture. Refrigerate until firm, about 1 hour (keep the rest of the chocolate warm and melted).

6. Arrange the cooled oranges, stem to stem, over the chocolate down the centre of the mould. Pour the rest of the chocolate on top, so that the oranges are completely covered. Refrigerate overnight.

---

7. To unmould the fondant: Run a small knife around the perimeter of the mould; invert the mould onto the serving platter, then pull on the ends of the paper to ease it out. Remove the paper and smooth the sides of the fondant with a spatula. Garnish the sides and top with candied orange zest. Cut into slices with a serrated knife.

8. Serve with orange, mint or Grand Marnier crème anglaise (page 209).

Dark Chocolate Mousse

A lighter than usual mousse, with the intense flavour of unsweetened chocolate.

Serves 6.

4 oz	**unsweetened chocolate**
³⁄₄ cup	**granulated sugar**
¹⁄₄ cup	**strong black coffee**
5	**egg yolks**
1 to 2 Tbs	**brandy** or **rum** or **Grand Marnier**
5	**egg whites**
2 Tbs	**granulated sugar**

FOR DECORATION

whipped cream (see page 31) or **candied orange zest** (see page 32) or **Toasted Sliced Almonds** (see page 39)

1. Combine the chocolate, sugar, and black coffee in a bowl that can go over hot water (or in the top of a double-boiler). Set over simmering, but not boiling, water, and heat until melted and smooth, stirring frequently.

2. Remove the bowl from the heat and beat in the egg yolks, one at a time, beating well after each one. Then, stir in the brandy (or rum or Grand Marnier — they all have a great affinity with chocolate), and set aside to cool to room temperature.

3. Beat the egg whites until frothy, add 2 Tbs sugar, and continue to beat to firm peaks (see page 31). Stir ¹⁄₃ of the whites into the cooled chocolate, then fold in the rest (see page 128).

4. Pour into wine glasses or individual soufflé dishes, cover with plastic wrap, and refrigerate for 4 hours, or longer. (May be made up to 24 hours ahead to this point.)

5. Decorate with whipped cream, candied orange zest, or toasted almonds, before serving.

CREME CHANTILLY
Named (because the Royal family once had a model dairy there that made excellent thick cream) after the town of Chantilly, northeast of Paris where race horses are trained and the crème de la crème sport the elegant country look. This is cream mixed with 2 or 3 tablespoons of sugar and beaten just to the soft-peak stage, then flavoured with a few drops of vanilla. In the French view, this is the de rigeur (i.e., the only) way to serve cream with dessert.

CRÈME FRAÎCHE CHOCOLATE TRUFFLES

Chocolate truffles should (so say the experts) look as much like their tuberous namesakes as possible — a smooth but not perfectly round shape, with a cocoa coating on the outside, as if the earth is still clinging to the surface.
Start the day before; the chocolate base needs to chill overnight.

Yields 24.

³/₄ cup	**Crème Fraîche** (see page 207)
1 tsp	**vanilla extract**
6 oz	**semi-sweet chocolate**
3 oz	**milk chocolate**
1	**egg yolk**
1 Tbs	**cognac**
¹/₂ cup	**unsweetened cocoa powder**

1. Rinse out a small saucepan with water but do not dry; pour in the crème fraîche and vanilla, and bring to a boil over medium heat. Coarsely chop the two chocolates, then place in a bowl and pour on the hot cream. Whisk until melted, then whisk in the egg yolk and cognac, and stir until smooth. Cool until tepid, then cover with plastic wrap and chill overnight.

2. With a melon-baller (or rounded teaspoon), scoop out small balls of the chocolate and roll them in the cocoa powder until completely coated. Place in little paper cups and refrigerate until 15 minutes before serving — chocolate has a fuller flavour at room temperature.

MACADAMIA SHORTBREAD TRUFFLES

A good addition to a Christmas or petit-fours tray.

Makes 60.

1 cup	**unsalted butter**, soft
¹/₂ cup	**icing sugar**
¹/₂ tsp	**vanilla extract**
2 cups	**all-purpose flour**
60 large	**roasted macadamia nuts** (approx. ³/₄ lb)
3 oz	**semi-sweet chocolate**

1. Preheat the oven to 350° F. Line a baking sheet with aluminum foil.
2. Using an electric mixer (may be done by hand), cream the butter well, then beat in the icing sugar until light and fluffy. Add the vanilla, and stir in the flour until well combined. Turn out the dough onto your work surface, flatten it into a disc and wrap in plastic. Refrigerate for 30 minutes (longer if you wish).
3. Pinch off ¹/₂ tablespoon pieces of dough and roll the dough evenly with your hands around a macadamia nut. Place 1" apart on the prepared baking sheet. Bake on the middle rack of the oven for 18 minutes, turning the cookie sheet halfway

through, until the cookies are barely golden. Remove from the oven and transfer to a rack to cool. Repeat until all the cookies are baked.
4. Place the chocolate in a bowl (or in the top of a double boiler) over a pan of simmering water, and allow to melt, stirring occasionally. Keep warm.
5. When the cookies are completely cool, drizzle the melted chocolate over them with a fork.

CHOCOLATE MOUSSE BOMBE WITH RASPBERRY CURD

Chocolate and raspberries make a pretty good combination.
Make the day before serving.

Serves 6 to 8.

8 oz	**unsalted butter**
8 oz	**semi-sweet chocolate**, chopped
4	**egg yolks**
5	**egg whites**
3 Tbs	**granulated sugar**
2 Tbs	**Raspberry Curd** (see page 208)

FOR DECORATION

2 oz	**semi-sweet chocolate**, chopped **shaved chocolate curls** (see box)
½ pint	**raspberries**

SHAVED CHOCOLATE CURLS
Easy when the chocolate is at room temperature. Find a good-sized chunk of chocolate, or a regular chocolate bar, and let it warm up. With a sharp vegetable peeler, shave long strips off the chocolate on to a plate. Transfer to the fridge and store until required.

---

1. Melt the butter in a saucepan over medium heat. When the butter comes to a boil, remove from the heat and add the chocolate. Stir until the chocolate has melted. Set the chocolate mixture aside and let stand for 10 minutes, until tepid.
2. With an electric mixer (or by hand), beat the egg yolks at high speed until thick and pale yellow. With the machine running, slowly pour in the chocolate mixture in a slow, steady stream. The mixture will become thick (like mayonnaise) – this is the way it should be.
3. In a separate bowl, whisk the egg whites until white and foamy, then add 3 tablespoons sugar and beat to stiff peaks (see page 24).
4. Stir ⅓ of the egg whites into the chocolate mixture to lighten it; then gently fold in another ⅓; when they are almost incorporated, fold in the rest (see page 128).
5. Line a small (4-cup) bowl with plastic wrap. Pour ½ of the chocolate mixture into the bowl, then swirl in the raspberry curd. Pour the rest of the chocolate mixture on top. Cover with plastic wap and refrigerate overnight.

---

6. To serve: Invert the chocolate bombe onto a serving plate and remove the bowl and the plastic wrap. Melt the chocolate in a small bowl set over simmering water, then pour it over the bombe. Decorate with shaved chocolate curls, and garnish with fresh raspberries.

CAKES

I used to think that a cake was just a cake, and that all cakes were created more or less equal (although some, like chocolate, were more equal than others), but I am beginning to realize the significance of their differences. Partly as a result of association and habit (eating fruitcake at Christmas) and partly because of their texture and character (a sponge cake somehow seems apter in the summer or at tea time, rather than as dessert), different cakes lend themselves to different occasions. I wrote in our first book that I make a cake only three times a year, for the children's birthdays; since then I have begun to realize how much I am missing by this limitation. Cakes are not only for special occasions (although nothing symbolizes such an occasion quite so well as a cake). Indeed there are cakes that are just not special enough for a birthday (unless you really like it and it's *your* birthday), but that are wonderful as a treat with a cup of coffee in the morning, or to come home to after a day outdoors in the winter. Some, like the Marjolaine, make as delicious a dessert as you will find anywhere; and the sweet spice smell of a coffee cake drifting up the stairs is enough to get even the laziest person out of bed.

Most cakes are simple enough to make; some are so quick and easy that you can make them for a last-minute dessert in little more than an hour (Hungarian Plum Cake, for example). Because the lightness and texture of a cake often depends on how well the batter is beaten, an electric mixer is an asset, but definitely not essential: our grandparents made very good cakes without electricity, and you can do the same — you just have to work a bit harder. A few cakes require a bit of technique; when making genoise, for example, melted butter has to be folded into the batter without knocking out all the air, which you have just spent 15 minutes beating in. But there is nothing in cake making (or in cooking in general, for that matter) of which you need be afraid. As with all things, practice will make you better; but there is no reason, if you follow the recipe carefully, that you should not make a very successful cake on your first attempt.

THE BEST CHOCOLATE FUDGE LAYER CAKE

A traditional chocolate fudge cake. (See photograph opposite page 46.)

Serves 8 to 10.

FOR THE CAKE

2 cups	**boiling water**
4 oz	**unsweetened chocolate**
4 cups	**all-purpose flour**
2¼ tsp	**baking soda**
½ tsp	**salt**
1½ cups	**sweet butter**
3½ cups	**brown sugar**
4	**large eggs**
3 tsp	**vanilla extract**
1 cup	**sour cream**

FOR THE ICING

2 cups	**whipping cream** (35%)
12 oz	**semi-sweet chocolate**, chopped
3-4 tbs	**Kahlua**

1. Make the cake first: Place the chocolate in a bowl and pour on the boiling water; stir until dissolved, then set aside to cool.

2. Preheat the oven to 325° F. Butter and flour two 9" cake pans (springform are easiest). Sift the flour, soda, and salt into a bowl.

3. In an electric mixer (you can do it by hand), cream the butter and sugar until light and fluffy — about 5 minutes. Then add the eggs, one at a time, and the vanilla. By hand, stir in half the flour, then half the sour cream, then repeat. Finally, stir in the chocolate mixture and pour half into each of the prepared pans.

4. Bake in the preheated oven for 50 to 60 minutes, until a tester comes out almost clean. Remove from the oven and allow to cool in the pans for 15 minutes; then turn out onto wired racks and cool completely.

5. Now, make the icing: Rinse out a saucepan with cold water but do not dry. Pour in the cream and bring almost to boiling over medium heat. Remove from the heat and set aside.

6. Chop the chocolate in fairly fine pieces, either by hand (which is hard work) or in a food processor. Pour the hot cream into the processor or bowl and mix with the chocolate. Mix in the liqueur and allow to cool to an iceable consistency — approximately 5 minutes in the fridge.

7. Ice the cake: Set one cake round on a serving platter (a cake board is fine; or a cardboard circle just a little smaller than the cake so it will not be seen). With a palette knife (or similar), spread about ¼ of the icing over the cake, then set the second round on top. Now, ice the top and sides of the cake, dipping the knife in hot water to do the final smoothing. Refrigerate until 20 minutes before serving. Serve with fresh berries and lightly whipped cream.

CHOCOLATE CAKE WITH CHOCOLATE ICING

*A good chocolate cake with a simple but delicious chocolate icing is not easy to find —
but this is one. The raspberry jam and cream filling make it a bit like a Black Forest
cake, only better!*

Serves 8 to 10.

FOR THE CAKE

2 oz	**unsweetened chocolate**
2 oz	**unsalted butter**
½ cup	**hot water**
½ tsp	**instant coffee powder**
1 cup	**granulated sugar**
¾ cup	**all-purpose flour**
¾ tsp	**baking soda**
⅓ tsp	**baking powder**
pinch of	**salt**
1	**large egg**
¼ cup	**sour cream**

FOR THE FILLING

2 Tbs	**raspberry jam**
1 Tbs	**lemon juice**
½ cup	**whipping cream (35%)**

FOR THE ICING

5 oz	**semi-sweet (or bittersweet) chocolate**
2 oz	**unsalted butter**
¾ cup	**icing sugar**
3 Tbs	**cold water**

1. Preheat the oven to 325° F. Lightly butter and flour a 8½" or 9" springform pan. Line the bottom with a circle of parchment paper (or waxed paper).
2. Place the chocolate, butter, water, and coffee powder in a double boiler (or in any bowl that can be set over a pan of very hot water). Set over simmering but not boiling water. Heat, stirring occasionally, until the chocolate is melted and the mixture is smooth.
3. Remove from the heat and whisk in the sugar; stir until dissolved, then set aside to cool slightly.
4. Sift together the flour, baking soda, powder, and salt. Set aside.
5. Mix the egg with the sour cream in a small bowl.
6. Whisk ½ of the egg mixture into the chocolate, then ½ of the flour. Add the rest of the egg, and then the flour, and stir until the batter is smooth.
7. Pour the batter into the prepared springform pan. Bake in the preheated oven for 30 to 40 minutes, until a tester comes out clean. The cake will still be slightly lower in the middle. Remove from the oven and allow to cool in the pan for 10 minutes. Then remove from the pan and cool completely.
8. When cool, cut the cake in half (so that you have two circles); a serrated knife works best. Choose the half that has a good smooth top and set it aside. Set the other half on a cake board or cardboard circle just about the same size as the cake (slightly smaller is best; it makes icing easier).
9. Melt the raspberry jam and lemon juice in a small saucepan. Whip the cream until quite stiff — it should be stiff enough to hold its shape firmly (normally, we would not ask you to whip cream this hard, but for a cake filling it works better).
10. Spoon the raspberry jam over the bottom cake layer (the one on the board) and let it sink in a bit. Now spread the whipped cream over the jam,

taking it almost to the edges. Set the other cake round carefully on top; if some of the cream comes out the sides, lift if off with a palette knife (or whatever you are using as a substitute). Set the cake aside while you make the icing.

11. Melt the chocolate in a double-boiler set over simmering water. When it is melted, add the butter and then the icing sugar. Stir until completely incorporated. The mixture will become very firm and slightly grainy; but it will come back together when you add the water. Remove from the heat and allow to cool slightly: the icing will spread much more easily when it is warm; but it should not be so warm that it runs all over the place.

12. Now add the cold water, one tablespoon at a time and stir until it is well mixed. The icing should have a thick pouring consistency.

13. Pour the icing over the top of the cake. If the icing is a good consistency, you should be able to pour around the perimeter in such a way that it runs down the sides and coats them with chocolate. If it is a bit too thick you will have to use your palette knife to spread it over the sides as well as top. If it is too thin, it will just run off onto the work surface; if this happens, let the icing cool a bit more. Use your palette knife to spread the chocolate as smoothly as possible on the sides and top of the cake. Dipping it in hot water will help to stop the chocolate sticking to the blade.

14. If you are ambitious (or the cake is for a birthday) you can use the left-over icing to pipe a decoration or birthday greeting on the top. (See page 63 for instructions on making a paper piping bag.) Making the writing the same colour as the icing makes a subtle and attractive decoration.

TOASTING ALMONDS

Sliced almonds are thin wafers of almond; slivered almonds are the little sticks. Either can be used for decoration, but they are both better toasted.

Heat the oven to 350° F. Spread the almonds out on a baking sheet. Toast until golden brown (it will take 5 to 10 minutes, the slices less time that the slivers). It is all but impossible to get them to brown evenly, but tossing every 2 or 3 minutes certainly helps. Watch carefully towards the end - they burn easily, especially the thin slices.

GYPSY JOHN CAKE

A rich very chocolatey cake.

Serves 8 to 10.

FOR THE FILLING

1½ cups	**whipping cream**
6 oz	**unsalted butter**
1 tsp	**vanilla extract**
12 oz	**semi-sweet chocolate**, chopped
2 large	**egg yolks**

FOR THE CAKE

6 oz	**semi-sweet chocolate**, chopped
1 oz	**unsweetened chocolate**, chopped
2½ oz	**unsalted butter**
4	**egg yolks**
⅓ cup	**granulated sugar**
½ tsp	**vanilla extract**
1 cup	**apricot jam**
2 tbs	**brandy**
6 oz	**semi-sweet chocolate**

1. Make the filling: Rinse out a medium saucepan with water, but do not dry it; pour in the cream, butter, and vanilla and bring to a boil over medium heat. Place the chocolate in a bowl and pour on the hot cream; stir until completely melted. Whisk in the egg yolks, then chill until the chocolate is the consistency of pudding. Set aside at room temperature until the cake is assembled.

2. Preheat the oven to 350° F. Lightly butter and flour two 8½" springform pans.

3. Place the two chocolates in a bowl that can go over hot water (or in the top of a double boiler). Set it over hot, but not boiling, water, add the butter and heat until melted and smooth, stirring occasionally. Remove from the heat and cool until tepid.

4. Using an electric mixer fitted with the whisk attachment (may be done by hand), beat the egg yolks with the sugar and vanilla until very pale and thick, 5 to 8 minutes. In a clean bowl, whip the whites to stiff but not dry peaks (see page 24). Fold ⅓ of the yolk mixture into the melted chocolate to lighten it. Fold the rest of the egg yolks into the chocolate. In 2 additions, fold the beaten egg whites into the chocolate-egg yolk mixture(see page 128). Divide the batter evenly between the two prepared pans. Bake in the preheated oven for 30 to 40 minutes, until a tester comes out almost clean. Set aside to cool; as they cool the cakes will deflate, but don't worry.

5. Assemble the cake: Make a collar out of parchment paper and fit it snuggly into a clean 8½" spring form. Fit one of the cake layers into the pan, inside the collar.

6. In a small saucepan, melt the jam with the brandy. Brush the cake inside the collar with half the jam. Whip the chocolate filling (from Step 1) to soft peaks; if it starts to separate, whisk in a little soft butter. Pour most of the filling over the bottom cake layer, reserving ½ cup. Place the second cake layer over the first, pressing down gently to remove any air bubbles; then brush with the rest of the jam. Cover with plastic wrap and refrigerate for 3 hours or overnight.

7. Release the springform and pull away the collar. Set the cake on the serving platter; or on a cake board or cardboard circle just slightly smaller than the cake. With a palette knife, spread the reserved chocolate filling evenly around the sides of the cake. Grate the 6 oz chocolate and press it onto the icing around the sides of the cake and around the top edge.

8. Refrigerate until 15 minutes before serving.

AUSTRIAN MARBLE CAKE

This recipe was given to Marc by an exceptional Viennese family: he has streamlined it for the food processor. The cake is rich and buttery, and will keep well for several days. Serve it at tea-time, sprinkled with icing sugar.

Makes one 10" cake, enough for 10 to 15 people.

4 oz	**bitter-sweet chocolate** (semi-sweet is OK)
1⅔ cups	**all-purpose flour**
1¼ cups	**granulated sugar**
1¼ cups	**unsalted butter**, room temperature
5	**eggs**
¾ tsp	**baking powder**
¾ tsp	**vanilla extract**
or 1 Tbs	**lemon juice** plus **zest of 1 lemon** (see page 210)

1. Preheat the oven to 350° F. Butter and flour a 10" cake pan. Chop the chocolate coarsely and place in a bowl set over simmering water (or in the top of a double boiler); heat, stirring occasionally, until melted, then set aside.

2. Combine the flour, sugar, soft butter, eggs, baking powder, and vanilla (or lemon juice and zest), in the workbowl of your food processor. Process, using the pulse action, until a smooth, creamy batter is formed. Pour half the batter into the prepared cake pan, leaving the rest in the bowl of the processor.

3. Pour the melted chocolate into workbowl with the rest of the batter and process until well blended. Spoon the chocolate batter over the white batter in the cake pan. Swirl the two batters lightly together with a fork; but not too much, as you want them to be quite distinct.

4. Bake in the preheated oven for 45 to 50 minutes, until a tester comes out clean. Remove from the oven and allow to cool for 10 minutes in the pan, then turn out and cool completely on a rack. Store in an air-tight container.

SHOWER CAKE

Actually a genoise filled with fresh fruit and whipped cream; rich without being heavy, and a very attractive cake for a special occasion.

Serves 8 to10.

FOR THE CAKE

7	**eggs**
1 cup	**white sugar**, fine is best but granulated is fine too
1 tsp	**vanilla extract**
1¾ cup	**all-purpose flour**
½ cup	**clarified butter**, warm but not hot

FOR THE FILLING

2½ Tbs	**corn starch**
½ cup	**white sugar**
¾ cup	**boiling water**
5-6 tbs	**fresh lemon juice**
1 Tbs	**Lemon Zest** (see page 210)
1	**egg**,beaten
1 tsp	**sweet butter**, softened
2 tsp	**sugar**
2 cups	**whipping cream** (35%)
½ pint	**raspberries**
1 pint	**strawberries**
½ pint	**blueberries**
½ cup	**orange segments** or any other fruit combination

1. Preheat the oven to 350° F. Butter and flour two 9" or 10" cake pans (springform are easiest to work with).

2. In a stainless-steel bowl (or other bowl that can go over hot water, but stainless is best), combine the eggs, sugar, and vanilla. Set the bowl over simmering, but not boiling water (don't let the bowl touch the hot water), and whisk the egg mixture until it is warm to your finger.

3. If you have an electric mixer, remove the batter from the heat and transfer it to the bowl of the mixer. Mix on medium-high speed until the batter is thick and fluffy or until it ribbons from a spoon (approximately 15 minutes) – see page 43. If you do not have an electric mixer, continue to whisk over simmering water until the mixture is quite hot to your finger and it has doubled or trebled in volume. Then remove from the heat and continue whisking until it has cooled again and is thick and fluffy. (*Note:* This takes quite a while — don't despair.)

4. Sift the flour into a bowl. Gently fold, first, half the flour, then, half the clarified butter into the batter, then repeat; try your best not to deflate the eggs in the process as it will affect the lightness of the finished cake (see page 128, on folding).

5. Pour the batter into the prepared pans. Bake in the preheated oven for 20 to 25 minutes. When ready, the centre of the cake should spring back to the touch of your fingers.

6. Make the filling: In a stainless-steel bowl, blend together the corn starch and sugar. Whisk in the boiling water, then set the bowl over a pan of simmering water (a double boiler may be used) and cook for approximately 10 minutes, stirring constantly or until the corn-starch mixture becomes clear.

7. Beat in the lemon juice, zest, and beaten egg and cook for another 3 minutes. Remove from heat and

FORMING A RIBBON
When egg yolks and sugar are beaten together, the sugar is dissolved by the liquid in the egg yolks (yolks are about 50% water), and the resulting foam is thick, pale yellow, and stable. It can be lifted by the beaters; as it falls back into the bowl, it forms a slowly dissolving ribbon on the surface. This is the stage that pastry chefs refer to when they talk about beating a foam "until it forms the ribbon". To achieve the best results, the sugar should be added a little at a time, allowing enough time for the sugar to dissolve.

beat in the butter. Cover the top of the filling with plastic wrap so as a skin does not form and set aside to cool.

8. Stir the sugar into the whipping cream, then beat to soft peaks (see page 31). Scoop out 1 cup of the whipped cream and set aside the rest for later. Once the filling has cooled, fold in the 1 cup of already whipped cream.

9. Assemble the cake: Place one of the baked cakes on your cake plate, or on a cake board or cardboard disk just a little smaller than the cake. Spread the filling over the top and sprinkle on an even layer of the fruit. Spread a little of the whipped cream over the fruit, then place the other layer of cake on top. Ice the top and sides with the remaining whipped cream and garnish with the rest of the fruit. Refrigerate.

10. Remove from fridge and allow to stand at room temperature for about 20 minutes before serving.

CARROT CAKE

Dead easy and deadly good.

FOR THE CAKE

2 cups	**all-purpose flour**
2 tsp	**baking powder**
½tsp	**baking soda**
1 tsp	**cinnamon**
½ tsp	**salt**
1½ cups	**vegetable oil**
2 cups	**white sugar**
4	**eggs**
2 cups	**grated carrots**
2 cups	**pecans**, chopped

FOR THE ICING

8 oz	**cream cheese**, softened
½ cup	**unsalted butter**
1 tsp	**vanilla extract**

FOR DECORATION

¼ cup	**pecans**, chopped

1. Preheat the oven to 350° F; butter and line with parchment (or waxed paper) one large or two standard loaf pans; or one 9" springform pan. Sift together the flour, baking powder, baking soda, cinnamon, and salt.

2. Using an electric mixer (may be done by hand), cream together the oil and sugar; then add the eggs one at a time. Stir in the sifted flour, then the grated carrots and pecans; do not over-stir or the cake will be heavy.

3. Pour into the pans lined with parchment paper. Bake in the preheated oven for 40 to 45 minutes, or until a tester comes out almost clean. Remove from the oven and allow to cool in the pans; turn out and remove the paper before icing.

4. Make the icing: Cream together the cream cheese, butter, and vanilla until smooth. Spread it over the cooled cake with a spatula or palette knife. Carrot cake is traditionally decorated with finely chopped pecans pressed into the icing around the sides.

CHOCOLATE ORANGE CAKE

The crème fraîche in the filling cuts the rich cake, and imparts a wonderful but slightly elusive tartness. This is a cake for a grand occasion.
Start the day before as it should sit overnight in the fridge.

Serves 10 to 12.

FOR THE CAKE

14 oz	**semi-sweet chocolate**, chopped
6 oz	**unsalted butter**
8	**egg yolks**
3 Tbs	**granulated sugar**
2 Tbs	**all-purpose flour**
	zest of 3 **medium oranges**, finely chopped
8	**egg whites**
3 Tbs	**granulated sugar**

FOR THE FILLING

12 oz	**semi-sweet chocolate**, in chunks
²/₃ cup	**whipping cream** (35%)
2 oz	**unsalted butter**
2 Tbs	**instant espresso powder** (or instant coffee powder)
1¹/₂ tsp	**water**
2 cups	**Crème Fraîche** (see page 207)

FOR THE TOPPING

10 oz	**bittersweet chocolate**, chopped (semi-sweet is all right if bittersweet not available)
²/₃ cup	**whipping cream** (35%)
2 Tbs	**unsalted butter**

FOR THE DECORATION

6	**candied orange slices** (see page 45)

1. Preheat the oven to 350° F. Butter 2 10" springform pans (but do not dust with flour).
2. In a bowl that can go over hot water (or in the top of a double boiler), combine the chocolate and butter and melt over simmering water, stirring occasionally. Remove from heat and set aside to cool to lukewarm.
3. With an electric mixer (may be done by hand), beat the egg yolks and 3 Tbs sugar until pale yellow and quite thick; add the orange zest.
4. Beat the egg whites to soft peaks, then add 3 Tbs sugar and beat to firm but not dry peaks.
5. Stir ¹/₃ of the egg yolks into the cooled chocolate, then gently fold in the rest. Fold in the beaten whites along with the flour. Divide the batter between the two pans, and bake in the preheated oven for 30 to 35 minutes, until a tester comes out almost clean. Remove from the oven and allow to cool in the pans for 10 minutes, then take out of the pans and cool completely on a rack.
6. Make the filling: Place the chocolate pieces in a large bowl. Rinse out a saucepan with water but do not dry; pour in the cream and the butter, and bring to a boil over medium heat. Pour the hot cream over the chocolate, and whisk until melted and smooth. Set aside to cool to room temperature.
7. Dissolve the coffee powder in the water. Pour into the chocolate.
8. Using an electric mixer at high speed (may be done by hand), beat the crème fraîche to soft peaks, then fold into the chocolate.
9. Wash one of the springform pans, then line it with a collar made of parchment or waxed paper, coming about 1" above the side of the pan. It may be helpful to butter the inside of the pan, so that the paper sticks to it.
10. Place one cake round on the bottom of the prepared pan, then pour ²/₃ of the crème fraîche

CANDIED ORANGE SLICES
Slice an orange crosswise into rounds about $1/8$" to $3/16$" thick. Bring a pot of water to a boil, throw in the orange slices and allow to cook for 1 minute. Drain and discard the water (this removes the bitterness from the orange).

Combine $1/4$ cup of water and 1 cup sugar in a small saucepan; bring to a boil over medium heat, then add the orange slices and allow to simmer for 10 minutes, until tender. Remove from the heat and allow to cool in the syrup.

Drain thoroughly on paper towel before using for decoration.

filling on top, add the second cake round, and mask the top with the remaining crème fraîche. Cover lightly with plastic wrap and refrigerate overnight.

---

11. At least 2 hours before serving: Place the chocolate pieces in a large bowl. Rinse out a saucepan with water but do not dry; pour in the cream and the butter, and bring to a boil over medium heat. Pour the hot cream over the chocolate, and whisk until melted and smooth. Set aside to cool until it reaches a good spreading consistency.

12. Remove the cake from the springform and peel off the collar; set it on a serving platter or on a cake board or cardboard circle just a little smaller than the cake (so it will not be seen). With a palette knife (or similar), ice the top and sides of the cake. For decoration you can pipe rosettes around the edge, and place half candied orange slices between them.

13. Store in the fridge until 30 minutes before serving.

HUNGARIAN PLUM CAKE

A simple cake with a nice texture that can be made in an hour.

Serves 8.

$1/2$ cup	**all-purpose flour**
$1/4$ tsp	**baking powder**
$3/4$ lb	**plums**
$5^{1}/_{2}$ oz	**unsalted butter**
$3/4$ cup	**granulated sugar**
4	**egg.yolks**
4	**egg whites**
2 Tbs	**granulated sugar**

1. Preheat the oven to 350° F. Butter and flour a 10" cake pan, or 9" springform pan. Sift together the flour and baking powder onto a plate.

2. Cut the plums in half, remove the pits, then cut into slices. Set aside in a bowl.

3. Cream together the butter and sugar until light and fluffy, then add the egg yolks one at a time, beating between each one. Fold in the sifted flour.

4. Beat the egg whites with 2 Tbs sugar to medium peaks (page 24); then gently fold them into the batter.

5. Pour the batter into the prepared pan; arrange the sliced plums on top.

6. Bake in the preheated oven for 15 minutes, then turn the oven temperature down to 325° F and bake for 20 minutes longer, until golden brown on top.

7. Allow to cool for 10 minutes in the pan, then turn out onto a rack and cool. Serve warm.

LEMON CAROUSEL CAKE

This is a very light and fresh cake, with the look of summer. Fresh strawberries line the sides, with lemon mousse and whipped cream on top.
It needs to set in the fridge for at least 3 hours; it works well if made the day before.

1 recipe	**Sponge Cake** (page 224)
1 recipe	**Lemon Mousse** (page 12)
1 recipe	**Sugar Syrup** (page 227)
1½ pints	**strawberries**
¾ cup	**whipping cream** (35%)

1. Make the sponge cake following the recipe; allow to cool, then trim it so that you have a 9" circle about ¾" to 1" thick — if it is much thicker the cake will dominate the rest of the ingredients.

2. Make the lemon mousse following the recipe on page 12. While it is cooling, make the sugar syrup (Step 3 below) and prepare the springform pan (Step 4). By the time you are ready to add the whipped cream to the mousse (Step 5 in the mousse recipe), you should be at Step 6 in this recipe.

3. Make the sugar syrup following the recipe. Set aside to cool.

4. Lightly butter a 9" springform pan. Cut a piece of parchment or waxed paper about 30" long and 5" wide; fit it inside the springform pan as a collar (it should stick up above the side of the pan) — the butter will stick it to the pan and help keep it in place.

5. Press the cake circle (from Step 1) firmly into the bottom of the pan. Brush with the sugar syrup (it doesn't matter if it is still a bit warm).

6. Hull the strawberries, then cut about 15 of the largest and best in half vertically. Stand these up around the edge of the cake, with the cut side of the berry pressed against the paper collar. Fill the middle with whole strawberries, so that you have a solid layer of strawberries on top of the cake. Reserve 4 large strawberries for decoration.

7. Pour the lemon mousse directly over the strawberries; it will come quite a way up the collar. Refrigerate for 3 hours (or longer). *(May be made up to 1 day ahead to this point.)*

8. Remove from the fridge, release the springform and remove, then gently peel off the paper collar.

9. Whip the cream to medium peaks (page 31); then spread it over the top of the cake, in a thick layer. You may pipe additional cream into rosettes around the top if you wish. Cut the 4 reserved strawberries in half, and set them on top of the cream, as decoration.

Opposite: *Best Chocolate Fudge Layer Cake (See recipe on page 37) and a Crunchie Bar Cheesecake with Chocolate Swirls (see recipe on page 74).*

DARLENE'S APPLE PECAN WALNUT CAKE

A moist and delicious cake, great for times when you need something sweet, yet wholesome. It is even better served warm.

Serves 12 to 14.

FOR THE CAKE

1½ cups	**vegetable oil**
1½ cups	**white sugar**
½ cup	**brown sugar**
3 large	**eggs**
3 cups	**all-purpose flour**
3 tsp	**cinnamon**
1 tsp	**baking soda**
¾ tsp	**nutmeg**
½ tsp	**salt**
4 cups	**diced apples**, peeled and cored
¾ cup	**chopped walnuts**
¾ cup	**chopped pecans**
3 tsp	**vanilla extract**

FOR THE TOPPING

4 Tbs	**sweet butter**
4 Tbs	**brown sugar**
4 Tbs	**white sugar**
4 Tbs	**whipping cream**
1 tsp	**vanilla extract**
¼ cup	**whole pecans**, for garnish

1. Preheat the oven to 325° F. Butter and flour a 10" or 12" bundt or angel-cake pan.

2. With an electric mixer (or by hand), beat together the oil and the two sugars. Then beat in the eggs one at a time and, finally, the vanilla.

3. Sift the flour, cinnamon, baking soda, nutmeg, and salt into a separate bowl, then stir them into the batter. Fold in the nuts and apples, pour it all into the prepared pan, and smooth the top evenly.

4. Bake in the preheated oven for 1¾ to 2 hours, or until a tester comes out clean. Remove from the oven and allow to cool for 30 minutes in the pan. Then loosen the edges with a knife and turn out onto a wire rack and allow to cool completely.

5. Make the topping: Combine the butter, the brown and white sugars, cream, and vanilla in a small saucepan and bring to a boil over medium heat. Allow to boil for a few seconds, then pour the glaze over the cake. Decorate the top with pecans.

WHITE CHOCOLATE CAROUSEL

This is a very attractive cake, with halved strawberries around the edge and the white-chocolate filling inside. (The look is similar to the Lemon Carousel Cake [page 46], but the sponge here is dark chocolate and the mousse, white chocolate.)

Serves 8.

1 recipe	**Chocolate Sponge** (see page 224)
1 recipe	**White Chocolate Mousse** (see page 31)
1 recipe	**Sugar Syrup** (see page 227)
1 Tbs	**Kirsch**
2 pints	**strawberries**
¼ cup	**whipping cream**

FOR DECORATION

6	**strawberries**, halved, stem intact
1	**whole strawberry**

1. Make the chocolate sponge following the recipe on page 224; bake it in a 8½" springform pan (or in the same size pan as you will use in Step 2 below) and let cool. Cut it in half horizontally (so that you have two circles) — if it's not very thick you can keep it whole. Wrap and freeze the other half for another day.

2. Set the rim (but not the base) of a clean 8½" springform pan on a serving plate (or cake board): this will serve as the mould inside which the cake is made. Cut a strip of parchment or wax paper about 30" by 3½"; this will line the pan and make a collar for the cake. Lightly butter one side of the paper (to serve as glue), then wrap it around the inside of the springform (glue side against the pan), making sure that the paper is sitting on the serving platter on the bottom and extends 1" above the pan at the top.

3. Place the chocolate sponge inside the paper collar, trimming to make it fit if necessary.

4. Make the sugar syrup, following the recipe on page 227; remove from the heat and allow to cool. Add 1 Tbs Kirsch to the syrup and brush it over the cake.

5. Hull the 2 pints of strawberries and cut them in half top to bottom. Choose the best-looking berries and line them up around the edge of the cake against the paper, cut-side facing outward. Then, fill in the centre with the rest of the berries, standing up.

6. Make the white chocolate mousse following the recipe on page 31; immediately pour into the cake mould, filling all the holes and crevices. Smooth the surface with a spatula and chill for 3 hours (or overnight).

7. Release the spring on the pan and carefully peel off the collar. Whip the cream to soft peaks. With a palette knife, spread a thin layer of cream on the top, making the edge as neat as possible. Place the 12 strawberry halves around the border of the cake (cut-side down, green end out) and the whole one in the centre.

8. Let the cake stand at room temperature for 20 minutes before serving.

CHOCOLATE DEVIL'S FOOD CAKE

Very chocolately and moist without being sweet. A snap to make.

Serves 8 to 10.

2 cups	**light brown sugar**, well packed
1¾ cups	**all-purpose flour**
¾ cup	**unsweetened cocoa powder**, sifted
2 tsp	**baking soda**
1 tsp	**baking powder**
¼ tsp	**salt**
1 cup	**buttermilk**
1 cup	**strong coffee** (room temperature)
½ cup	**vegetable oil**
2 large	**eggs**

Optional:
1 recipe **Chocolate Buttercream** (see page 206)
or
1 recipe **Basic Chocolate Icing** (see page 212)

1. Preheat the oven to 350° F. Lightly butter two 8½" springform pans.

2. Sift flour, cocoa, baking soda, baking powder, and salt into a large bowl; add the sugar and stir to combine. In a separate bowl, beat the eggs, then pour in buttermilk, coffee, and oil. Pour the wet ingredients over the dry ingredients and whisk until smooth. Divide the batter evenly between the two pans.

3. Bake in the preheated oven for 25 to 30 minutes, until a cake tester inserted in the centre of each comes out almost clean. Remove and cool completely.

4. Make the chocolate buttercream, following the recipe on page 206 if you are using it; if not proceed to Step 5.

5. To assemble: Place the cake round on a cake stand (or on a cakeboard or cardboard circle just a little smaller than the cake). Scoop about ¾ cup of buttercream over and spread it evenly with a palette knife. Set the second cake on top. Spread the buttercream over the sides and top of cake, as smoothly and evenly as possible. Pipe a decorative pattern on top of the cake with the rest of the buttercream. It is important to let the cake stand at room temperature for 30 minutes before serving, to allow the butter to soften; eaten straight from the fridge the effect of the hard butter is to make the cake seem stale.

6. If you are using the basic chocolate icing, follow the recipe for Chocolate Cake with Chocolate Icing (page 38) for filling and icing the cake; the same raspberry filling would be good.

MARJOLAINES

These are good. Ours is not exactly the classic recipe, developed by Fernand Point (see page 51), but a modification by Daphna for one of the dinners we catered at the Toronto Economic Summit.

Makes one 8" cake, serving 6 to 8 people.

1 recipe **White Chocolate Mousse** (page 31)

FOR THE MERINGUE
³/₄ cup   **finely ground hazelnuts**
1 Tbs   **cornstarch**
¹/₂ Tbs   **flour**
2 Tbs   **granulated sugar**
7   **egg whites**
³/₄ cup   **granulated sugar**

FOR THE CHOCOLATE CREAM
1 cup   **whipping cream** (35%)
2 oz   **bittersweet chocolate**, in chunks (use semi-sweet if not available)
2 Tbs   **unsweetened cocoa powder**
1 cup   **whipping cream** (35%)

1. Make the white chocolate mousse, following the recipe on page 31. Chill in the refrigerator.
2. Preheat the oven to 250° F. On a piece of parchment paper, draw three 8" circles in pencil. Turn the paper over (so that the meringues do not pick up the marks as they cook) and lay them on 1 or 2 baking sheets.
3. Combine the hazelnuts, cornstarch, flour, and sugar in a bowl and toss well. Set aside.
4. Combine the egg whites and sugar in a large bowl, and whisk to mix. Set over a pan of simmering water and whisk until barely warm to your finger.
5. Transfer the whites to the bowl of an electric mixer (may be done by hand) and beat on medium-high speed to stiff peaks. Fold in the hazelnuts by hand, then scoop the meringue into a piping bag fitted with a medium plain tip. Pipe out 3 circles, using the pencil marks as a guide.
6. Bake in the preheated oven for 1 hour 20 minutes, then remove and allow to cool.
7. Make the chocolate cream: Rinse out a saucepan with water but do not dry, pour in 1 cup cream and bring to a boil over medium heat. Combine chocolate and cocoa in a bowl; pour in hot cream, and whisk until melted. Set aside to cool.
8. Beat the other cup of cream to soft peaks (page 31), then fold into the cooled chocolate.
9. Assemble the cake: Set one layer of meringue on the serving platter (or a cake board, or a cardboard circle just a little smaller than the cake). With a palette knife, spread an even layer of chocolate cream over it (use about ¹/₃). Set the second meringue on top, and cover this with white chocolate mousse (use most of it). Finish with the last meringue, smooth out any filling coming out at the sides, then cover the top and sides with the rest of the chocolate cream.
10. For the decoration: Pipe any remaining chocolate cream in rosettes around the top of the cake, and the last of the white chocolate mousse around the base. Sprinkle some ground hazelnuts in the centre on top.

AFTERNOON TEA SPONGE CAKE

Once in a while, you have to throw caution to the winds and have a real afternoon tea; this light, white and simple cake is just the thing.

5	**eggs**
1½ cups	**granulated sugar**
1 cup	**all-purpose flour**

FOR THE FILLING

2 Tbs	**raspberry jam** (or any other good jam)
1 Tbs	**lemon juice**
½ cup	**whipping cream** (35%)

1. Preheat the oven to 350° F. Lightly butter and flour a 9" springform pan.

2. Combine the eggs and sugar in a medium bowl and whisk to combine. Set the bowl over a pan of simmering water and whisk steadily until they are just warm to your finger.

3. Scoop the eggs into the bowl of your electric mixer (if you don't have one, all this can be done by hand, or with a hand mixer) and beat on medium-high speed until tripled in volume and quite cool. The eggs should be beaten to the point where you can draw your initial in the batter, and it only slowly disappears.

4. Gently fold the flour into the batter (see page 128), then pour it into the prepared pan. Bake in the preheated oven for 25 to 30 minutes, until the top springs back when pressed and the sides have started to come away from the pan.

5. Remove from the oven and allow to cool for 5 minutes in the pan; then take it out of the pan and cool completely.

6. Cut the cake in half horizontally, so that you have two circles of equal thickness. Place one of the cirlces on a serving plate or cake board.

7. Melt the jam and lemon juice in a small saucepan. Whip the cream to firm peaks (it should be stiff enough to hold its shape).

8. Spoon the jam over the bottom cake layer (the one on the board) and let it sink in a bit. Now spread the whipped cream over the jam, taking it almost to the edges. Set the other cake round carefully on top; if some of the cream comes out the sides, lift if off with a palette knife.

9. Refrigerate until 15 minutes before serving; dust the top of the cake with icing sugar.

FERNAND POINT

Fernand Point was the chef-owner of La Pyramide, in Vienne, just south of Lyon. It was he who began the move away from the heavy food and formal meals towards what is now called "nouvelle cuisine". Many of the great French chefs of the second half of the twentieth century – Chapel, Troisgros, Bocuse, Outhier – trained in Point's kitchens. He instilled in his apprentices the respect for ingredients that is so important a part of modern cooking; and he emphasized simplicity (albeit luxurious) over complex and elaborate dishes and presentations. The Marjolaine took him years to perfect, and it has been further developed by many of his pupils. To us it may seem complex; but it really uses a few luxurious ingredients supremely well.

Point did not trust thin chefs: "Whenever I go to a restaurant I don't know, I always ask to meet the chef before I eat. For I know that if he is thin, I won't eat well. And if he is thin and sad, there is nothing for it but to run."
Quoted in *Great Chefs of France*, Blake and Crewe, p.38.

SOUTHERN SPICE CAKE WITH CARAMEL BOURBON PECAN SAUCE

Great with French vanilla ice cream.

Serves 8 to 10.

FOR THE CAKE
2½ cups	**all-purpose flour**
1 tsp	**baking soda**
2½ tsp	**ginger**
¾ tsp	**nutmeg**
1 pinch	**ground cloves**
2 pinches	**salt**
1 cup	**unsalted butter**
1 cup	**granulated sugar**
3 large	**eggs**
1 cup	**light molasses**
¾ cup	**warm water**
1 tsp	**vanilla extract**
¾ cup	**pecans**

FOR THE CARAMEL BOURBON PECAN SAUCE
3¾ cup	**whipping cream**
½ cup	**butter**
½ cup	**brown sugar**
3 tsp	**vanilla extract**
4 tbs	**bourbon**
¼ cup	**pecans**

1. Preheat the oven to 375° F. Butter and flour a 9" cake pan (springform is best). Sift together the flour, baking soda, ginger, nutmeg, and cloves into a bowl.

2. Using an electric mixer (may be done by hand), cream the butter and sugar until light and fluffy, beat in the eggs one at a time, then the molasses, warm water, and vanilla. Finally, stir in the sifted ingredients.

3. Pour the batter into the prepared pan, then sprinkle the pecans over the top. Bake in the preheated oven for 30 to 40 minutes, or until a tester comes out clean.

4. Make the sauce: Combine the whipping cream, butter, sugar, vanilla, bourbon, and pecans in a small saucepan. Heat over medium heat until thoroughly blended. Keep warm until ready to serve the cake.

5. To serve: Cut the cake into servings, but leave it in a round. Scoop French Vanilla ice cream on top and pour on the Caramel Bourbon Pecan Sauce. The cake may also be served warm, with unsweetened, lightly whipped cream.

Angel Food Cake

Ideal for a light summer dessert. Use tart berries, as they act as nice foil for the sweetness of the cake.

Makes one 10" tube cake, serving 10 people.

1³/₄ cups	**egg whites**, about 14 whites.
1 tsp	**cream of tartar** (see page 67)
¹/₈ tsp	**salt**
1³/₄ cups	**granulated sugar**
1¹/₄ cups	**cake flour**
1³/₄ cups	**granulated sugar**
1¹/₂ tsp	**vanilla extract**
¹/₂ tsp	**almond extract**
³/₄ tsp	**fresh lemon juice**

TO SERVE

1 cup	**whipping cream** (35%)
1 cup	**strawberries**
1 cup	**blackberries**

1. Preheat the oven to 300° F. You will need a tube pan or angel-cake pan with a removable bottom.
2. In the bowl of an electric mixer (or by hand) combine the egg whites, cream of tartar and salt. Beat on high speed to very soft peaks (see page 24). Sprinkle 2 Tbs of the sugar over the egg whites and fold in very gently with a spatula. Continue to add the sugar and fold it in, 2 Tbs at a time, until all the sugar is thoroughly folded in (see page 128), being as gentle as possible so as not to deflate the egg whites.
3. Now sift 2 Tbs of the flour over the egg whites and carefully fold it in. Repeat, adding 2 Tbs at a time, until all the flour is incorporated. Gently fold in the vanilla, almond extract, and lemon juice.
4. Pour the batter into the tube pan. Smooth the top with a spatula. Rap the pan against the counter to eliminate any air bubbles.
5. Bake in the preheated oven for about 1 hour and 10 minutes, until pale brown and springy to the touch. Invert immediately and cool, upside down, in the pan for 1 hour.
6. Remove cake from pan by loosening it around the edges wth a long thin spatula.
7. Whip the cream to soft peaks (see page 31). Serve the cake with fresh berries and the whipped cream.

DUNDEE CAKE

A very simple to make fruit cake; just the thing for tea in the afternoon.

This recipe makes two loaves, which will serve up to 25 people.

1¹/₂ cups	**all-purpose flour**
¹/₂ tsp	**salt**
1¹/₂ tsp	**baking soda**
¹/₂ tsp	**ground cinnamon**
¹/₈ tsp	**ground nutmeg**
1 cup	**unsalted butter**, at room temperature
²/₃ cup	**granulated sugar**
4 large	**eggs**
¹/₃ cup	**blanched chopped almonds**
¹/₃ cup	**lemon peel**, grated
¹/₃ cup	**orange peel**, grated
1 cup	**seedless raisins**
1 cup	**currants**
1 Tbs	**orange juice**
1 Tbs	**brandy**

1. Preheat oven to 325° F. Have ready two regular bread pans — they do not need to be buttered. Sift together the flour, salt, baking soda, cinnamon, and nutmeg into a bowl.
2. Using an electric mixer (may be done by hand), cream the butter and sugar together until fluffy. Add the eggs, one at a time, beating well after each addition. Mix in the sifted flour and the dried fruit and nuts, then the orange juice and brandy. The dough should be quite stiff.
3. Divide the dough between the 2 bread pans and bake in the preheated oven for 1 to 1¹/₂ hours, until a tester comes out clean. Cover with foil as soon as the cake starts to brown. Remove from the oven and allow to cool for 15 minutes in the pans, then turn out and cool completely. Stored in an airtight container, this cake will keep for several weeks.

POPPY SEED CAKE

Basic but good.

Serves 12.

2²/₃ cups	**all-purpose flour**
1¹/₄ tsp	**baking powder**
1 tsp	**baking soda**
¹/₂ tsp	**salt**
1 cup	**unsalted butter**
1¹/₂ cups	**granulated sugar**
5	**egg yolks**
2 Tbs	**lemon juice**
1 cup	**buttermilk**
¹/₂ cup	**poppyseeds**
2 Tbs	**lemon zest**, finely grated (page 210)
5	**egg whites**
¹/₂ cup	**granulated sugar**

1. Preheat the oven to 325° F; butter a 10" bundt or angel-cake pan. Sift together the flour, baking powder, baking soda, and salt into a bowl and set aside.
2. Using an electric mixer (may be done by hand), cream the butter and sugar until light and fluffy. Beat in the egg yolks one at a time and then the lemon juice.
3. Stir in half the flour, then half the buttermilk; then repeat. Add in the poppy seeds and lemon rind; and set aside.
4. In a clean bowl, beat the egg whites until white and foamy (see page 24), then add the sugar and beat until soft peaks form. Fold gently into the batter.
5. Pour into the prepared pan; bake in the

preheated oven for 55 minutes or until a tester comes out almost clean.

6. Remove from the oven and allow to cool in the pan for 5 minutes. Then loosen cake carefully and invert on a rack until completely cool.

7. Serve sprinkled with sugar, accompanied by fresh raspberries and lightly whipped cream.

Fresh Ginger cake with Rhubarb Compote and Creme Fraiche

This moist cake is delicious with the rhubarb compote — but perhaps even better on its own with butter and marmalade and a quiet cup of tea.

Serves 10.

³/₄ cup	**unsalted butter,** softened
¹/₂ cup	**dark brown sugar**
2	**eggs**
1 cup	**molasses**
4 Tbs	**fresh ginger**, finely grated
1 cup	**all-purpose flour**
1 cup	**whole-wheat pastry (soft) flour**
2 tsp	**baking soda**
1 cup	**Crème Fraîche** (see page 207) or **sour cream**

TO SERVE WITH IT (if you like)

2 cups	**Rhubarb Compote** (see page 13)
1 cup	**Crème Fraîche**

1. Preheat the oven to 350° F. Butter and flour a 10" round cake pan (springform is best).

2. Using an electric mixer, cream the butter and sugar until light and fluffy. Beat in the eggs one at a time, then the molasses and ginger. The mixture will look curdled — this is as it should be.

3. Sift the flour and baking soda together into a bowl. Fold ¹/₃ of the flour into the batter, then ¹/₃ of the crème fraîche or sour cream; repeat until all the flour and cream has been folded in.

4. Pour the batter gently into the prepared pan. Bake in the centre of the preheated oven for 50 minutes, or until a cake tester comes out clean. Set it on a rack to cool for about 10 minutes, then turn it out of the pan. Allow to cool completely before cutting. The cake will fall a bit in the centre — this, too is as it should be.

5. Serve with rhubarb compote and crème fraîche.

SEMOLINA RUM CAKE

This is an unusual cake, but surprisingly good considering the prosaic nature of its ingredients. The cake has four layers of quite crispy pastry sandwiching a rum-flavoured filling. The chocolate glaze provides the touch of class. Start the work the day before, as it should rest overnight in the fridge.

Makes about 40 squares.

FOR THE FILLING

3 cups	**milk**
9 Tbs	**semolina**
³/₄ cup	**butter**
1 cup	**sugar**
1 tsp	**vanilla extract**
¹/₄ cup	**rum** or **brandy**

FOR THE CAKE

1 tsp	**baking powder**
4 cups	**all-purpose flour**
³/₄ cup	**sugar**
¹/₂ cup	**butter**
4 Tbs	**honey**
2	**eggs**
4 Tbs	**milk**
1 tsp	**vanilla extract**

FOR THE GLAZE

¹/₂ lb	**bittersweet chocolate**, finely chopped
¹/₂ cup	**whipping cream**

1. Make the filling: Rinse out a medium-size sauce pan with water, but do not dry it. Pour in the milk and bring it to a boil over medium heat; then remove from the heat and slowly whisk in the semolina. Return to the stove, lower the heat to a simmer, and cook stirring constantly for 3 to 4 minutes. Remove and pour into a shallow bowl to cool. Spread a tablespoon of butter over the top to prevent a skin from forming (spear a lump of butter with a fork, then push it all over the surface). Let cool completely.

2. Preheat the oven to 350° F. You will need a 9" by 13" rectangular cake pan (but two would be even better). Sift the flour and baking powder together into a bowl.

3. Using an electric mixer (or by hand if you are energetic), cream the butter and sugar together until light and fluffy. Gradually beat in the honey, then the eggs, one at a time, then the milk and vanilla, and finally the flour.

4. When the mixture is too stiff to beat, turn it out onto the counter and knead until smooth. Divide the dough into four equal pieces. It will be baked on the back of the baking sheet so it can be removed without breaking when it is cooked. Spray the underside of the 9" X 13" pan with no-stick spray, and set it upside down; then roll out one piece of dough to fit the bottom of the pan, trimming off any overlapping edges. (If you have another pan, roll a second piece of dough onto it while the first is baking.)

5. Bake on the lower rack of the preheated oven for 8 minutes; then remove from the oven and let the pastry cool on the back of the pan until it is firm enough to remove. Detach it with a long-bladed spatula and place on a cooling rack. Roll out and

bake the remaining dough until all 4 pieces are
baked and cool.

6. While the pastry is baking, finish off the filling:
Using an electric mixer (may be done by hand),
cream the butter and sugar until light and fluffy.
Slowly beat in the cooled semolina mixture;
continue beating for 3 to 4 minutes. Beat in the rum
and vanilla.

7. Set one of the pastry layers on your work surface;
spread $\frac{1}{3}$ of the filling on it, taking it all the way to
edges. Cover with another pastry layer, then another
$\frac{1}{3}$ of the filling, another layer of pastry, the last of
the filling, and finally the fourth layer of pastry.
Wrap the pastry securely and refrigerate over night,
to allow it to soften.

8. Make the glaze: Rinse out a saucepan with water,
but do not dry. Pour in the whipping cream and
bring to a boil over medium heat. Remove from the
heat and add the chocolate. Stir until the chocolate
is completely melted. Let the glaze cool to a
spreadable consistency. With a spatula or palette
knife, spread it over the top of the cake. Place in the
refrigerator to set the glaze.

9. To serve: Cut into small rectangles with a serrated
knife.

HAZELNUT GENOISE WITH CARAMEL BRANDY BUTTERCREAM

A classic cake; a butter-enriched sponge with real buttercream. Let the cake stand at room temperature for at least half an hour before serving, to allow the butter to soften up. If it is eaten straight from the fridge the butter will be hard, the cake will seem stale, and your work will be wasted. This recipe will give your electric mixer a good workout — but it can be done by hand if you are in the mood.

Serves 8.

FOR THE GENOISE

2 Tbs	**cornstarch**
$^1/_2$ cup	**all-purpose flour**
6 Tbs	**unblanched hazelnuts**, finely ground
5 large	**eggs**, at room temperature
2 large	**egg yolks**, room temperature
1 cup	**granulated sugar**
1 Tbs	**brandy**
1/2 tsp	**salt**
5 Tbs	**unsalted butter**, melted to the noisette stage and cooled

FOR THE FILLING

1 recipe	**Caramel Brandy Buttercream** (page 205)

BEURRE NOISETTE

Butter that has been heated (carefully, so that the milk solids do not burn) until it is a mid- to dark-brown colour is called "beurre noisette" (nut butter) or "beurre noir" (black butter). The name comes from its sweet, slightly nutty flavour. It is for this flavour that chefs use it instead of plain melted butter. Melted butter is an essential feature of a genoise, and to give the cake a little extra flavour we use "beurre noisette".

"Beurre noisette" is traditionally served with sautéed, mild-flavoured fish and meat dishes, such as brains with black butter and capers.

1. Preheat the oven to 350° F. Lightly butter and flour a $8^1/_2$" or 9" springform pan. Sift the flour and cornstarch into the hazelnuts and toss to combine.

2. In a large bowl that can go over hot water, combine the eggs, egg yolks, sugar, brandy, and salt. Whisk together until well mixed, then set the bowl over a pan of barely simmering water and continue whisking until quite hot to your finger and very thick. Transfer the mixture to an electric mixer and beat until it has tripled in volume and cooled to room temperature (the whisking can be done by hand).

3. In a small saucepan melt the butter and cook until just beginning to brown (the "noisette" stage; see box). Immediately remove from the heat and set aside to cool.

4. One third at a time, sprinkle the flour and hazelnut over the batter and gently fold together. Repeat twice more, until all the flour has been folded in. Drizzle 2 Tbs of the noisette butter over the mixture and fold in carefully. Repeat until all the butter has been incorporated; the more gently you work at this stage the lighter you cake will be.

5. Transfer the mixture to the prepared pan and bake in the centre of the preheated oven for 20 to 25 minutes, until golden and springy to the touch. Remove and allow to cool in the pan.

6. Make the buttercream following the recipe on page 205.

7. To assemble the cake: Cut the genoise in half horizontally (so that you have two circles); a serrated knife works best. Set one circle on the serving plate or a cakeboard (or cardboard circle just a little smaller than the cake): spread $^1/_3$ of the buttercream over the cake, making it as even as possible. Place the second genoise layer on top. Spread the rest of the buttercream over the sides and top of the cake, smoothing it off with a (palette) knife dipped in hot water. Pipe rosettes around the top of the cake and place a whole hazelnut on top of each rosette.

8. Chill until 30 minutes before serving time.

Oatmeal Spice Cake with Caramel Cashew Icing

Homey and delicious just as it is; or dress it up with some sautéed apples and ice cream.

Serves 8.

¹/₂ cup	**all-purpose flour**
1 tsp	**baking soda**
1 tsp	**cinnamon**
¹/₂ tsp	**allspice**
2 cups	**rolled oats** (quick-cooking are fine)
²/₃ cup	**butter**, softened
1 cup	**brown sugar**
1¹/₄ cup	**boiling water**
2	**egg yolks**
2	**egg whites**
¹/₄ tsp	**salt**

FOR THE ICING

1 cup	**brown sugar**
¹/₂ cup	**butter**
¹/₂ cup	**whipping cream**
1 cup	**roasted cashew pieces**
1¹/₂ cup	**unsweetened coconut** (large-flake)

1. Preheat the oven to 325° F. Butter and flour a 9" springform pan. Sift together the flour, baking soda, cinnamon, and allspice.

2. Combine the oats, butter, and sugar in a bowl. Pour the boiling water over them, then allow to cool completely, stirring occasionally.

3. Stir in the sifted flour, then beat in the egg yolks. In a clean bowl beat the egg whites to stiff peaks (see page 24); stir ¹/₃ of the whites into the batter until well incorporated, then gently fold in the rest.

4. Pour the batter into the prepared pan, then bake in the preheated oven for 35 to 40 minutes, or until a tester inserted in the middle comes out clean.

5. Make the icing: Combine the brown sugar, butter, and whipping cream in a saucepan. Bring to a boil and cook, stirring occasionally, for 3 minutes. Remove from the heat, then stir in the cashews and coconut. Allow to cool slightly, then spread over the top of the cake.

6. Heat the broiler; then set the cake about 4 inches from the heat and broil until the icing is brown and bubbly. Allow the cake to cool completeley before removing it from the springform pan.

MOROCCAN PRESERVED LEMON POUND CAKE

A lemon pound cake is a good workhorse of a cake, suitable for serving on many occasions. The preserved lemons bring it into the thoroughbred class.

2½ cups	**all-purpose flour**
1 tsp	**baking soda**
1 tsp	**baking power**
½ tsp	**salt**
1 cup	**unsalted butter,** softened
1½ cup	**granulated sugar**
4	**egg yolks**
1 cup	**plain yogurt**
¾ cup	**preserved lemon peel,** finely diced (see page 210)
4	**egg whites**
¾ cup	**fresh lemon juice**
½ cup	**fragrant honey**

1. Preheat oven to 350° F. Butter and flour a 10" bundt or tube pan. Sift together the flour, baking soda, baking powder, and salt into a bowl.
2. Using an electric mixer (may be done by hand), cream the butter and sugar together until light and fluffy. Beat in the egg yolks, one at a time. Fold ⅓ of the flour into the batter; then ⅓ of the yogurt. Repeat twice with the remaining flour and yogurt. Stir in the preserved lemon peel.
3. Beat the egg whites to stiff but not dry peaks (see page 24); stir ⅓ of them into the cake batter, then gently fold in the rest. Spoon the batter into the pan and smooth the top.
4. Bake in the centre of the preheated oven for 1 hour, or until a cake tester comes out clean.
5. Meanwhile, combine the lemon juice and honey in a small saucepan. Stir over low heat until the lemon and honey are well mixed. Let cool.
6. When you remove the cake from the oven, pour the lemon and honey mixture evenly over the top. Let the cake cool completely before removing it from the pan.

BRAZIL NUT TORTE AND CREME FRAICHE

Easy and impressive; and it can be made 2 days in advance.

Makes one 9" torte, serving 6 or 8 people.

3 cups	**all-purpose flour**
1½ tsp	**baking powder**
¼ tsp	**salt**
1½ cups	**butter,** softened
1⅛ cups	**sugar**
1	**egg**
1	**egg yolk**
FOR THE FILLING	
3 cups	**Crème Fraîche** (page 207) or **sour cream**
1½ cups	**icing sugar**
1½ cups	**sliced brazil nuts**

1. Preheat oven to 350° F. Butter and flour a large cookie sheet. Sift the flour, baking powder, and salt together into a bowl.
2. In an electric mixer (or by hand), cream the butter and sugar together until light and fluffy. Beat in the egg and egg yolk, then stir in the sifted flour.
3. Place a 9" cake pan on the baking sheet and trace around the pan. (This will give you a guide for patting out the dough.) If you have 2 or 3 cookie sheets, draw a circle on them too.
4. Divide the dough into 3 equal pieces. Pat out one piece into the circle on each of the cookie sheets.

Bake one at a time in the preheated oven for 20 to 25 minutes, until golden brown. Remove from the oven and cool slightly before removing from the pan. Place on a rack to cool. Repeat with the remaining pieces of dough.

5. Mix the crème fraîche or sour cream together with the icing sugar and set aside. When the three pieces of pastry are completely cool, lay one of them on a serving plate, or on a cake board (or cardboard circle just slightly smaller than the cake) and spread with ⅓ of the crème fraîche mixture, then sprinkle with ⅓ of the brazil nuts. Place another pastry circle on top of the first; again spread with ⅓ of the crème fraîche mixture and ⅓ of the brazil nuts. Do the same with the last disk.

6. Cover loosely with plastic wrap and refrigerate for at least 12 hours before serving.

HEIDI'S SOUR CREAM COFFEE CAKE

This is my birthday cake every year, always made by Heidi, and I love it.

Serves 10 to 12.

FOR THE FILLING & TOPPING

1 cup	**brown sugar**
4 tsp	**cinnamon**
1 cup	**shredded coconut**
1½ cups	**semi-sweet chocolate chips**

FOR THE CAKE

2 cups	**unbleached white flour**
4 tsp	**baking powder**
2 cups	**whole-wheat flour**
2 Tbs	**milk**
2 cups	**sour cream**
2 tsp	**baking soda**
8 oz	**unsalted butter**
2 cups	**brown sugar**
4	**eggs**

1. Preheat the oven to 350° F. Find a 10" bundt pan.

2. Make the topping: Mix the sugar, cinnamon, coconut, and chocolate chips together in a bowl and set aside.

3. Sift the white flour and the baking powder together into a bowl; add the whole-wheat flour and mix well together.

4. Mix the milk, sour cream, and baking soda together in a small bowl, and set aside to rise.

5. Using an electric mixer (or by hand), cream together the butter and the sugar until light and fluffy. Add the eggs one at a time, beating after each. Add half the flour, mix briefly, then half the sour cream; then repeat.

6. Pour half the batter into the bundt pan, then sprinkle on half the topping. Pour in the rest of the batter, then finish off with the rest of the topping.

7. Bake in the pre-heated oven for 1 to 1¼ hours; test after one hour. Remove from the oven and allow to cool in the pan.

SPICE CAKE WITH MAPLE BUTTERCREAM

This cake is very moist, so is not usually split and iced in the middle. Icing just on top gives it an informal feel — and makes it easier to prepare. Remember to take it out of the fridge 15 to 30 minutes before serving to allow the buttercream to soften up.

Serves 10.

2½ cups	**soft cake flour**
or	
2¼ cups	**all-purpose flour**
1 tsp	**baking powder**
1 tsp	**baking soda**
½ tsp	**salt**
1 tsp	**cinnamon**
½ tsp	**nutmeg**
¼ tsp	**mace**
1 cup	**granulated sugar**
¾	**unsalted butter**, softened
⅔ cup	**brown sugar**, well packed
1	**buttermilk**
2	**eggs**
2 Tbs	**buttermilk**
1 recipe	**Maple Buttercream**(see page 206)

Optional Decoration:

10	**pecan halves**

1. Preheat the oven to 325° F. Lightly butter and flour a 10" square baking pan. Sift together the flour, baking powder, baking soda, salt, cinnamon, nutmeg, and mace into a bowl.

2. Using an electric mixer (may be done by hand), cream the two sugars and the butter together until light and fluffy. Stir in the sifted flour, then 1 cup buttermilk, and mix for 1 minute. Add the eggs and 2 Tbs buttermilk, then mix for 1 minute more.

3. Pour the batter into the prepared pan and bake in the centre of the preheated oven for 25 to 30 minutes, until a tester comes out clean. Remove from the oven and allow to cool in the pan.

4. Prepare the maple buttercream following the recipe on page 206.

5. Turn the cake out of the pan, and set right side up on the serving platter. Ice the sides and top with the maple buttercream, smoothing out the icing with a spatula or knife dipped in hot water. Decorate the top with the pecan halves.

White Butter Cake with Mocha Frosting

A butter cake is a richer, denser, cake than a sponge. It is important to bring the cake to room temperature to let the butter soften before serving, or it may appear hard and slightly stale. At the right temperature, it is delicious.

2½ cups	**soft (cake) flour** (or all-purpose)
1 Tbs	**baking powder**
½ tsp	**salt**
1 cup	**unsalted butter**, softened
1½ cups	**granulated sugar**
¾ cup	**milk**
2 large	**eggs**
¼ cup	**milk**
1 tsp	**vanilla extract**
1 recipe	**Mocha Frosting** (see page 213) or **Orange Cointreau Buttercream** (see page 206)

1. Preheat the oven to 350° F. Butter and flour a 8½" springform pan. Sift together the flour, baking powder, and salt into a bowl.

2. Using an electric mixer fitted with the paddle (may be done by hand), cream the butter and sugar until light and fluffy. Add the sifted flour and mix until thoroughly crumbly.

3. Add ¾ cup milk and beat for 2 minutes on low speed. Add the eggs, ¼ cup milk, and vanilla extract, and beat for 1 minute more, until completely smooth.

4. Pour the batter into the prepared pan and bake in the preheated oven for 20 to 25 minutes. Remove from the oven and allow to cool in the pan for 5 minutes; then turn out and cool completely on a rack.

5. Prepare the mocha frosting according to the recipe on page 213.

6. Cut the cake in half horizontally, so that you have two circles. Set one on a serving plate, or on a cake board or cardboard circle just a little smaller than the cake. Spread ⅓ of the frosting on top, place the other cake on top and ice the top and sides of the cake. Dip the knife or spatula in hot water to for a smooth finish.

PAPER CONES FOR CAKE DECORATING

A very useful little trick. You will need a triangular piece of paper (waxed or parchment is best) with a right angle at one of the corners (i.e., one corner should be square). The side opposite the right angle (the hypotenuse) should be 10" to 12"; one of the other sides, 8" to 10"; and the short side, 5" to 6" long. With the thumb and forefinger of your left hand, hold the paper on the hypotenuse at a point opposite the right angle (i.e., at the point on that side closest to the right angle). The long point should be pointing away from you. With your right hand, lift the corner closest to you up towards you and then away from you, pulling the point towards the right angle, and folding the surface of the paper right over so that it forms a complete circle. With luck you should see the beginnings of a cone.

Continue to roll up the paper towards the long point; the point in your left hand will become the point of the cone. When it is all rolled up you will have a cone with two points sticking up from the open end; they may even be in more or less the same place. Fold these over inside the cone to lock it.

There will be a small opening at the point end; if it is not large enough, cut it straight across with scissors or a sharp knife.

Fill the cone about half way with icing, then press the top together and fold it over to prevent the icing coming out the wrong way.

This is the point at which Art takes over from Science: you are on your own.

PETITS FOURS

These are really professional-looking little iced cakes. They can be served for an elegant tea or as part of a dessert table. Serving them at the end of a gargantuan dinner with the coffee, as used to be the custom, has fortunately gone the way of the passenger pigeon. (Ingredient quantities are given in weight as well as volume, since we expect that if you are going to make these you are experienced with working by weight. HOWEVER, they are really not hard to make — you need to be more careful than skilled — and, as in all things, the desire to succeed counts for at least as much as experience!)

Makes about 24.

17 oz	**almond paste**
³/₄ cup	**granulated sugar**
1	**egg**
6 oz (165 gr)	**butter**, soft
4	**eggs**
1 cup	**all-purpose flour**
1 cup	**raspberry jam**
8 oz	**semi-sweet chocolate**, chopped
8 oz	**white chocolate**, chopped

1. Preheat the oven to 350° F. Line an 11" by 17" cookie sheet (with ½" sides) with parchment paper.
2. Using an electric mixer fitted with the paddle, cream the almond paste with the sugar. Add one egg and beat until completely smooth, stopping to scrape down the sides. Add the soft butter and cream together thoroughly. Add the remaining eggs, one at a time, beating well after each addition. Scrape down the sides of the work bowl. Add the flour and mix until smooth.
3. Scoop into the prepared baking sheet and spread evenly. Bake in the preheated oven until just turning golden, 15 to 18 minutes, and a tester comes out clean. Remove from the oven and allow to cool completely in the pan.
4. When cool, cut the cake in half (the short distance); lift one half of the cake out of the pan. Spread the half of the petits-fours sheet still in the pan with the raspberry jam; set the other half on top. Put in the freezer for 20 minutes, still in the pan.
5. Meanwhile, put the dark ckocolate in a bowl and set over a pan of gently simmering water. In a separate bowl, do the same with the white chocolate. Stir both chocolates until melted and smooth. Keep warm over the water until ready to use.
6. Remove from the freezer and lift the cake out of the pan. Using small cookie cutters, cut out shapes — squares, diamonds, and rounds. Leave half of them on your work surface, and cover the other half with a damp cloth. With a fork, spear the petits

fours through the top (which will now become the underside); dip in the dark chocolate (they do not need to be covered on the underside) and then place on a rack to dry. Chill. In the same way, dip the other half of the petits fours in the white chocolate, remove to a rack and chill.

7. Make 2 paper cones (see page 63). Fill one with melted dark chocolate and the other with white chocolate. Remove the petits fours from the refrigerator. Pipe white chocolate designs on the dark chocolate coated petits fours and dark chocolate designs on the white chocolate ones. Remove from rack, place in petits-four cups and chill until set.

8. Allow petits fours to sit at room temperature for 20 minutes before serving.

Low Cholesterol Chocolate Cake

Very quick to make — and, if not exactly good for you, not nearly as bad for you as it could be.

Makes two 8" round cakes; or one rectangle 9" by 13"

FOR THE CAKE

2 cups	**all-purpose flour**
2 cups	**granulated sugar**
½ tsp	**salt**
1 tsp	**baking soda**
1 cup	**margarine** (low polyunsaturated)
¼ cup	**cocoa powder**
1 cup	**water**
2	**eggs**
½ cu	**buttermilk**
1 tsp	**vanilla extract**

FOR THE ICING

½ cup	**margarine**
¼ cup	**cocoa powder**
6 Tbs	**milk** (2%)
1 lb	**icing sugar**
1 tsp	**vanilla extract**

1. Preheat the oven to 350° F. Butter and flour your cake pan(s); either two 8" or 9" round; or one rectangle. Sift together the flour, sugar, salt, and baking soda.

2. Melt the margarine, cocoa, and water together in a fairly large saucepan over medium heat. Remove from the heat and pour in the sifted flour. Stir in the vanilla, salt, eggs, and buttermilk, and mix well.

3. Pour the batter into the prepared pans; bake in the centre of the preheated oven for 40 to 45 minutes. Remove and allow to cool in the pan for 10 minutes; then turn out of the pan and cool completely.

4. Make the icing: Melt margarine in a small saucepan and add the cocoa; remove from the heat and beat in the milk, icing sugar, and vanilla.

5. Spread the icing over the cake with a spatula or palette knife. Do **NOT** serve with lightly whipped cream!

CHERRY PRALINE UPSIDE DOWN CAKE

A very simple and delicious cake; the slight tartness of the sour cherries is balanced by the sweet and crunchy praline. When serving, Karen pours unwhipped cream over it , which gets absorbed by the cake and adds the finishing touch.

³/₄ lb	**fresh sour cherries**
¹/₂ cup	**unsalted butter**
1 cup	**brown sugar**
³/₄ cup	**pecan halves**
2	**eggs**
²/₃ cup	**white sugar**
1 tsp	**vanilla extract**
6 Tbs	**milk**
1 cup	**all-purpose flour**
¹/₂ tsp	**baking powder**
¹/₄ tsp	**salt**

Optional:

3 drops	**almond extract**

1. Preheat the oven to 350° F. Spray a 9" (square or round) cake pan with non-stick spray (if you approve; otherwise, oil it well).

2. Remove the stones from the cherries.

3. Melt the butter in a small saucepan and pour into the cake pan; sprinkle the brown sugar on top, then the pecans, followed by the cherries. Set it aside while you make the batter.

4. Using an electric mixer (or by hand), whisk the eggs until frothy, then gradually beat in the sugar, until it is light in colour. Add the vanilla, almond extract (if you like it and want to enhance the sour cherry flavour), and milk, and beat until smooth.

5. Mix together the flour, baking powder, and salt until well blended. Mix the flour into the eggs, but mix only enough to blend — the batter should not be at all smooth; if you mix too much the cake will be tough. Pour the batter into the pan, and gently smooth the top.

6. Bake in the preheated oven for 25 to 30 minutes, until the top springs back when pressed.

7. Remove from the oven and allow to cool for 10 minutes in the pan, then turn out onto a plate. Serve warm or at room temperature, with (unwhipped; or very lightly whipped) heavy cream. Heavenly.

PLUM AND BLACKBERRY SHORTCAKES

A tart variation on the more traditional strawberry shortcakes.

Serves 6.

FOR THE CAKE

1½ cups	**soft cake flour**
1 Tbs	**baking soda**
½ tsp	**cream of tartar** (see box)
pinch of	**salt**
3 Tbs	**granulated sugar**
1½ Tbs	**Lemon Zest**, finely grated (page 210)
1¼ cups	**whipping cream** (35%)
⅓ cup	**all-purpose flour**

FOR THE FILLING

5 firm	**plums**, quartered and pitted
½ cup	**water**
3 Tbs	**granulated sugar**
¼ cup	**crème de cassis**
2 pints	**ripe blackberries**
2 Tbs	**unsalted butter**
1 cup	**whipping cream** (35%)

CREAM OF TARTAR
Cream of tartar is fine white acidic powder that helps to increase the volume of beaten egg whites and make them more stable. The acid reacts with the protein in the whites, strengthening the cell walls and so making a collapse of the whole mass less likely.

---

1. Preheat the oven to 425° F. You will need a large cookie sheet (two would be even better).
2. Sift the cake flour, baking soda, cream of tartar, and salt into a large bowl, add 3 Tbs sugar and the grated lemon zest, and toss lightly to combine. Make a well in the centre and pour in the cream. With a fork, work everything together until a soft dough has been formed.
3. Sprinkle your work surface with flour and turn the dough on to it. Dust with more flour. Pat or gently roll out onto a large square, about ½" thick. Cut out rounds with a 3" cookie cutter and place on the ungreased cookie sheet (or you may simply cut the dough into squares, for a more traditional look).
4. Bake in the preheated oven for 15 minutes, until golden brown. Cool on a rack. Leftover scraps of dough may be rerolled, but they will not be as tender as the first batch.
5. Cut the plums into thick slices. In a medium-sized saucepan (preferably with a heavy bottom), combine the sugar, crème de cassis, and water; cook over medium heat until the sugar is dissolved. Then, put in the plum slices and cook until almost tender, about 4 minutes. Add the blackberries and cook 30 seconds longer. Remove from the heat and stir in the butter.
6. Stir in the remaining 1 cup cream to soft peaks.
7. To serve: Cut the shortcake in half horizontally, so that you have two circles. Spoon the plum and blackberry compote over and top with the second half. Place a dollop of whipped cream on top of the fruit cake and drizzle a bit of the compote juice over the cream.

RASPBERRY HAZELNUT MERINGUE

If a torte is a cake without flour (this is the generally accepted definition), then this is a torte — and a very good one too.

FOR THE MERINGUE

8	**egg whites**
pinch of	**cream of tartar** (not essential if not available — see page 67)
pinch of	**salt**
2 tsp	**white vinegar**
2¹/₂ cups	**granulated sugar**
2 cups	**ground hazelnuts** (or **almonds** if not available)
2 tsp	**almond extract**

FOR THE FILLING

1 Tbs	**granulated sugar**
2 cups	**whipping cream** (35%)
1 pint	**raspberries**
1 pint	**blackberries** (or more **raspberries**)
1 tsp	**almond** or **hazelnut liqueur** (again not essential; but good)

FOR DECORATION

2 Tbs	**icing sugar**
¹/₄ cup	**toasted hazelnuts** (see page 153) or **sliced almonds**

1. Preheat the oven to 325° F. Butter and flour two 8¹/₂" springform pans.

2. Using an electric mixer (or by hand), beat the egg whites with the cream of tartar and salt until very soft peaks form. Add the vinegar (another acid, reinforcing the action of the cream of tartar), and beat to almost-stiff peaks. Quite gently, fold in the sugar ¹/₂ cup at a time (the gentler you are, the less likely your meringue will stick to the pans; if you beat the sugar too much, it forms a syrup with the egg whites, which becomes an indestructible glue as it cooks). Finally, fold in the ground nuts, and the liqueur if you are using it.

3. Spread the meringue over the bottom and sides of the prepared pans, leaving a slight depression in the middle. Bake in the preheated oven for 1 hour to 1¹/₂ hours, until pale brown. Remove from the oven and allow to cool before removing from the pans.

4. Whip the cream to soft peaks (see page 31), then add the sugar and beat a little more, but not to firm peaks.

5. Place one of the meringue shells the right way up on the serving plate. Fill it with the whipped cream and fruit, mounding it up in the centre. Place the second meringue upside down over the first, making the whole thing look as neat as possible. Sift the icing sugar over the top, then decorate with the hazelnuts or almonds.

6. Refrigerate for at least 1 hour (up to 6) to allow the meringue to soften. Cut with a serrated knife.

CHEESECAKES

Cheesecakes are some of the richest desserts there are. Despite this (perhaps because of it), they continue to be very popular. There is quite a range to choose from: we include the traditional New York–style recipe, as well as few more whimsical cheesecakes — made with Oreo cookies and Crunchie Bars. At the extremely rich end of the scale, there is a double-chocolate cheesecake, and, at the other, a cake made with Quark cheese that has a considerably lower fat content. None of these cheesecakes is hard to make; the crusts are simplicity itself; and the only aspect of the filling that requires caution is allowing them plenty of time to cool and set after the cake has been baked — you will get the best results if you leave them overnight in the fridge.

Pumpkin Frangelico Cheesecake

The cake should be made the day before you want to serve it.

Serves 10.

FOR THE CRUST

24	**gingersnap biscuits**
3 Tbs	**granulated sugar**
½ cup	**unsalted butter**, melted

FOR THE FILLING

16 oz	**cream cheese**, soft
16 oz	**pumpkin purée** (if canned use unsweetened) (2 cups)
5	**eggs**
¾ cup	**brown sugar**, well packed
½ cup	**Frangelico liqueur**
¾ tsp	**ground cinnamon**
½ tsp	**ground ginger**
¼ tsp	**ground nutmeg**
⅛ tsp	**ground cloves**
1 tsp	**vanilla extract**

FOR THE TOPPING

2 cups	**sour cream**
¼ cup	**granulated sugar**
¼ cup	**Frangelico liqueur**
10	**whole hazelnuts**

1. Preheat the oven to 350° F.

2. Make the crust: Combine the gingersnaps and sugar in the workbowl of your food processor; process until very fine. With the machine running, pour the melted butter down the feed tube; process until the batter is evenly moistened. Pat the mixture into the bottom of a 9" springform pan. Freeze for 20 minutes.

3. In a food processor, electric mixer, or even by hand, blend the cream cheese, pumpkin purée, eggs, sugar, ½ cup Frangelico, cinnamon, ginger, nutmeg, cloves, and vanilla extract until completely smooth. Pour the filling over the crust in the prepared springform pan. Bake in the preheated oven for about 45 minutes, until the surface is starting to brown lightly and the filling is almost set; it should still be somewhat jiggly (it will be cooked some more in Step 4).

3. In a medium bowl whisk together the sour cream, sugar, and ⅓ cup Frangelico. Carefully, pour it over the top of the hot cake. Work from the outside to the centre; spread with a spatula until smooth and evenly distributed. Bake the cake for 10 to 15 minutes longer, until the edges begin to bubble. Remove from the oven, allow to cool completely then refrigerate overnight.

4. Run a small knife around the edge of the cake, then release the springform; it should come off easily. Transfer the cake to a serving platter. You may have to leave it on the base, as the crust is not very strong. Decorate with whole hazelnuts. The cakes tastes best if brought to room temperature before serving; 45 minutes out of the fridge should do it.

CHOCOLATE ALMOND CHEESECAKE (WITH QUARK CHEESE)

A bit lighter than your average cheesecake, and considerably lower in fat.

Serves 10.

FOR THE CRUST

³/₄ cup	**chocolate wafers**
¹/₄ cup	**ground almonds**
3 tsp	**sugar**
3 Tbs	**butter** or **margarine**, melted

FOR THE FILLING

1 lb	**Quark cheese**
¹/₄ cup	**granulated sugar**
4	**eggs**
1 ¹/₂ oz	**Amaretto**
¹/₂ tsp	**almond extract**
3 oz	**semi-sweet chocolate chips** or **carob**
2 Tbs	**cream** or **milk**

FOR THE TOPPING

1 oz	**chocolate** or **carob**
2 Tbs	**butter** or **margarine**
1 Tbs	**Amaretto**
1 cup	**low-fat sour cream**

1. Preheat the oven to 350° F. Butter an 8¹/₂" spirngform pan.

2. Make the crust: Combine the chocolate wafers, almonds, and sugar in the workbowl of your food processor. Pulse until reduced to fine crumbs, then transfer to a bowl. Melt the butter in a small saucepan and pour over the crumbs; mix until the crumbs are moistened, then turn into the prepared springform pan and press evenly over the bottom. Refrigerate while you prepare the filling.

3. Using an electric mixer (or by hand), cream together the Quark, sugar, eggs, amaretto, and almond extract.

4. In a small bowl set over simmering water, melt the chocolate and cream together.

5. Pour the Quark mixture into the springform pan, then pour over the melted chocolate in a spiral pattern. Bake in the preheated oven for approximately 30 minutes, until just about set — it may still be a little loose in the centre. Remove from the oven and cool completely, then refrigerate overnight. *(May be made one day ahead to this point.)*

6. Make the topping: Melt the butter, chocolate, and amaretto in a small bowl set over simmering water. Spread the sour cream on top of the cooled cheesecake, then swirl the melted chocolate on top of the cream.

New York Cheesecake

Makes a 10" cheesecake, serving up to 12.

1¼ cups	**graham cracker crumbs**
2 lbs	**cream cheese**
5 large	**eggs**
1⅓ cups	**sugar**
¼ cup	**lemon juice**
⅓ cup plus 1 Tbs	**all-purpose flour**
½ cup	**whipping cream (35%)**
½ cup	**sour cream**

1. Preheat the oven to 275° F. Butter (or spray with no-stick, if you approve: it works better) the inside of a 10" springform pan. Press a good even layer of graham cracker crumbs onto the bottom.

2. Using an electric mixer fitted with the paddle (or may be done by hand), beat the cream cheese until soft, then add the sugar and beat until light and fluffy. Add the eggs one at a time, then the lemon juice, flour, and cream, and beat well. Pour the filling into the prepared pan.

3. Bake in the preheated oven for 2 to 2½ hours, until set. Remove and allow to cool completely in the pan.

4. Remove the cake from the pan; you may want to leave it on the base as the cake is not that strong.

5. Spread the sour cream over the top and serve with fruit.

FROMAGE BLANC AND QUARK

These are both fresh cheeses (in the sense that they have not been matured for any length of time) made from skimmed milk that has been soured by the addition of a culture. They have a smooth and creamy consistency that belies their low fat content, which is in the 5% to 10% range. Quark originates in Germany, and Fromage Blanc in France, but they are both cottage cheeses made, originally on farms, from surplus milk from which the cream had been skimmed.

FRAMBOISE CHEESECAKE

Great raspberry flavour. Make the cake the day before you plan to serve it.

Serves 10.

FOR THE CRUST

1 cup	**flour**
¼ cup	**white sugar**
½ cup	**butter**

FOR THE FILLING

1 lb	**cream cheese**
¾ cup	**white sugar**
2	**eggs**
1	**egg yolk**
2 Tbs	**framboise liqueur**
1 cup	**Raspberry Purée** (see page 211)
½ cup	**Créme Fraîche** (see page 207) or **sour cream**

FOR DECORATION

a few	**raspberries** **grated rind** of 1 **lemon** (see page 210)

1. Preheat the oven to 350° F. Lightly butter a 8" springform pan (or spray with no-stick if you approve: it does work better).

2. Prepare the crust: Combine the flour and sugar in the workbowl of your food processor and pulse to mix. Roll the butter in flour (it makes it easier to handle), then cut into cubes; distribute them over the flour, then process until the mixture resembles coarse meal. Press the dough into the bottom of the prepared springform pan.

3. Make the filling: Using an electric mixer fitted with the paddle (or may be done by hand), beat the cream cheese with the sugar, eggs, egg yolk, and framboise liqueur until completely combined. Stir in ⅔ cup of the raspberry purée, reserving the rest to swirl in (Step 4).

4. Pour the filling into the pan; then pour over the reserved raspberry purée in a spiral pattern. Bake in the preheated oven for approxmately 30 minutes, or until almost set (it may still jiggle a little in the centre: a little jiggle is OK; a lot is not).

5. Remove from the oven and allow to cool completely, then refrigerate overnight. *(May be made one day ahead to this point.)*

6. Spread the top with créme fraîche (or sour cream) and fresh raspberries.

CRUNCHIE BAR CHEESECAKE

A light-hearted cheesecake with a seriously good taste (how could it fail to have when Crunchies are involved?). Prepare it the day before you plan to serve. (See photograph opposite page 46.)

Serves 8 to 10.

FOR THE CRUST

1¹/₃ cups	**Oreo Cookie crumbs** (about 15 cookies, centres removed — and presumably eaten!)
¹/₃ cup	**melted unsalted butter**
¹/₂ cup	**granulated sugar**

FOR THE FILLING

1 lb	**cream cheese**
3	**eggs**
¹/₂cup	**granulated sugar**
2 tsp	**vanilla extract**
2 Tbs	**lemon juice**
¹/₂ cup	**whipping cream** (35%)
2	**Crunchie Bars**

FOR THE CARAMEL SWIRL

¹/₃ cup	**brown sugar**
¹/₄ cup	**corn syrup**
¹/₄ cup	**unsalted butter** (2 oz)

FOR THE CHOCOLATE SWIRL

¹/₂ cup	**semi-sweet chocolate**
¹/₄ cup	**whipping cream**

FOR THE CHOCOLATE RUFFLE DECORATION

8 oz	**semi-sweet chocolate**

1. Preheat the oven to 325° F. Butter an 8 ¹/₂" springform pan.

2. Prepare the crust: Place the Oreo crumbs in a bowl and pour on the melted butter. Add the sugar and stir to mix well. Press into the bottom of the prepared springform pan.

3. Prepare the filling: Using an electric mixer (or by hand), cream together the cream cheese, eggs, sugar, vanilla, lemon juice, and cream.

4. Chop the Crunchie Bars into medium chunks; set them aside.

5. Make the caramel swirl: Combine the sugar, corn syrup, and butter in a small saucepan, bring to a boil over medium heat, then cook for 1 minute. Remove from the heat and set aside.

6. Make the chocolate swirl: Melt the chocolate and cream in a small saucepan over medium-low heat, stirring constantly, then set aside.

7. Assemble the cheesecake: Pour ¹/₂ the batter in the prepared pan; sprinkle the chopped Crunchie Bars over the top, then pour on ¹/₂ the caramel and ¹/₂ the chocolate, in a spiral pattern. Pour on the rest of the batter, then swirl in the rest of the caramel and chocolate. Bake in the preheated oven for 1 hour; when gently shaken the filling should be set all the way to the centre. Bake a little longer if necessary. Remove from the oven and allow to cool; then refrigerate overnight to set completely.

8. Make the chocolate ruffles: Melt the chocolate in a bowl set over a pan of simmering water, then pour and spread it very thinly over the back of a clean baking sheet. Let the chocolate set, then shave it off with a palette knife or egg lifter so that it comes off in long strips that curl as they are lifted off. The key is to get the chocolate to just the right temperature: too cold and it cracks and flakes off; too warm and the curls collapse and stick together. Trial and error (putting it in the freezer and taking it out) will lead you to the right temperature. It is a bit of an aggravation, but the results are very impresssive.

OREO COOKIE CHEESECAKE

A very succesful cheesecake, maybe even better than eating Oreos just as they are.

Serves 8 to10.

FOR THE CRUST

2½ cups **Oreo Cookie crumbs** (about 25 Oreo cookies, from which you or a small assistant may be obliged to eat the centres, leaving only the cookie part).

2 oz **unsalted butter** (¼ cup), melted

FOR THE FILLING

1½ lbs **cream cheese**, at room temperature

1 cup **granulated sugar**

2 Tbs **all-purpose flour**

4 **large eggs**,

3 **egg yolks**

½ cup **whipping cream** (35%)

1 tsp **vanilla extract**

18 **Oreo cookies**, broken into pieces

¼ cup **granulated sugar**

2 cups **sour cream**

1. Preheat the oven to 425° F. Lightly butter a 9" springform pan.

2. Place the Oreo cookies in the workbowl of your food processor and pulse until reduced to fine crumbs. Transfer to a bowl, add the melted butter, and toss to moisten the crumbs. Press the crumbs evenly over the bottom and two-thirds up the sides of a springform pan. Set in fridge to chill while the filling is made.

3. Using an electric mixer fitted with the paddle (or by hand), beat the cream cheese until smooth. Add the sugar and beat until fluffy. Scrape down the sides, then add the flour and blend well. Add the eggs and yolks, one at a time, and beat briefly between additions. Pour in the whipping cream and vanilla, scrape down the sides, and beat until smooth.

4. Pour half of the batter into the prepared crust. Sprinkle the Oreo crumbs over the top, then pour on the remaining batter and smooth the surface with a spatula.

5. Bake in the preheated oven for 15 minutes, to set the cake; then reduce the temperature to 225° F and bake for 50 minutes longer.

6. Remove the cake from the oven. Turn the temperature up to 350° F.

7. Mix the sour cream and sugar together in a small bowl. Carefully pour the sour cream over the cake and smooth the surface gently. Bake for 10 more minutes, until the sour cream begins to set.

8. Remove from the oven and allow to cool to room temperature; then place in the refrigerator and chill for 3 hours or overnight before removing the springform.

DOUBLE CHOCOLATE CHEESECAKE

Prepare the day before; it needs to be refrigerated overnight.

Makes one 10" cake, serving up to 12 people.

FOR THE CHOCOLATE CRUST

2 cups	**chocolate wafer crumbs**
5 oz	**butter**, melted

FOR THE FILLING

4 oz	**semi-sweet chocolate**
4 oz	**white chocolate**
2 lbs	**cream cheese**
³/₄ cup	**granulated sugar**
2	**eggs**
2	**egg yolks**
1 tsp	**vanilla extract**
³/₄ cup	**whipping cream** (35%)

FOR THE TOPPING

2 cups	**sour cream**
¹/₄ cup	**sugar**

OPTIONAL DECORATION

1 oz	**semi-sweet chocolate**

1. Place the wafer crumbs in a bowl; melt the butter in a small saucepan. Line the bottom and sides of a 10" springform pan with parchment paper. Lightly brush the paper with the melted butter; this helps the crust adhere to the pan. Wrap the outside of the springform pan with tin foil to prevent leaking during baking.

2. Mix the butter into the crumbs until well moistened. Press the chocolate crust into the bottom and up the sides of the springform pan. Set aside.

3. Preheat the oven to 325° F.

4. Place the dark chocolate in a medium bowl that can go over hot water; set over simmering water and heat until melted. Set aside. In a separate bowl melt the white chocolate, then set aside.

5. Using an electric mixer fitted with the paddle (or by hand), beat the cream cheese and sugar together until smooth. Beat in the eggs and yolks one at a time, beating between additions. Mix in the vanilla and cream.

6. Pour half the filling into the melted dark chocolate and mix to incorporate. Pour the other half into the white chocolate and mix.

7. Pour the dark chocolate filling into the prepared crust; gently pour the white chocolate filling on top. Bake in the preheated oven for 1 hour, until the filling is set.

8. While the cake is baking, mix together the sour cream and sugar in a small bowl. *IF NOT DOING THE DECORATION:* As the cake comes out of the oven, pour the sour cream over the top and smooth it out. *FOR THE DECORATION:* Melt the chocolate in a small bowl set over simmering water; remove from the heat and stir in ¹/₄ cup of the sour-cream topping. Pour the 1³/₄ cups of sour cream over the cake as it comes out of the oven, and smooth it over. Make a paper icing cone (see page 63) and fill with the chocolate mixture. Pipe a spiral decoration on top of the cake, taking it all the way out to the

edge. As if cutting a slice, lay the edge of a knife on top of the cake, and draw it about $^3/_8$" towards the centre; the effect is to cut the chocolate lines and curve the cut ends inwards. For the adjacent slice, draw the knife towards the outside edge, pulling the ends outwards. Repeat all the way round the cake.
9. Let the cheesecake cool at room temperature, then refrigerate for 8 hours or overnight.

BLUEBERRY LEMON YOGURT CHEESECAKE

This cake is rich, but the lemon zest makes it seem less so.

Serves 10.

FOR THE GRAHAM CRUST
$^1/_2$ cup	**unsalted butter** (4 oz)
$1^1/_2$ cups	**graham cracker crumbs**
$^1/_4$ cup	**granulated sugar**

FOR THE FILLING
$1^1/_2$lbs	**cream cheese**
$^1/_2$ cup	**granulated sugar**
2	**eggs**
2	**egg yolks**
1 tsp	**vanilla extract**
$^3/_4$ cup	**yogurt**
$^3/_4$ cup	**blueberries**
zest of 1	**lemon**, finely chopped (see page 210)

FOR THE TOPPING
2 cups	**sour cream**
$^3/_4$ cup	**granulated sugar**

FOR THE DECORATION
$^3/_4$ cup	**honey**
$^3/_2$cup	**sliced almonds**

1. Preheat the oven to 325° F. Line the bottom and sides of a 10" springform pan with parchment paper (or lightly butter them if you don't mind serving the cake from the springform base).
2. Melt the butter in a small saucepan and set aside. Combine the graham crumbs and sugar in a small bowl, then pour on the butter and toss to mix. Press the crust into the bottom of the prepared pan. Refrigerate while you prepare the filling.
3. Using an electric mixer (or by hand), cream together the cream cheese and sugar; beat in the eggs and yolks, one at a time, then mix in the vanilla, yogurt, and lemon zest.
4. Place the blueberries into a medium bowl, then pour on half the filling and fold together (see page 128). Pour into the prepared crust.
5. Gently pour in the rest of the filling, and smooth the top. Bake in the preheated oven for 1 hour, until set.
6. While the cake is baking, mix the sour cream and sugar together in a small bowl. As soon as the cake comes out of the oven, pour the topping over the top. Allow to cool at room temperature, then refrigerate for 8 hours or overnight.
7. Release the springform and unmould the cheesecake (if you did not line it with parchment, slide a thin knife around the cake before opening the springform).

PASTRIES

The pastry category includes some of the most glorious desserts of all, from the airy lightness of Napoleons to the opulence of Gâteau Saint-Honoré and the towering *croquembouche*. They are desserts that belong at a party—creations in the grand style, a memory from an earlier day when formal set-pieces were in fashion and a large "corps de cuisine" was on hand to do the work. Today pastries such as these creations are found in traditional pastry shops and in large hotels—and in a few other places that, like our shops, try to combine the best of the old with new creations.

Unfortunately the quality is not always what it might be. These pastries became part of the basic repertoire of any self-respecting pastry cook (and of a good many who had not enough respect, either for their art or their own integrity); over the years, appearance has taken precedence over quality, so that it is not always wise to inquire what a particular pastry is made from: the answer is all too likely to be frozen pastry and commercial filling mixes and icings.

The fact that it is mostly well-staffed kitchens that make these pastries today should not deter you from doing them at home (with a kitchen staff of one, and that includes the dishwasher!). Pastry making is basically a question of assembly; this calls for a certain preciseness and a designer's eye, but it is not hard. The more time-consuming part is getting all the components ready; a Gâteau Saint-Honoré, for example, requires you to have ready puff pastry, choux pastry, and pastry cream, making any one of which is enough to put off some aspiring dessert makers. It is being organized enough get the components ready in good time that is the real challenge in pastry making.

There is no point pretending that making puff pastry, choux pastry, and pastry cream (for example) does not take time; or that your technique in making them will not improve with practice. But I do want to assure you that, if you have the inclination and are prepared to take the time, you can and will produce beautiful pastries, at least as good as you can find in most stores and hotels—and very likely a good deal better, because yours will not be made with commercial mixes or frozen pastry and will have the secret ingredient of tender, loving care—something that is all too often lacking in kitchens where they are forced, for economic reasons, to place productivity ahead of quality.

The key to success is organization; make all the components (or as many of them as can be made ahead) the day before you plan to serve the pastry. Once you and your kitchen have recovered from this work, the task of making the final components (choux pastry, for example, is best made when you need it) and doing the assembly will seem much more manageable, and you will be able to enjoy your work. The rewards are considerable, because few desserts

Opposite: *Fresh Figs in Phyllo (See recipe on page 96.)*

are quite so impressive as a good-looking pastry, particularly to those of your friends who know enough to appreciate what it took to make it.

We have also included some pastries that are simplicity itself to make, such as Figs in Phyllo (see photograph opposite page 78); and others, such as Ginger Pinenut Springrolls, which are definitely not part of the classical tradition. Even if you are not inclined to tackle some of the more intimidating creations at first, you can cut your teeth on these simpler ones.

NAPOLEONS

Puff pastry layered up with pastry cream and fresh berries; a very classic pastry, also called millefeuille (a thousand leaves). In this recipe, there are in fact 2,000 leaves of fine pastry—but don't let that put you off. It is a classic showcase for puff pastry, and is not difficult. The quick puff pastry works particularly well here because it is very light and flaky, and does not puff quite so much as the classic version; but either will do very well.

Make the puff pastry the day before (or longer).

Serves 6 to 8.

½ recipe	**Quick Puff Pastry** (page 216)
1 recipe	**Pastry Cream** (page 222)
⅔ cup	**whipping cream** (35%)
½ pint	**raspberries**
½ pint	**blueberries**
3 oz	**semi-sweet chocolate**, in pieces
1 Tbs	**light corn syrup**
2 oz	**white chocolate**, in pieces
Optional:	**raspberries and blueberries** to serve with it

1. Make the puff pastry following the recipe on page 216; it is best done the day before, to give it time to rest. (Puff pastry freezes well, so make a full recipe and keep the rest for another day.)

2. Make the pastry cream following the recipe on page 222. Cover with plastic wrap and set aside to cool.

3. Preheat the oven to 450° F.

4. Divide the puff pastry into thirds. Roll out each third into a strip 4" wide and ⅛" thick; they will be about 10" long. Trim them so that they are all an even size, lay them on a baking sheet that you have wiped with a damp cloth (this makes the pastry stick lightly to the sheet and hold its rectangular shape), then prick the tops with a fork and chill for 30 minutes.

5. Bake in the preheated oven for 20 minutes until golden brown and nicely puffed. This is one recipe where it is better if the pastry does not puff too much; they should puff to between ½" and ¾" thick. If they are puffing more than this, you can prick them with a fork during baking to deflate them or, when they are almost baked, place a second baking sheet directly on top of them to hold them down (the second method results in a more even puff). Remove from the oven and cool completely.

6. Whip the cream to stiff peaks, then stir 2 Tbs of the pastry cream into it.

7. Set one strip of the puff pastry on a serving platter. Spread ½ the pastry cream over it (about ⅓" thick). Place raspberries evenly on top of the pastry cream. With a palette knife spread, ½ the whipped cream on the underside of the second layer of puff pastry, then place it over the raspberries and press down gently, being careful not to break the pastry. Spread more pastry cream over the pastry, again about $1/3$" thick, and place the blueberries over the top. Spread the rest of the cream on the top of the last layer of puff pastry (it is easier to spread on the chocolate if you have the bottom of this layer of pastry facing up), and place on top of the blueberries and again press down gently. Refrigerate while the topping is made.

8. Combine the semi-sweet chocolate with the corn syrup in a bowl that can go over hot water (or in the top of a double boiler); set it over simmering water, and heat until melted, stirring occasionally. In a separate bowl, melt the white chocolate, stirring carefully until smooth (white chocolate is a lot more temperamental). Cool both chocolates slightly.

9. Remove the Napoleon from the fridge. With a palette knife, spread dark chocolate evenly over the top pastry layer. Fill a small paper cone (see page 63) with the white chocolate. Pipe parallel lines of white chocolate over the dark chocolate, about $1/3$" apart (it doesn't matter which direction). Then draw a toothpick, fine skewer, or the blade of a knife across these lines at right angles, about 1" apart, first in one direction and then the other, creating a feathered effect. Return to the refrigerator for 20 minutes.

10. Let the millefeuille sit at room temperature for 15 minutes before serving. Cut with a serrated knife and serve with more raspberries and blueberries, if you wish.

PUFF PASTRY AND APRICOT SQUARES WITH APRICOT PURÉE

This has the real flavour of dessert from a French patisserie—freshly poached apricots with rich pastry cream and flaky puff pastry.

Serves 8.

½ recipe	**Classic** or **Quick Puff Pastry** (page 214 or 216)
1 recipe	**Pastry Cream** (page 222)
2 Tbs	**Grand Marnier**
24	**apricots**, ripe but still firm
2 cups	**water**
1½ cups	**granulated sugar**
1	**egg**
1 Tbs	**whipping cream**

1. Make the puff pastry, following the recipe on pages 214 or 216; it should be made the day before (or longer; up to 5 days in the fridge; and 3 months if frozen).

2. Make the pastry cream, following the recipe on page 222; cover with plastic wrap and allow to cool.

3. Preheat the oven to 400° F.

4. On a lightly floured work surface, roll the puff pastry out to approximately ³⁄₁₆" thick. Cut the dough into 8 squares (each one about 4" by 4"). Place them on a cookie sheet lined with parchment paper (or on a baking sheet wiped with a damp cloth) and refrigerate for 30 minutes.

5. Combine the water and sugar in a heavy medium sized saucepan. Heat gently until the sugar dissolves, then add the apricots and simmer until the apricots are tender but not mushy—about 15 to 20 minutes. Carefully remove the apricots, using a slotted spoon, reserving the poaching liquid. Set aside the 8 best-looking apricots; halve and pit the others, then purée them in a food processor. If the purée is too thick, add a bit of the poaching liquid to thin it out. Set both the purée and the whole apricots aside. (You do not need the poaching liquid any more; but it will keep, covered, in the fridge for weeks—and can be used to poach other fruit or to soak a cake.)

6. Whisk the egg and the cream together. With the tip of a sharp knife, score a design (anything will do; diagonal lines or diamonds look good) in the top of the puff-pastry rectangles; do not cut too deep—¹⁄₁₆" is fine. Brush them with the egg glaze; then bake in the preheated oven for 10 minutes. Reduce the oven temperature to 375° F and bake for an additional 15 to 20 minutes, until golden brown.

Remove from the oven and cool completely.

7. To assemble: Cut each rectangle in half horizontally and spread some pastry cream over the bottom of each. Halve the good-looking apricots and place 2 halves on top of the pastry cream. Top with the upper half of the pastry rectangle. Place on individual dessert plates and spoon apricot purée around. Serve with a sprig of fresh mint.

CHERRY FRITTERS

Individual cherries in a light batter; a good item for stand-up desserts.

Serves 4 to 6.

FOR THE BATTER

1	**egg yolk**
¹⁄₂ cup	**milk**
¹⁄₂ tsp	**melted butter**
¹⁄₂ cup	**all-purpose flour**
2 Tbs	**icing sugar**
2	**egg whites**
10 oz	**cherries**, pits removed
	vegetable oil for deep frying (see box)
	icing sugar

DEEP FRYING IN OIL
The best temperature for deep frying is between 320° F and 360° F. Clearly the best way to check the temperature is with a thermometer; but if you don't have one, there are two ways to be sure that you are in the right range. (1) When oil reaches frying temperature a blue haze will rise from the surface; as the temperature continues to rise, it will start to smoke; it is now close to burning and will spoil if heated any more. So watch for the blue haze. (2) Cut a cube of day-old bread and drop it into the oil; it should turn golden in about a minute. If it browns faster, the oil is too hot; if it just sits there and looks greasy, it is not hot enough.

1. In a measuring jug or small bowl, beat together the egg yolk, milk, and butter.

2. Sift the icing sugar and flour together into a large bowl; make a well in the centre and pour the egg mixture into it. With a whisk or a large spoon, mix the egg mixture quite vigourously, gradually widening your mixing circle and drawing in more and more of the flour, until it is all incorporated and the batter is completely smooth.

3. Beat the egg whites almost to the firm peak stage (page 24) and fold them into the batter.

4. Heat 3" of oil in a heavy pan to about 365° F (see box).

5. Stick a toothpick into each cherry and dip it in the batter, making sure that it is completely covered.

6. Deep fry a few at a time, being careful not to crowd the pan (if too many are put in at once, the temperature of the oil will drop, and the batter will be greasy).

7. Drain on paper towels; dust with icing sugar and serve immediately.

GINGER AND PINENUT SPRING ROLLS
WITH APRICOT SAUCE

An interesting way to end an Oriental dinner; or a great sweet snack any time.

FOR THE SAUCE

¼ lb	**unsulphured sour Turkish apricots**
2 cups	**water**
2 to 3 Tbs	**granulated sugar** or to taste
¼ tsp	**salt**

FOR THE FILLING

2 Tbs	**crystallized ginger**, finely minced
½ cup	**semolina flour**
2 cups	**milk**
4 Tbs	**sugar**
2 Tbs	**butter**
½ tsp	**vanilla extract**
¼ cup	**toasted pinenuts** (see box)
36	**spring-roll wrappers** (available in Oriental stores)
2 Tbs	**all-purpose flour**
2 Tbs	**water**
	vegetable oil for deep frying (see page 83)

TOASTING PINENUTS
Preheat the oven to 350° F. Spread the pinenuts on a baking sheet and toast in the oven for 5 minutes, or until lightly browned, stirring once so that they brown evenly. Pinenuts have a tendency to burn, so watch them carefully if they need longer than 5 minutes.

---

1. Make the sauce: Place the apricots and water in a saucepan; bring to a boil then reduce the heat to a simmer. Cook for 10 minutes, then remove from the heat and allow to cool.

2. Place the cooked apricots, sugar, and salt in a food processor and blend until smooth. Cover and refrigerate. *(May be prepared 5 days ahead to this point.)*

---

3. In a heavy saucepan, combine the crystallized ginger, semolina, milk, and sugar together. Bring to a boil over high heat, stirring constantly. Reduce the heat to low and cook, still stirring, for 3 to 4 minutes. Remove from the heat and stir in the butter, vanilla, and pinenuts. Scrape into a bowl and cool completely. Cover and store in the refrigerator. *(May be prepared 3 days ahead to this point.)*

---

4. Spinkle a baking sheet lightly with cornstarch. Separate the spring-roll wrappers. Mix the flour and water together to form a paste. Place one wrapper on a flat surface with one of the corners pointing towards you. Place a scant tablespoon of the filling in the middle of the wrapper and spread it out into a log shape, about 3" long. Fold the bottom point tightly over the filling. Fold the side points over the filling. Firmly roll up the spring roll, keeping the ends even, seal with the flour and water paste. (Don't be discouraged by your first attempt: remember to roll firmly and tightly.) Place on the cornstarch-sprinkled sheet. Continue with the remaining wrappers and filling. Cover with damp paper towels and refrigerate. *(May be prepared 1 day ahead to this point.)*

---

5. Pour three inches of oil into a heavy deep pot or frying pan. Heat to 325°F (see page 83). Slip the spring rolls into the oil a few at a time; don't overcrowd the pan. Deep fry until golden brown, then drain on paper towels. Serve hot or at room temperature with the apricot sauce.

6. To reheat: Preheat the oven to 325° F; place the spring rolls directly on the oven rack and bake for 8 to 10 minutes.

APPLE STRUDEL IN PHYLLO

This is a simple way of making strudel, but it produces a good result. It should be made the day before you plan to serve it.

Makes 12 servings.

2 lbs	**tart apples** (e.g., Granny Smith)
2 Tbs	**lemon juice**
³/₄ cup	**granulated sugar**
2 tsp	**ground cinnamon**
¹/₂ cup	**dried currants**
10 sheets	**phyllo**
¹/₂ lb	**unsalted butter**
1¹/₂ cups	**chopped pecans**

1. Peel, quarter, and core the apples, then cut them into slices. Toss them in a bowl with the lemon juice, sugar, cinnamon, and currants. Set aside.

2. Butter a cookie sheet.

3. Lay the phyllo in one corner of your work surface. Cover with plastic wrap and a damp cloth: this prevents them drying out while you work. Melt the butter in a small sauce pan; then set the pan to the side of your work surface; find a pastry brush and put it in the butter.

4. Peel off one sheet of phyllo and lay it down on the work surface. Brush all over with melted butter; then sprinkle 2 Tbs of chopped pecans on top. Lay a second sheet of phyllo over the pecans; brush with butter, then sprinkle another 2 Tbs of pecans over it.

5. Repeat this process until there is only one sheet of phyllo left, and all the pecans have been used up. Take this last layer of phyllo and lay it on top, but do not brush with butter or sprinkle with nuts. Instead arrange the apple slices in a 3" wide strip running top to bottom on the phyllo. Leave a border without apples about 2" along each side, and 1" at top and bottom. Fold over one side flap and both top and bottom flaps onto the apple filling; brush the open flap with the melted butter.

6. Roll up the strudel in a jelly-roll fashion, starting with the long side that has been folded over, and seal it with the open flap that has melted butter on it. Carefully transfer the strudel to the prepared cookie sheet. Brush completely with melted butter, then refrigerate for several hours, or overnight.

7. Preheat the oven to 375° F.

8. Bake the strudel in the preheated oven for 30 minutes, until crisp and golden brown. Serve warm for the best taste.

GATEAU PITHIVIERS

Traditionally this is an Epiphany cake, served on Twelfth Night; our variation includes apples and raspberries in the filling, and is delicious any time.
The pastry should be made the day before (in fact, the whole cake may be made a day ahead, if you wish, and refrigerated; but it should be baked on the day of serving.)

Serves about 10.

1 recipe	**Classic** or **Quick Puff Pastry** (page 214 or 216)

FOR THE FILLING

4 oz	**unsalted butter**
²/₃ cup	**granulated sugar**
1	**egg**
1	**egg yolk**
1 cup	**finely ground almonds**
2 Tbs	**all-purpose flour**
2 Tbs	**rum**
2	**tart apples** (e.g., Granny Smith)

Optional:

½ pint	**raspberries**

FOR THE GLAZE AND DECORATION

1	**egg**
½ tsp	**salt**
	icing sugar
½ cup	**whipping cream** (35%)

1. Make the pastry following the recipe on page 214 or 216. Refrigerate for several hours or overnight.
2. Using an electric mixer (or by hand), cream the butter and sugar until light and fluffy; add the egg and the yolk and beat well. Then stir in the almonds, flour, and rum; set aside.
3. Peel, quarter, and core the apples, then cut them into slices. Set aside.
4. Divide the puff pastry in half. On a lightly floured work surface, roll out one half to a circle about 11" in diameter; then, using a 10" cake pan or tart tin bottom as a guide, cut out a 10" circle with a sharp knife. Wipe a baking sheet with a damp cloth, and transfer the pastry to the centre of the sheet (the moisture makes the pastry stick slightly to the sheet and so hold its shape while baking).
5. Roll out the other half of the pastry to a slightly larger circle, and cut out an 11" circle; this is the lid. Set it aside.
6. Mound the almond filling onto the base, leaving a 1" border all around, and building it up towards the centre. Press the apple slices into the filling around the outside, leaving the centre clear. Fill this area with raspberries, if you are using them; press them slightly into the filling.
7. Beat the egg with the salt to make the glaze, then brush it over the pastry border.
8. Lay the pastry lid carefully over the cake, pressing the two sheets of pastry gently but firmly together all the way around. Scallop the edges with the back of a knife (see page 215); the indentations should be about 2" apart. Cut a small hole right in the centre as a vent, then brush the whole cake with the egg glaze.
9. The traditional decoration for a Pithiviers is a series of curved lines that go from the centre vent to

the edge; each line curves about ¼ the way around the cake. (If you are facing the cake, one line begins at the edge of the vent closest to you, then curves down the side of the cake and to the left, so that it meet the border at the extreme left hand side of the cake.) These lines are scored on the pastry with the tip of a sharp knife, but do not cut through to the filling; they are about ¹/₁₆" deep. Refrigerate the cake for 30 minutes—or longer; (*may be made up to 1 day ahead to this point*).

---

10. Preheat the oven to 425° F.
11. Brush the Pithiviers with left-over egg glaze. Bake in the preheated oven for 20 minutes, then turn the heat down and bake for 10 to 15 minutes longer, until it is puffed and golden brown. Allow to cool a bit, then sprinkle with icing sugar; serve warm with lightly whipped cream.

IS BUTTER BETTER THAN MARGARINE IN BAKING?
Many people no longer eat butter as part of their regular diet, because of concerns about cholesterol. Margarine or other butter substitutes are recommended by doctors and dieticians, not because they contain less fat than butter (they do not: both contain about 8.1% fat, the balance being water, salt, and in the case of margarine, flavourings), but because they are made with oils that promote a lower rate of formation of cholesterol in the bloodstream. Shortenings are used in baking to provide colour, flavour and improved texture. All shortenings made of soft fat will coat the strands of gluten, causing them to slip against each other, and slow down the development of glutens; the finished product will be more tender as a result. There is no reason to prefer butter to margarine in this respect. Since margarine generally has carotene added to make it look like butter, margarines will give much the same colour as butter to your baking. The reason to prefer butter, if there is one, is for its flavour. Some people are more sensitive than others to the flavourings added to margarine to make it taste like butter; if you are happy with this flavour, then you will be happy with the results when you bake with it.

Paris-Brest

A cake named after a train, which, as you might guess, went between Paris and Brest. It is a choux-pastry ring filled with praline-flavoured pastry cream and whipped cream—here with the addition of an orange flavouring. One of the very best of the classic French pastries.

Serves 8.

1 recipe	**Choux Paste** (page 220)
1	**egg**
4 Tbs	**sliced almonds**

FOR THE PRALINE

1 cup	**granulated sugar**
3 Tbs	**water**
1/2 cup	**blanched almonds**
1 recipe	**Pastry Cream** (page 222)
	zest of 2 oranges
2	**oranges**
2 cups	**whipping cream** (35%)
2 Tbs	**granulated sugar**
2 Tbs	**dark rum**

1. Preheat the oven to 400° F. Butter and flour a baking sheet, or line it with parchment paper. Using a cake pan or tart bottom as a guide, draw a 10" diameter circle on the flour or parchment (turn the parchment over so that the cake does not pick up the mark as it cooks).

2. Make the pastry cream, following the recipe on page 222. Cover with plastic wrap and set aside to cool.

3. Make the choux paste, following the recipe on page 220. Scoop the pastry into a pastry bag fitted with a large star or plain tip. Following the circle, pipe a 10" circle onto the baking sheet; then pipe a second circle inside the first, but touching it. Finally, pipe a third circle on top of the first two, in the groove between them.

4. Beat the egg well to make a glaze, then brush the choux-paste rings with the glaze. Sprinkle the sliced almonds on top, pressing if neccessary to make them stick on.

5. Bake in the preheated oven for about 45 minutes, until well browned and nicely puffed up. If it is browning too fast, turn the oven down.

6. Remove from the oven, and turn it off. Make 5 or 6 slits in the cake all around with a skewer or sharp knife; then return the cake to the turned off oven for 10 minutes. Choux paste has to dry out completely in the oven, or it will collapse as it cools. Remove from the oven and allow to cool.

7. While the pastry is baking, make the praline: Lightly oil a cookie sheet. Combine the sugar and water in a small heavy saucepan, and bring to a boil over medium heat, stirring frequently until the sugar has dissolved; then turn up the heat and cook to a golden caramel (see page 11). Quickly add the blanched almonds to the caramel, then turn out onto the oiled pan, and allow to cool completely.

8. When the praline is cool, break it into pieces then grind to a fine powder in a food processor or blender. Set aside about $\frac{1}{3}$ cup of the praline, then fold the rest into the pastry cream.

9. Remove the zest from the oranges (see page 210), then chop if finely. Fold it into the praline cream.

10. Peel the oranges as you would an apple, taking off all the skin and white pith (see recipe for Caramelized Oranges, page 10). Cut them across into thin circles, then the circles in half. Set aside to drain.

11. Whip the cream with the sugar and rum to firm peaks (page 31).

12. To assemble the Paris-Brest: With a serrated knife, cut the pastry ring in half horizontally (so that you have two circles). Try to cut it in such a way that the top and bottom are the same width (i.e., do not cut off the narrower top; cut lower down, close to the base). Spoon or pipe the praline pastry cream into the bottom half. Place the drained orange slices on top, pressing slightly into the cream.

13. Scoop the whipped cream into a pastry bag fitted with a star tip; pipe a layer of cream over the pastry cream, then fit the top of the cake over the bottom.

14. You may pipe rosettes of cream on top of the cake, and sprinkle the reserved praline over them if you wish. Finally dust the cake with icing sugar.

CROQUEMBOUCHE

Literally "Crunch in the mouth"; traditional at New Year in France; but good for a party any time.

Enough for 8 to 10; a bigger one, double or more in size, would be more impressive.

2 recipes **Pastry Cream** (page 222)
1 recipe **Choux Paste** (page 220)
1 **egg**
2 Tbs **water**

FOR THE CARAMEL
1½ cups **granulated sugar**
½ cup **water**

1. Make the double recipe of pastry cream, following the instructions on page 222; cover with plastic wrap and cool completely.

2. Preheat the oven to 400° F. Line a baking sheet with parchment (or butter and flour it if you don't have any).

3. Make the choux paste, following the recipe on page 220. Scoop the dough into a pastry bag fitted with a medium plain tip. Pipe 1" mounds of dough onto the baking sheet, about 2" apart (they need room to puff).

4. Beat the egg with 2 Tbs water to make a glaze, then gently brush the little mounds with it.

5. Bake in the preheated oven for 20 to 30 minutes, until well puffed and golden brown. Remove and turn the oven down to 350° F.

6. Pierce the side of each puff with a skewer or the point of a sharp knife, then return to the oven to dry out the insides for 5 or 10 minutes, until quite firm. Then remove and allow to cool completely.

7. Pierce a hole in the bottom of each puff with the point of a sharp knife; the hole should be large enough to take the piping-bag tip you will use to fill them (Step 8).

8. Scoop the pastry cream (in batches) into a piping bag fitted with a small plain tip, and fill all the puffs through the hole in the bottom. Set them aside.

9. Combine the sugar and water in a heavy-bottom saucepan and bring to a boil over medium heat, swirling the pan frequently until the sugar has melted. Then increase the heat to high and cook the syrup to a medium caramel (see page 11 on cooking a sugar syrup). While the syrup is cooking, fill a pan or sink with cold water. When the syrup is caramelized enough, remove the pan from the heat and dip the base in the pan of water, just until the sizzling stops (this will prevent it cooking any more, and perhaps burning).

10. Assemble the *croquembouche* not more than 4 hours before serving, or the sugar may melt. You can build it up freehand, or on a jig; to make a jig, wrap a medium flower pot in aluminum foil and set it uspide down on the serving plate or cake board. Whichever way you choose, this is construction (for as Carème, arguably the greatest chef of all time, said: "The pastry cook of the present day should possess the skill of the architect"): the puffs are the bricks, and the caramel is your mortar.

11. Set the pan of syrup on an angle, so the syrup flows to one side (this makes dipping the puffs easier). One at a time, dip the base of the puffs in the caramel and stick them to the serving platter in a circle; they should also be stuck to each other. When the bottom row is done, dip the puffs on the sides as well as the bottom, and build a second row on top, angled slightly inwards. Continue like this until you have a tall cone, and all the puffs are used up (with luck these events coincide). If the caramel gets too cool and sticky at any point, just return it to the heat until it reaches the right consistency.

12. To make the final decoration of spun sugar strands around the *croquembouche*, the caramel must be at just the right point. When you dip a fork in and pull it out, it should bring with it a thin strand of sugar that will stretch anywhere you move your fork. You can start just before this stage (i.e., when the sugar is still a bit warm and the caramel no longer drips from the fork in drops but is just able to form a strand). Use your fork to wrap these strands around and around the *croquembouche*, until it is completely encased in spun sugar (or until you run out of caramel, and you think it looks pretty good anyway).

13. Store your *croquembouche* in a cool dry place; the air in the fridge is too moist, and the sugar will melt. In summer it is not easy to find such a place—perhaps that is why the French serve it at New Year!

STRAWBERRY GATEAU SAINT-HONORÉ

People often confuse Gâteau Saint-Honoré with Croquembouche; in fact, they are quite different. The classic Saint-Honoré is a puff-pastry base with choux-pastry sides, filled with a pastry cream lightened with beaten egg whites. Most of the ingredients may be made the day before; in fact, the puff pastry must be, to allow it time to rest.

Serves 6 to 8.

½ recipe	**Classic** or **Quick Puff Pastry** (pages 214 or 216)
1 recipe	**Pastry Cream** (page 222)
1 recipe	**Choux Paste** (page 220)
1	**egg**
2 Tbs	**water**
1 cup	**whipping cream** (35%)
1½ pints	**fresh strawberries**
1 cup	**granulated sugar**
¼ cup	**water**

Optional:

1 Tbs	**Kirsch**

1. Make the puff pastry, following the recipe on page 214 or 216. Wrap it in a plastic bag and refrigerate for several hours or overnight. (*May be made 5 days ahead to this point.*)

2. Make the pastry cream, following the recipe on page 222. Stir in the Kirsch if using, cover with plastic wrap and cool completely, then refrigerate. (*May be made 2 days ahead to this point.*)

3. On a lightly floured surface, roll out the puff pastry to a circle about ¼" thick. Using a plate or a tart tin bottom as a guide, cut out an 8" circle. Transfer carefully to a baking sheet lined with parchment paper, or an unlined sheet wiped with a damp cloth (this helps the cake to hold its shape as it bakes). Prick the pastry all over with a fork and return to the refrigerator.

4. Preheat the oven to 400° F. Line a second baking sheet with parchment, or butter and flour it (this is for the choux-paste puffs).

5. Make the choux paste, following the recipe on page 220, and allow to cool slightly, then scoop into a pastry-bag fitted with a medium plain tip.

6. Beat the egg with the water to form a glaze. Remove the puff-pastry circle from the fridge, and brush the outer ½" of the circle with the glaze. Pipe a ring of choux paste around the perimeter of the puff pastry, on top of the glaze.

7. Pipe about 15 little mounds of choux paste onto the prepared baking sheet; see recipe for Profiteroles (page 94). (If you have a star tip, it makes an attractive finish to use it for the puffs—although changing tips is a messy business if you only have one bag.)

8. Brush the choux-paste circle, and the puffs, with the egg glaze. Bake both the base and the puffs in the preheated oven for 20 to 30 minutes, until golden brown and quite crisp. Remove both trays from the oven, and reduce temperature to 350° F.

9. Pierce a hole in the side of the choux-paste puffs, then return them to the oven for 5 to 10 minutes, to let the insides dry out. Remove and allow to cool completely.

10. With a skewer, make a hole in the base of each puff large enough to accommodate the tip of the piping-bag. Scoop half the pastry cream into the piping bag, and fill all the puffs (12 to 15).

11. Set the gâteau base on a serving platter. Hull and halve the strawberries, reserving 4 large, good-looking ones for decoration. Arrange half the strawberries over the bottom of the base, inside the choux-paste ring. Cover them completely with the remaining pastry cream, then arrange the rest of the strawberries on top.

12. Whip the cream to medium peaks (see page 31). Spread or pipe the cream over the strawberries.

13. Make a caramel to stick the puffs onto the choux-paste ring: In a small heavy-bottom saucepan, combine the sugar and water and bring to a boil over medium heat, brushing down the sides occasionally (see page 11). Then turn up the heat to high and cook to a dark golden caramel. Remove from the heat and cool the base in a sink or bowl of cold water, just until the hissing stops. Allow the caramel to cool slightly, so that it is slightly sticky. Tilt the pan so that the caramel runs to one side, and dip the bottom of each puff in the caramel. Then, set it securely on top of the choux-paste ring. Continue until the perimeter is lined with puffs.

14. Cut the 4 reserved strawberries in half, and arrange them on top of the whipped cream. Then dip a fork into the remaining caramel, and drizzle and spin a caramel cage over the cake (see Step 12 of the Profiteroles recipe for directions).

15. High humidity will melt the caramel (particularly the cage) so a fridge is not the best place to store it. If you have to make the cake ahead, *EITHER* leave off the caramel cage or add the cage two hours or so before serving and leave the dessert in a cool place, but out of the fridge.

PROFITEROLES

An old favourite, and not difficult—although a bit time-consuming (but what that is worthwhile is not?). Serve with ice cream and Raspberry Purée (page 211); or with Chocolate Coffee Sauce (page 223).

Serves 8 (approximately).

2 recipes	**Pastry Cream** (page 222)
1 recipe	**Choux Paste** (page 220)
1	**egg**
1 Tbs	**water**
4 oz	**semi-sweet chocolate**
2 oz	**semi-sweet chocolate**

1. Make the double recipe of pastry cream, following the recipe on page 222; cover with plastic wrap and allow to cool.

2. Preheat the oven to 400° F. Line a baking sheet with parchment (or butter and flour it if you don't have any).

3. Make the choux paste, following the recipe on page 220. Scoop the pastry into a piping bag with a large star tip. Pipe small mounds onto the baking sheet, making them as round and even as possible.

4. Beat the egg with the water to make a glaze, then brush the tops and sides of the choux-paste mounds lightly. Bake in the preheated oven for 25 to 30 minutes, then remove and turn the oven down to 350° F.

5. With a skewer or the point of a sharp knife, pierce a small hole in the side of each puff, then return to the oven and allow to dry out for 10 minutes, until completely firm and dry. Remove from the oven and allow to cool.

6. Cut the Profiteroles in half horizontally with a serrated knife.

FOR PROFITEROLES FILLED WITH BOTH CHOCOLATE-FLAVOURED AND PLAIN PASTRY CREAM : Follow Steps 7 And 8. *IF YOU ARE HAPPY WITH PLAIN PROFITEROLES* : Go straight to Step 9.

7. Place 4 oz chocolate in a bowl that can go over hot water (or in the top of a double boiler); set it over simmering water and heat until melted. Remove from the heat and allow to cool a little.

8. Divide the pastry cream between two bowls. Stir the cooled chocolate into one, and leave the other plain. Scoop the chocolate pastry cream into a piping bag. Pipe the chocolate cream into half the profiterole bottoms, then fit the tops on; pastry-cream filling should be visible between the two halves.

9. Scoop the plain pastry cream into a pastry bag and fill the rest of the profiterole bottoms, then put the lids on.

10. Place the 2 oz chocolate in a bowl that can go over hot water (or in the top of a double boiler); set it over simmering water and heat until melted. Remove from the heat and allow to cool a little. With a fork, drizzle the melted chocolate over the profiteroles.

11. Serve with ice cream and raspberry purée; or with chocolate coffee sauce.

FIGS IN PHYLLO WITH ORANGE BLOSSOM CREME ANGLAISE

Different but very elegant; and very simple to make.
If you use the simple Crème Anglaise method (see page 209), it is best made the day before you plan to serve (see photograph opposite page 78).

Serves 3 or 6, depending on whether you and your guests can eat one or two figs.

1 recipe	**Crème Anglaise** (page 208 or 209)
4 oz	**unsalted butter**
6	**fresh figs**
3 Tbs	**finely ground walnuts**
3 Tbs	**marzipan**
¼ tsp	**cinnamon**
6 sheets	**phyllo pastry**
2 tsp	**orange flower water**

OPTIONAL :

fresh raspberries for decoration

1. Make the crème anglaise, using whichever method you prefer (see pages 208 and 209). Set aside to cool (or refrigerate overnight).

2. Preheat the oven to 325° F. Melt the butter in a small saucepan and set aside in a warm place. Find a baking sheet.

3. Cut each fig in quarters, top to bottom, but not all the way through (just enough that you can open them like a flower).

4. Mash the marzipan with a spoon in a small bowl until soft, then mix in the walnuts and cinnamon. Stuff 1 Tbs of this stuffing into each fig, then gently press together until it looks like a fig again.

5. Lay the phyllo in one corner of your work surface and cover with a damp cloth to prevent it from drying out. Spread one sheet out on the work surface, and brush it with melted butter, then lay a second sheet over the first. Cut them in half the short way, so that you have two rectangles (close to squares).

6. Place a stuffed fig in the centre of each phyllo rectangle and bring the corners up over the fig, as if making a pouch. Press the phyllo together where it meets, to enclose the fig, and brush the outside with melted butter. As you can see from the photograph (opposite page 78), a free-form approach can look quite good, so they do not have to be perfect. Continue until all the figs are bundled up on the baking sheet.

7. Bake in the preheated oven for 15 to 20 minutes, until golden brown. Cool to room temperature before serving.

8. Stir the orange flower water into the crème anglaise.

9. Set one or two figs on each plate, spoon the crème anglaise around, and serve. A few raspberries would not go amiss as garnish.

PIES AND TARTS

A fruit pie, with its crust nicely browned and still warm from the oven, conjures up an image of a country kitchen in the fall, full of sunshine and the smell of leaves. And an open-faced strawberry tart, glistening under its glaze with the yellow pastry cream peeking through here and there, surrounded by a thin layer of delicate pastry, we expect to see in a good French pastry shop or bakery. We do not associate them with our own kitchens (unless they arrived in a nice box wrapped with the store ribbon); or with being able to make them, given the way that most of us live these days.

Quite frankly, our business depends on the fact that most people no longer have the time nor the inclination to bake for themselves, and we would be in deep trouble if suddenly everyone decided to do all the cooking at home. However, we are fairly confident that this is not going to happen, because the vital missing ingredient in most people's lives is time, and no amount of cook books will give you more of that.

The trick is to use the time that you do have well. And making pies and tarts, working with pastry in general, is, if you like the feel and texture of food, a very rewarding way to spend a little of it, precisely because of the associations it has for us of pure natural food in a simpler and slower era when nature was part of daily life. Even if your own past was not exactly like that, the magic of pastry is that it allows you share the collective memory of such a time and believe that it was.

Unfortunately, there are many people who would love to indulge in a bit of bucolic nostalgia, but who will skip this section because of a deep-seated conviction that they cannot make pastry. Just because you have not so far made a pastry that your friends considered edible does not mean that you are condemned to a life of avoiding pastry-based desserts or buying the stuff from the freezer section of your supermarket. With a food processor, anyone who can read, and who wants to do it, can make excellent pastry — and open up for themselves the whole world of desserts (and savouries, for that matter) whose glory lies in the pastry that encases them. And for those who are already accomplished pastry makers, but who have not yet discovered the speed and convenience that a food processor brings, please try some of our pastry recipes. Once you have adjusted to the new technique, you will find that the prospect of making a pie or tart for family or friends is much less daunting than it ever was before, and that you will make one much more often, and on much shorter notice, than you would have in the days when you did all the work by hand.

The aspect of pastry making that has always deterred me (not absolutely; but has certainly decreased the frequency of my baking) is the process of blind baking the pastry shell: lining it with aluminum foil or parchment, filling it with dried beans or weights and baking for 10 or 15 minutes to set the pastry, then removing the weights and paper and baking another 10 minutes to dry it out. In the recipes that follow, we have completely eliminated this process by the very simple technique of thoroughly chilling the pastry-lined tart or pie tin (or freezing it, if you are in a hurry) and then baking it in a hotter oven than normal until the pastry is set. What happens is that chilling the pastry hardens the butter and holds it in the shape of the pie tin; then the hot oven cooks and sets it before the butter has a chance to melt completely — there is no longer any need to support it while it is setting.

It is true that some pastries are easier to work with than others. In general the sweet pastries are the harder work because the large amount of sugar they contain makes them quite sticky; with patience, a very generously floured work surface, and a long, thin-bladed knife to slide under the pastry and release it where it has stuck to the surface you will succeed every time. And the rewards of success are very sweet; for no dessert looks quite so good, or inspires quite so much pleasurable aniticipation in your family and guests, as a well-made pie.

This was a feeling clearly shared by Lord Dudley, who lived and dined in the early years of the nineteenth century. The story is told (by Abraham Hayward in *The Art of Dining,* 1852) that "Lord Dudley could not dine comfortably without an apple pie, as he insisted on calling it, contending that the term 'tart' only applied to open pastry. Dining, when Foreign Secretary, at a grand dinner at Prince Esterhazy's, he was terribly put out on finding that his favourite delicacy was wanting, and kept on muttering pretty audibly, in his absent way: 'God bless my soul! No apple pie.'"

KEY LIME PIE

Not difficult; and it has a wonderfully fresh taste.

1 recipe	**Sweet Pastry** (see page 218)
1 can	**condensed milk**
5	**egg yolks**
¾ cup	**fresh lime juice**, preferably from Key limes

OPTIONAL:

	green food colouring

1. Make the pastry, following the recipe on page 218. Chill for half an hour before rolling out. You will need an 8" or 9" tart pan with a removable bottom.
2. Sprinkle your work surface very generously with flour as this pastry has a tendency to stick. Roll out the pastry in a circle to a thickness of ⅛" to ³⁄₁₆". A long thin knife (or palette knife) is useful to slide beneath the pastry to free the parts that have stuck. Carefully roll the pastry up round your rolling pin, then unroll over the tart pan. It will be delicate and sticky, and will not go into the pan without breaking; but fortunately this pastry is very forgiving. If it falls apart, just patch and press together until the pan is completely lined. Trim the pastry off around the edges and refrigerate the pastry-lined pan for about 30 minutes (or freeze if you are in a hurry).
3. Preheat oven to 375° F. Remove pie shell from fridge and bake in the preheated oven for to 20 to 30 minutes, until golden brown. Remove from the oven and allow to cool. Reduce oven to 350° F.
4. Whisk together condensed milk, egg yolks, lime juice, and food colouring in a bowl. Pour into the prebaked pie shell and bake at 350° F for 15 to 18 minutes. Remove from the oven and cool completely.
5. Cover the top with whipped cream and candied lime zest or with chiffon topping

CHIFFON TOPPING

1½ tsp	**gelatine**
2 Tbs	**cold water**
2	**egg yolks**
½ cup	**granulated sugar**
¼ cup	**fresh lime juice**
1 tsp	**lime zest**, finely grated (see page 210)
2	**egg whites**
½ cup	**whipping cream**

1. Sprinkle the gelatine over the cold water in a small saucepan, and set aside to dissolve. Mix together the egg yolks, sugar, and lime juice in a small stainless-steel bowl. Set the bowl over a pan of simmering water and warm the mixture slightly. Transfer to the bowl of an electric mixer and whip until light and ribbony.
2. Carefully warm the gelatine over a low heat, stirring until melted: add it to the yolks. Whip the whites to stiff, but not dry, peaks (see page 24), and fold them into the yolk mixture (see page 128).
3. In a clean bowl, whip the cream to soft peaks. Fold into the egg-yolk mixture. Pipe or spoon the filling on top of the pie. Chill until completely set.

TARTE TATIN

(UPSIDE-DOWN APPLE TART — see page 101)

There are many versions of the recipe, but this is the one still used at the hotel — and it is also the most reliable.

This recipe is for a 10" or 11" round pan; it will serve 10 people.

FOR THE PASTRY

1¾ cups	**all-purpose flour**
3 Tbs	**granulated sugar**
5 oz	**unsalted butter**, chilled
1	**egg yolk**
4 Tbs	**cold water**

FOR THE APPLE FILLING

4 oz	**unsalted butter**
1 cup	**granulated sugar**
8	medium **apples**

1. Make the pastry: Combine the flour and sugar in the workbowl of your food processor. Pulse once or twice to aerate. Cut the butter into slices about ⅓ " thick, then roll them in the flour and sugar. Cut the floured slices into sticks, then across into cubes. Distribute the cubes over the top of the flour and sugar. Process briefly until the mixture resembles coarse meal; don't overprocess or the pastry will be tough.

2. Beat together the egg yolk and cold water. With the motor running, pour the egg mixture down the feed tube and process until just incorporated. Turn out onto a work surface, and knead just enough to bring the dough together. Wrap in plastic and refrigerate for at least 30 minutes.

3. Preheat the oven to 400° F. Choose a sauté pan or frying pan about 10" across that can go both on top of the stove and into the oven. Set the pan over medium-low heat and put in the butter; when it melts, add the sugar. Shake the pan so that all the sugar is covered with butter, and allow it to cook and start to caramelize (turn golden brown).

4. Peel and core the apples, then cut them into quarters. Have them ready to add to the caramel when it is ready.

5. As the sugar starts to turn colour, watch it carefully. Shake the pan if the browning is not even — you want to reach a deep golden colour, but to avoid burning it (obviously!). When it reaches the right colour, put in the apples; this will stop it colouring any more. They should be quite crowded as they will shrink during cooking. Turn up the heat to medium; after a while turn the apples gently so that they become evenly browned. As the apples cook, their juices start to run and form a syrup with the caramel. Some of this liquid evaporates, but

TARTE TATIN

"La tarte des desmoiselles Tatin" has been famous for over 100 years, ever since the two Tatin sisters opened their hotel in the small town of Lamotte-Beuvron, in the Loire valley not far from Orléans, and started baking this delicious dessert. No one knows if the tart was their own invention (either planned or accidental), or whether it was simply a local dish for which they gathered the credit when they introduced it to a wider public. A collection of Scottish recipes includes one for a very similar tart, named after a village not far from Lamotte-Beuvron. Whatever its origins, it is an excellent apple tart; the caramelized butter and sugar permeates the apples; and the crust stays crisp because it is baked on top of the apples, and only turned the right way up – or upside down, depending on your point of view – just before serving.

more is absorbed by the apples. Continue to cook over medium heat for about 20 minutes; the juice will become quite syrupy, but not all of it will be absorbed. The apples should be soft, but still retain their shape. You may find that it takes a little longer to reduce the apples to this stage. Remove the pan from the heat and set aside.

6. Roll the pastry into a circle a little larger than the pan, and about $^1/_8$" to $^3/_{16}$" thick. Roll up the pastry round your rolling pin and unroll it over the cooled apples. Trim the edges, cut a few slits to allow steam to escape, then bake in the middle of the preheated oven for about 30 minutes. Have a look at the pastry after 20 minutes; if it is getting too brown, drape a piece of foil loosely over it. Remove from the oven and allow to cool.

7. Tarte Tatin is best eaten within 4 hours of baking; it should be served warm — or, at least, not refrigerated. If you can, leave it in the pan until ready to serve. To unmould, set a serving plate over the pan, then flip pan and plate over. The tart should come out without sticking, which it almost certainly will do if it is still warm. If it has become cold, reheat gently over low heat or in a warm oven, then unmould. Serve with lightly whipped cream.

TART LEMON TART

A good lemon tart is hard to find; one that is good and easy to make, harder still. This one satisfies both requirements.

For one 8" or 9" tart, serving 6 people.

1 recipe	**Sweet Pastry** (see page 218)

FOR THE FILLING

³/₄ cup	**granulated sugar**
2 oz	**unsalted butter**
4	**eggs**
zest of 1	**lemon**
³/₄ cup	**lemon juice** (juice of about 4 lemons)
¹/₄ cup	**orange juice**

FOR THE OPTIONAL DECORATION

1	**lemon** cut into thin rounds
¹/₂ cup	**water**
¹/₂ cup	**sugar**
¹/₄ cup	**icing sugar**

1. Make the pastry following the recipe. Chill for at least ¹/₂ hour before using. You will need an 8" or 9" tart pan with a removable bottom.

2. Sprinkle your work surface very generously with flour as this pastry has a tendency to stick (because of all the sugar in it). Roll out the pastry in a circle to a thickness of ¹/₈" to ³/₁₆". A long thin knife (or palette knife) is useful to slide beneath the pastry to free the parts that have stuck. Carefully roll it up round your rolling pin, then unroll over a 8" or 9" tart pan with a removable bottom. It will be delicate and sticky, and will not go into the pan without breaking; but fortunately this pastry is very forgiving. If there are holes, or it falls apart, just patch and press together until the pan is completely lined. Trim the pastry off around the edges and refrigerate the pastry-lined pan for about 30 minutes (or freeze if you are in a hurry).

3. Preheat the oven to 375° F.

4. Prepare the filling: Cream together the soft butter and the sugar until light and fluffy. Add the eggs one at a time, beating before adding the next; then add the lemon zest and beat again. Now pour in the lemon and orange juices and beat so that they are thoroughly incorporated. Set aside.

5. Set the cold pastry-lined tart pan in the centre of the preheated oven and bake for 15 minutes. Remove, and set aside to cool. Turn the oven down to 325 °F.

6. When the tart has cooled a little, check that there are no holes in the shell. If there are, use left-over scraps of pastry to seal them. Beat the filling again so that it is smooth and pour it into the tart shell. Carefully transfer to the hot oven and bake for 25 to 30 minutes, or until the filling is set. If the top is browning too much, cover loosely with aluminum foil. Remove from the oven, allow to cool a little, then add the lemon decoration if you wish.

7. For the decoration: While the tart is baking, slice a lemon carefully into thin rounds. Bring ½ cup of water and ½ cup of sugar to a boil in a small saucepan, and add the lemon slices. Simmer gently for 10 minutes, then remove from the heat and allow to cool in the syrup. When the tart has cooled a little, carefully arrange the lemon slices around the edge of the tart, so that each serving will have a lemon slice on it when it is cut. Put the icing sugar in a small sieve and sprinkle it over the top of the tart. It will stay on most of the tart, but melt on the lemon slices so that they show through.

MERINGUES

Meringues are made of beaten egg whites and sugar, and are then usually baked. The amount of sugar added to the beaten whites, and whether the sugar is plain or cooked, determine the type of meringue.

MERINGUE TOPPINGS for Lemon Meringue Pie (page 104) or Baked Alaska (page 144) are made with the least amount of sugar, generally about 2 Tbs per egg white. Beat the egg whites to Stage 2 (page 24), then gradually start adding the sugar until the meringue is shiny and reaches the soft-peak stage. Spread the meringue over the pie, smoothing the top gently. Bake in a 350° F oven for about 15 minutes (5 to 8 minutes at 500° F for Baked Alaska, but this is exceptional).

HARD MERINGUES for tortes and meringue cakes use twice as much sugar as soft meringues, about 4 Tbs per egg white. This is a large amount of sugar for the egg whites to absorb, and an acid stabilizer, such as lemon juice or vinegar, is often added to assist the process. Again, beat the whites to Stage 2, add the stabilizer, then gradually start to add the sugar, until it is all absorbed and the meringue is glossy and quite stiff. If traces of sugar granules remain, add a little water and beat some more to melt the undissolved sugar — you can add up to 1 Tbs of water per egg white.

FRENCH MERINGUE is a type of hard meringue, in that it uses the same 4 Tbs of sugar per egg white, with the difference that the sugar is not beaten in gradually, but added all at once after the egg whites have been beaten to stiff peaks and then folded in gently. The end product has a slightly soft inside, but a crisp outside, and it makes a much better eating meringue than the hard meringue used for tortes.

All of the above types of meringue are baked in the oven after the sugar has been added. The cooking of ITALIAN MERINGUE is accomplished by adding a hot sugar syrup to the beaten egg whites. Afterwards it may be browned in the oven to improve the appearance, but this is not necessary (see page 104 for the recipe for Italian Meringue)

LEMON MERINGUE PIE

This takes the "Tart Lemon Tart" one step further, with the addition of a meringue topping; you can make either the simple meringue, or the more challenging, but richer, and more stable, Italian meringue if you have an electric mixer.

1 recipe	**Tart Lemon Tart** (see page 102)

FOR THE MERINGUE TOPPING

4	**egg whites**
⅓ cup	**granulated sugar**

FOR THE ITALIAN MERINGUE

4	**egg whites**
2 Tbs	**granulated sugar**
1 cup	**granulated sugar**
¼ cup	**water**

1. Make the tart lemon tart following the recipe (page102) to the middle of Step 6. The tart should be fully baked. Remove from the oven while you make the meringue. Turn the oven to 350° F.

2. For the regular meringue topping: Beat the egg whites until white and foamy; add 2 tablespoons of sugar and beat some more. Beat to the firm-peak stage (see page 24), gradually adding the rest of the sugar; the meringue will be thick and glossy, and all the sugar granules should have dissolved. Spread the meringue over the pie (which should still be warm — see page 105), piling it up so that it looks like a real lemon meringue pie. Set in the centre of the preheated oven and bake for 15 minutes, until golden brown. Remove and allow to cool.

3. To make the Italian meringue: Using an electric mixer, beat the egg whites until white and foamy, add 2 Tbs sugar then continue beating to firm peaks (see page 24). Make a sugar syrup: Combine the sugar and water in a heavy-bottom saucepan, bring to a boil (see page 11) and continue to cook until the water has evaporated (the surface will be covered with bubbles). Continue to cook, bringing the syrup to the hard-ball stage (260° F on a sugar thermometer; or see page 11 for ways to test without a thermometer). Immediately remove from the heat, turn on the mixer with the beaten egg whites, and pour the syrup in a thin stream into the whites. The hot syrup will cook the whites and form an indestructible, firm white meringue. Continue to beat after all the syrup has been added, until the meringue has cooled to room temperature. You may pipe or spread this meringue onto the pie, then return to the centre of a 450° F oven and cook for 10 minutes, until golden brown. (You can brown it under the broiler.)

HOW TO AVOID A WEEPY AND A SLIPPY MERINGUE

There are two kinds of weeping that you may notice on a less-than-perfect meringue. If the sugar has not completely dissolved in the egg whites, the sugar granules will melt during baking, and beads of syrup will form on the surface. To prevent this, add the sugar gradually, and continue to beat the meringue until all the sugar has dissolved.

The second, and more serious, kind of weeping is caused by moisture draining out of the meringue as it bakes, and collecting between the filling and the meringue. The solution to this is to beat the meringue thoroughly, and to make sure that the meringue is fully baked. If the problem persists, you can take the belt-and-braces approach, and beat some cornstarch ($\frac{1}{2}$ tsp per egg white) into the meringue at the very end.

The problem of the slipping topping is also caused by moisture between the meringue and the filling. The things suggested to prevent weeping will help here, and there are two other ways to deal with it. As you spread the meringue over the pie, make sure that you push it into any indentations or cracks in the pie-crust, to lock it in position. Meringue will also slip much less if it is spread onto a hot pie filling; this cooks the underside of the meringue, and reduces weeping.

WALNUT TART

A good and simple nut tart. Serve warm, with cold lightly whipped cream.

1 recipe	**Sweet Pastry** (see page 218)
$\frac{1}{2}$ lb	**unsalted butter**
1$\frac{1}{2}$ cups	**firmly packed brown sugar**
4 large	**eggs**
2 tsp	**vanilla extract**
pinch of	**salt**
$\frac{3}{4}$ cup	**walnuts**, whole or chopped

1. Make the pastry, following the recipe on page 218. Proceed to the point where you have a 9" pie pan lined with pastry chilling in the fridge.

2. Preheat oven to 350° F. Cream together the butter and sugar (either by hand, or using an electric mixer), then add the eggs, one at a time, beating between each addition. Add the vanilla and salt then stir in the walnuts.

3. Remove the cold pastry shell from the fridge and pour in the filling. Bake in the centre of the preheated oven for 1 hour and 15 minutes or until set. Remove and allow to cool

4. Serve warm with whipped cream.

Pumpkin Pecan Pie

Depending on how the pecans are arranged, either in neat concentric circles or more abstractly, this can be either a formal or an informal dessert.

1 recipe	**Sweet** or **Flaky Pastry**(see page 218 or 219)
2½ cups	**pecan halves**
¼ cup plus 2 Tbs	**light brown sugar**
3½ Tbs	**unsalted butter**, melted
1½ cups	**unsweetened pumpkin purée**
1½ tsp	**ground ginger**
½ tsp	**ground cinnamon**
½ tsp	**ground allspice**
3 large	**eggs**
⅓ cup	**molasses**
2 tsp	**granulated sugar**
1 cup	**sour cream**
⅓ cup	**whipping cream** (35%)

1. Make pastry following the recipe on page 218 or 219. Refrigerate for at least an hour. Flour your work surface generously (sweet pastry tends to stick because of the high sugar content). Roll out to a thickness of ¼" to ³⁄₁₆" and about 12" diameter, turning it frequently to prevent sticking. Now, roll the pastry up around your rolling pin (slide a long, thin knife under it first to loosen it from the surface); then unroll over a 10" tart shell with a removable bottom. Gently press the pastry into the shell, then trim off the excess around the top. Press in scraps to fill any holes. Refrigerate for 30 minutes (or freeze for 10) while you prepare the filling.

2. Preheat the oven to 350° F.

3. In a bowl, toss the pecan halves with the brown sugar. Pour over the melted butter and toss again to ensure even coating. Set aside.

4. In a large bowl, whisk together the pumpkin purée, ginger, cinnamon, and allspice; then whisk in the eggs one at a time. Add the molasses, sugar, sour cream, and whipping cream, and whisk until blended. Pour into the chilled tart shell, and bake in the middle of the preheated oven for 30 minutes.

5. Remove the tart from oven: it will not yet be completely set so you must work gently to avoid puncturing the filling. Arrange the pecan halves in tight concentric circles, covering the entire surface. (Alternatively, you can simply sprinkle them on top in a more haphazard manner.) Return to the oven and bake for an additional 30 minutes, until the top is brown and crusty. Remove and allow to cool completely.

6. Serve on its own or with lightly whipped cream. A warm tart with cold whipped cream is a great combination.

LINZER CHERRY PIE

The name comes from the European type of pastry, and the traditional lattice-work decoration; but the filling is pure North American cherry pie.

FOR THE PASTRY

2 cups	**all-purpose flour**
1 tsp	**cinnamon**
½ cup	**sugar**
1 cup	**ground almonds**
7 oz	**butter**, chilled
1 large	**egg**

FOR THE FILLING

2 lbs	**fresh dark cherries**, stones removed
⅓ cup	**sugar**
1 cup	**water**
2 tbs	**kirsch**
1 tbs	**corn starch**
1	**egg white**, beaten

1. To make the pastry: Combine the flour, cinnamon, sugar, and almonds in the workbowl of your food processor. Pulse once or twice to aerate. Cut chilled butter into slices, roll in flour, then cut into sticks, and then into cubes (rolling in flour makes them easier to handle). Distribute the cubes over the flour in the food processor, then process briefly until the mixture resembles coarse meal: do not overprocess. With the motor running, drop the egg down the feel tube and process again just enough to mix it in. Turn the dough out onto your work surface and knead to bring it all together.

2. Divide the dough into two parts, one with ⅔ of the mixture and the other with ⅓. Roll out the larger between 2 pieces of parchment (or waxed) paper into a circle large enough to line a pie dish, then refrigerate. Wrap the other lump of dough in plastic and refrigerate as well.

3. Combine the pitted cherries, sugar, and water in a saucepan. Bring to a boil and simmer for 10 minutes. In a small bowl, mix together the kirsch and corn flour until smooth, add to cherries and boil for 1 minute more. Remove from heat and allow to cool.

4. Preheat the oven to 375° F. Remove the rolled out pastry from the fridge and lay it in the pie dish (without the paper), but do not trim off the edges.

5. Beat the egg white in a small bowl until white and frothy, then brush the inside of the pastry shell with it. Pour the cherry filling into the shell.

6. Remove the other pastry from the fridge and roll out to a rectangle. With a pastry cutter if you have one, or with a knife, cut the pastry into ½" to ¾" strips to make a lattice over the top. Seal the edges where the pieces of pastry join with more egg white. Trim off any excess.

7. Bake the pie in the centre of the preheated oven for 15 minutes, then turn down the heat to 325° F and coook for 40 minutes longer. Remove from the oven and allow to cool.

8. Serve warm (or at room temperature) with whipped cream.

Sweet Potato Pie — No. 1

A little more time-consuming than pie No.2, and a bit lighter because the egg whites are beaten before being folded in; but still delicious.

Serves 6.

1 recipe	**Sweet Pastry** (see page 218)

FOR THE FILLING

2 lbs	**sweet potatoes**, peeled and cut into 1" cubes
1 cup	**unsalted butter**, softened (8 oz)
3	**egg yolks**
$^1/_3$ cup	**corn syrup**
$^1/_2$ cup	**whipping cream**
1 tsp	**vanilla extract**
$^1/_2$ tsp	**salt**
3	**egg whites**

TO SERVE

$^1/_4$ cup	**whipping cream**

Optional:

3 Tbs	**bourbon**

1. Make the pastry, following the recipe on page 218. Chill for at least $^1/_2$ hour before using. You will need an 8" or 9" tart pan with a removable bottom.

2. Sprinkle your work surface very generously with flour as this pastry has a tendency to stick . Roll out the pastry in a circle to a thickness of $^1/_8$" to $^1/_{16}$". A long, thin knife (or palette knife) is useful to slide beneath the pastry to free the parts that have stuck. Carefully roll the pastry up round your rolling pin, then unroll over the tart pan. It will be delicate and sticky, and will not go into the pan without breaking; but fortunately this pastry is very forgiving. If there are holes, or it falls apart, just patch and press together until the pan is completely lined. Trim the pastry off around the edges and refrigerate the pastry-lined pan for about 30 minutes (or freeze if you are in a hurry).

3. Preheat the oven to 375° F. Bring a large pot of water to a boil on top of the stove, put in the sweet-potato cubes and cook until tender to the fork — about 20 minutes. Drain, then mash the sweet potatoes, either pressing them through a fine sieve while still warm or puréeing them in your food processor.

4. Beat in the butter into the potatoes until totally incorporated — again either by hand or in the processor. Beat in the brown sugar, then the egg yolks. Stir in the corn syrup, whipping cream, vanilla, and salt.

5. Transfer the chilled pie shell to the centre of the preheated oven and bake for 20 minutes, until pale golden brown. Remove from the oven, allow to cool, then check that there are no holes in the pastry; if there are, use scraps of left-over pastry to plug them up. Turn the oven down to 350° F.

6. Beat the egg whites until stiff, but not dry (see page 24), and fold into the sweet-potato mixture. Pour gently onto the baked pie shell, gently smoothing out the top. Bake for 40 minutes, then remove. The centre will still be jiggly. Let the pie set for 1 hour on a cooling rack before cutting. Serve with lightly sweetened whipped cream to which you've added some bourbon, if you like the taste.

Sweet Potato Pie — No. 2

Quick, easy, and delicious.

Serves 6.

1 recipe	**Sweet Shortcrust Pastry** (see page 221)

FOR THE FILLING

1½ cups	**whipping cream** (35%)
1 cup	**brown sugar**
½ tsp	**salt**
1 tsp	**cinnamon**
½ tsp	**nutmeg**
2 large	**eggs**
14 oz can	**sweet potato purée**

TO SERVE

³⁄₄ cup	**whipping cream** (35%)

Optional: **chopped pecans**

1. Make the pastry following the recipe on page 221, then refrigerate for at least 1 hour. Remove from the fridge and roll out the pastry to a circle large enough to line a pie dish. Trim the edges flush with the side of the pie dish, then set the lined dish in the fridge to chill completely.

2. Rinse out a heavy-bottom saucepan with cold water, but do not dry. Pour in the cream and heat over medium heat to just below boiling. Remove from the heat and set aside.

3. Beat together the brown sugar, salt, cinnamon, nutmeg, eggs, and sweet-potato purée, then blend in the cream and mix well. Allow to cool to room temperature.

4. Preheat the oven to 425° F. Pour the filling into chilled tart shell, and bake in the middle of the oven for 20 minutes. Then reduce the heat to 350° F and bake for another 25 minutes. Remove from the oven and allow to cool.

6. Serve with whipped cream and chopped pecans.

APPLE AND CREME FRAICHE TART

From Normandy where orchards and cows grow side by side comes this delicious combination of apples and crème fraîche.

1 recipe	**Sweet Pastry** (see page 218)
5	**tart apples**, peeled, quartered, and cored
½ cup	**granulated sugar**
½ cup	**Crème Fraîche** (see page 207) (or ½ cup **whipping cream** plus 2 Tbs **sour cream**)
2 large	**eggs**, room temperature
¾ cup	**ground almonds**

1. Make pastry as described in the recipe on page 218. After chilling, roll out the dough on a lightly floured surface to a 9" circle. Gently fit into an 8" tart shell with a removable bottom. Patch and press with scraps of pastry to fill any holes as necessary. Chill for 30 minutes.

2. Preheat oven to 375° F. Slice the apples more or less evenly. In a small bowl, whisk together the sugar, crème fraîche, eggs, and ground almonds. Arrange the apples in the chilled (unbaked) tart shell. Pour the filling mixture over apples.

3. Bake in the preheated oven for 30 to 35 minutes, until the pastry is golden and the filling has puffed and browned slightly. Serve warm for the best flavour.

RASPBERRY AND BLUEBERRY CREME FRAICHE TART

Not exactly traditional, but really good none the less.

1 recipe	**Apple and Crème Fraîche Tart** (see above)

Replace apples and almonds with 1 pint fresh blueberries and 1 pint fresh raspberries.

Opposite: *Fresh Strawberry Tart (see recipe on page111).*

Strawberry and Fresh Fig Tart with Caramel Pastry Cream

An unusual and interesting variation on the traditional fresh-fruit tart.

Serves 6 to 9.

1 recipe	**Sweet Shortcrust Pastry** (see page 221)
1 recipe	**Caramel Pastry Cream** (see page 223)
1 pint	**fresh strawberries**, hulled
2 or 3	**fresh figs**, stemmed

FOR THE GLAZE

4 Tbs	**apricot jam**
2 Tbs	**water**

1. Prepare the shortcrust pastry, following the recipe on page 221. When the dough has rested, knead together small pieces of dough with your fingers and press them onto the bottom and sides of a 9" tart pan with a removable bottom. Try to make the thickness of the dough as even as possible. Trim off the edge to make it level. Chill for 30 minutes.

2. Prepare the pastry cream, following the recipe on page 223. Allow to cool.

3. Preheat the oven to 375° F. Prick the bottom of the chilled tart with the tines of a fork. Bake in the centre of the preheated oven until golden brown (about 20 to 30 minutes). Remove from the oven and cool completely.

4. Gently remove the pastry crust from the pan. Spoon or pipe the pastry cream into the shell: it should be about 1/2" deep. Cut the figs into quarters (or eighths if they are large) and arrange around the edge of the tart. Cut the strawberries in half from top to bottom and lay them point-end up, overlapping one another all the way to the centre.

5. Boil the apricot jam and water together until the glaze becomes thick and sticky — it should drop in sticky drips from the spoon, not in a thin stream. Spoon or brush the glaze over the fruit.

Fresh Strawberry Tart

This is the tart in the cover photograph and opposite page 110.

1 recipe	**Strawberry and Fresh Fig Tart** (see above)
OPTIONAL: SUBSTITUTE	**Vanilla Pastry Cream** (see page 222) for the Caramel Pastry Cream
LEAVE OUT:	**Figs**
INCREASE:	**Strawberries** to 2 pints

1. Follow the recipe for Strawberry and Fresh Fig Tart, using the Vanilla Pastry Cream if you wish. Decorate the tart with the strawberries, following the pattern in the photograph.

COCONUT CREAM PIE

The way desserts used to taste — rich, sinful, and really good.

1 recipe	**Sweet Pastry** or **Sweet Shortcrust Pastry** (see page 218 or 221)
1½ cups	**shredded unsweetened coconut**
2½ cups	**milk**
4	**egg yolks**
½ cup	**granulated sugar**
2 Tbs	**all-purpose flour**
⅛ tsp	**salt**
2 tsp	**gelatine**
½ tsp	**vanilla extract**
1½ cups	**whipping cream**

FOR THE TOPPING

1 cup	**whipping cream**
1 Tbs	**icing sugar**
3 Tbs	**shredded unsweetened coconut**, toasted
3 Tbs	**shredded unsweetened coconut**

1. Prepare the pastry, following the recipe on page 218 or 221. The sweet pastry will give a sweeter crust; the shortcrust a shorter and slightly ligher one: the choice is yours. Follow the recipe to the point where you have a fully baked pie shell. Set it aside to cool.

2. Rinse out a heavy saucepan with water, but do not dry (this helps to prevent the milk solids sticking on the bottom of the pan). Pour in the milk and coconut and bring to a boil, stirring occasionally. Take off the heat and set aside until cool.

3. Using an electric mixer if you have one (or by hand), beat the egg yolks well. Gradually add ½ cup sugar and beat until thick and lemon-coloured. Then beat in the flour, salt, and gelatine.

4. Place the cooled coconut-milk mixture in a blender or food processor. Blend until the coconut is finely chopped. Pour the mixture through a sieve lined with a double thickness of cheesecloth. Gather up the cheesecloth and squeeze hard to extract all the milk from the coconut. If you don't have cheesecloth, just press hard with the back of a spoon to squeeze out all the liquid. Measure out 2 cups of milk; add more milk to make it up if necessary.

5. Rinse out a heavy saucepan with water again, pour in the coconut milk and bring to a boil over medium heat. Remove from the heat and pour in a thin stream into the egg-yolk mixture, whisking all the time. Make sure that the bottom of the saucepan is clean (wash out if necessary) and pour the mixture back into the pan.

6. Place over medium-low heat (see pastry cream method on page 222), stirring constantly with a rubber scraper until the mixture just comes to a boil. Remove from the heat and scrape into a bowl. Place the bowl in a large basin filled with cold water (make sure the bowl can still rest on the bottom of the basin — I find that the sink is the most convenient thing to use), whisking occasionally until completely cool. The mixture will be thick like pudding. Stir in the vanilla.

7. Beat $1\frac{1}{2}$ cups whipping cream in a chilled bowl with chilled beaters until it forms soft peaks (the colder it is the easier to whip). Fold it carefully into the cooled coconut mixture. Pour into the baked pie shell and smooth the top. Chill for 2 hours.

8. When ready to serve, beat 1 cup whipping cream with the icing sugar until it forms soft peaks. Spread over the top of the pie, and sprinkle the two coconuts over as decoration. Serve.

CHOCOLATE WALNUT CARAMEL TART

This is a completely delicious tart, very rich and dense — which is just as well because it takes a fair amount of work. None of it is terribly difficult, but it does require care, particularly in cooking the caramel cream and in spreading the chocolate icing.

Serves 8 to 10.

FOR THE SWEET PASTRY

2 cups	**cake flour**, sifted
$\frac{1}{4}$cup	**granulated sugar**
$\frac{1}{2}$ cup	**unsalted butter**, chilled
1 large	**egg yolk**, room temperature
1 tbs	**whipping cream**

FOR THE FILLING

$\frac{1}{4}$ cup	**water**
1 cup	**granulated sugar**
1 cup	**whipping cream**
2 cups	**walnuts**, chopped
$3\frac{1}{2}$ oz)	**unsalted butter**, in pieces
1	**egg yolk**
2 tsp	**water**

FOR THE CHOCOLATE ICING

4 oz	**semi-sweet chocolate**
$\frac{1}{4}$ cup	**whipping cream**
2 Tbs	**unsalted butter**

FOR DECORATION

10	**walnut halves**

1. First make the pastry: Combine the flour and sugar in the workbowl of your food processor fitted with the steel blade. Pulse once or twice to aerate. Cut the chilled butter into slices, then roll them in flour (it makes them easier to handle), then cut the slices into sticks and, finally, into cubes. Distribute these over the flour and process briefly until the mixture resembles coarse meal. Combine the egg yolk with the cream. With the machine running, add the egg/cream through the feed tube and process just until dough starts to come together. Be careful not to overprocess. Turn the dough out onto your work surface and divide into two parts, one slightly larger than the other. Flatten slightly, cover with plastic wrap, and refrigerate for 1 hour.

2. Combine the sugar and water in a heavy-bottom saucepan. Cook over medium heat until the sugar has dissolved, then increase the heat and boil until sugar has caramelized to a light golden colour (see page 11). Remove the pan from the heat, and slowly pour in the cream, being careful to avert your face. Stir in the walnuts and the butter. Return the saucepan to the heat and continue cooking over high heat, stirring constantly until the syrup is reduced and a deep caramel colour. This will take about 15 minutes. The point you want to reach is where all the water has evaporated; the best way to judge is when the surface is covered with bubbles and the liquid falls from the spoon in a very sticky stream. Remove from the heat, pour into a clear bowl, and cool to room temperature.

3. Remove the larger disc of pastry from the refrigerator. On a lightly floured surface, roll the dough out to $\frac{1}{8}$" thickness. Press into a 9" tart pan with a removable bottom; use scraps to fill any holes that appear. Chill for 20 minutes.

4. Preheat the oven to 375° F. When the caramel is

completly cool, mix the egg yolk with 2 tsp water.
Remove the tart shell from the refrigerator and
brush egg wash around the top edge (to seal on the
top pastry). Carefully fill the shell with the
caramelized walnut mixture: it should be flat across
the top.

5. On a lightly floured surface, roll out the smaller
pastry disc to $1/8''$ thickness and about 9" wide.
Gently place this over the tart shell and pinch top
and bottom crust together. Trim the edge. Bake in
the centre of the preheated oven for 40 minutes,
until crust turns a golden brown. Remove from the
oven and cool completely.

6. To make the topping: Melt the chocolate, cream,
and butter in a bowl set over simmering, but not
boiling, water. Stir until smooth.

7. Carefuly invert the cooled tart onto a serving
platter. With a palette knife (or any knife with a long
flexible blade) spread the chocolate ganache over
the top. This is easier said than done, but with
patience and a passion for perfection you can do it.
Set a walnut half at the outer edge of each slice.

FUDGE TRUFFLE TART

Makes one 11" tart, serving 8 to 10 people.

1 recipe	**Chocolate Pastry** (see page 214)
1 cup	**unsalted butter**
¼ cup	**very strong coffee**
9 oz	**semi-sweet chocolate**, finely chopped
1¾ cup	**granulated sugar**
½ tsp	**salt**
6 large	**egg yolks**, room temperature
2 tbs	**brandy**
¾ cup	**whipping cream**

1. Preheat the oven to 350° F. Make chocolate pastry, following the recipe on page 214. After it has rested for 30 minutes, knead together small pieces of dough with your fingers and press them onto the sides and bottom of an 11" tart pan with a removable bottom. Try to make the pastry an even thickness. Chill 30 minutes. Prick the base with a fork, then bake in the preheated oven for 15 to 20 minutes, until the pastry has set and dried out. Cool completely.

2. Combine the butter and coffee in a small saucepan and bring to a boil. Place the chocolate and sugar in a bowl, pour over the hot butter mixture, and whisk vigorously until melted and smooth. If all the chocolate has not melted, place the bowl over a pot of simmering water and whisk until it does. Add the egg yolks and brandy, and whisk until smooth. Allow to cool to room temperature.

3. Set aside ½ cup of the mixture in the fridge until it is thick enough to pipe. Spread half of the remaining chocolate mixture over the bottom of the chocolate pastry shell.

4. Whip the cream to soft peaks (see page 31) and fold it into the remaining chocolate; it may help to stir about ⅓ of the whipped cream into the chocolate to lighten it up, and then fold in the rest (see page 128). Spread this over the first layer. Scoop the chilled chocolate into a pastry bag fitted with a star tip. Pipe a decorative band around the border of the tart, with rosettes delineating the slices to be served. Chill uncovered until set. Tart will keep for 2 days refrigerated or up to 1 month frozen.

5. Allow to stand at room temperature for 20 minutes before serving, to allow the flavour to develop.

TREACLE TART

You probably had to be raised in Britain to appreciate this; and even if you were, you wouldn't want it every Sunday. But every now and then, after a good piece of roast beef, it'll take you right back — at a fraction of the cost of the airfare.

1 recipe	**Sweet Shortcrust Pastry** (see page 221)
1	**lemon**
1 large	**apple**
1 cup	**brown breadcrumbs** (white are fine too)
¼ cup	**golden syrup**

1. Make the pastry, following the recipe on page 221; proceed to the point where you have a tart tin or pie plate lined with pastry, chilling in the fridge. Allow to chill for at least 30 minutes (or freeze for 10). Wrap the left-over pastry in plastic and chill — it will be used in Step 7.

2. Preheat the oven to 375° F.

3. Bake the pastry shell in the centre of the preheated oven for 15 minutes, until set: it should not be fully cooked.

4. Remove the zest from the lemon and chop it finely (see page 210). Put into a medium bowl.

5. Grate the apple into the bowl — it should be quite coarse.

6. Add the breadcrumbs and syrup to the bowl and stir everything together well. Spoon this mixture into the baked pie shell.

7. Roll out the left-over pastry on a lightly floured board to ⅛" thickness; with a pastry cutter or sharp knife, cut into strips about 1½" wide. Make a lattice pattern on top of the pie with these strips, sealing the ends to the pie crust as well as you can.

8. Bake in the preheated oven for 20 to 30 minutes, until set and golden brown.

9. Serve with vanilla ice cream, or lightly whipped cream.

APPLE AND RASPBERRY PIE

I used to think that it was a waste of good raspberries to cook with them, but this pie has changed my mind.

Serves 6.

2 recipes	**Sweet Pastry** (see page 218)
7-8 tart	**apples**, peeled, halved, and cored
³/₄ cup	**granulated sugar**
2¹/₂ Tbs	**all-purpose flour**
1 tsp	**ground cinnamon**
¹/₈ tsp	**ground nutmeg**
2¹/₂ pints	**raspberries**, fresh
1 Tbs	**unsalted butter**

FOR THE GLAZE

1	**egg** mixed with
1 Tbs	**water**

1. Make the double recipe of pastry as described on page 218, to the point where the dough is resting in the fridge (Step 3). Remove from the fridge and cut it in half. On a well-floured surface, roll out one half (the larger) to an 11" circle. Carefully roll up the pastry around your rolling pin and unroll onto a 9" pie plate, leaving a ¹/₂ " to 1" overhang all around. Now, roll out the second half to a 12" circle; place it on a cookie sheet and refrigerate both pie shell and upper crust.

2. Preheat the oven to 375° F. Slice the apples into a bowl. Sprinkle the sugar, flour, cinnamon, and nutmeg over and toss well, until the apples are thoroughly coated. Add the raspberries and toss gently together.

3. Pile the apple mixture high on the pie shell and dot with the butter. Brush the egg glaze over the edge of the pastry; this will act as glue for the upper crust. Drape the 12" circle over the filling. Trim the crust so that the edges are even, then tuck them under and crimp decoratively. Using a small sharp knife or scissors, cut small vents in the upper crust (cutting a small apple shape is a nice touch). Brush with remaing egg glaze

4. Bake in the preheated oven for 40 to 45 minutes, until the juices inside are thick and bubbling, and the crust is a deep golden colour.

Blackberry and Apple Pie

One of the classics of England in September, when the apples are ripe and the hedgerows are full of blackberries. It will bring a tear to the eye of even the most hardened expatriate.

1 recipe **Apple and Raspberry Pie** (see page 118)

1. Follow the recipe, *SUBSTITUTING* 2 pints **blackberries** for the raspberries. Serve warm with thick cream (or lightly whipped cream if you can't find it thick enough).

Plum and Raspberry Pie

Another very good combination.

1 recipe **Apple and Raspberry Pie** (see page 118)

SUBSTITUTE:
1 lb **plums**, stoned and sliced, for the apples

INCREASE:
Raspberries to 3½ pints

Proceed as for original recipe.

Plum and Blackberry Pie

1 recipe **Apple and Raspberry Pie** (see page 118)

SUBSTITUTE:
1 lb **plums**, stoned and sliced, for the apples
3½ pints **blackberries** for the raspberries

Proceed as for original recipe.

APPLE AND STRAWBERRY PIE

1 recipe	**Apple and Raspberry Pie** (see page 118)

SUBSTITUTE:

2 pints	**strawberries**, hulled and halved, for the raspberries.

Proceed as for original recipe.

DRIED FRUIT PIE

A perfect winter dessert when fresh fruit is scarce and you want a filling, cosy dessert.

1 recipe	**Sweet Pastry** (see page 218)
2 cups	**pitted prunes**
2 cups	**dried apricots**
1 cup	**golden raisins**
$^1/_2$ cup	**dried apples**
$^3/_4$ cup	**granulated sugar**
$^1/_2$ cup	**chopped almonds**
$^1/_2$ cup	**unsalted butter**, melted
$^1/_2$ lb	**puff pastry**, either **Quick** (page 216), or **Classic** (page 214)

FOR THE GLAZE:

1	**egg**, beaten slightly **cinnamon**

1. Make the sweet pastry, following the recipe on page 218. Proceed to the point where you have a pie plate or tart tin lined with sweet pastry, ready to be filled. Put it in the fridge to chill while you make the filling.

2. Preheat the oven to 425° F. Combine the prunes, apricots, raisins, and dried apples in a large heavy-bottom saucepan. Cover with water, bring to a boil over medium heat, then simmer for 10 minutes. Drain the fruit and pat it dry with paper towels. Coarsely chop all the fruit, then transfer to a large bowl, and add the sugar, almonds, and melted butter. Toss gently to combine.

3. On a lightly floured work surface roll the puff pastry out to a circle about 12" across and $^1/_8$" thick. Remove the pie shell from the fridge and fill with the fruit filling, mounding it slightly. Beat the egg with a pinch of cinnamon, and brush the edges of the sweet-pastry base with this glaze. Drape the puff pastry over the fruit, trim the edges to meet the sweet paste, then seal and crimp the edges decoratively. Now, brush the exposed pastry with the glaze. Return to the fridge and chill for 15 minutes. Cut 2 or 3 vents in the top of the puff pastry. Bake in the preheated oven for 25 minutes, then reduce the temperature to 375° F and bake for an additional 20 to 30 minutes, until the pastry is golden brown.

4. Serve the pie warm with lightly whipped cream.

LOUISIANA PECAN PIE

The classic pie from deep in the heart of Dixie.

Makes one 8" pie, serving 6.

1 or 2	**sweet potatoes,** large or medium
1 recipe	**Sweet Pastry** (see page 218)

FOR THE SYRUP

½ cup	**granulated sugar**
½ cup	**corn syrup**
2	**eggs**
¼ tsp	**salt**

FOR THE FILLING

¼ cup	**brown sugar**
2 Tbs	**granulated sugar**
1	**egg yolk**
1 Tbs	**whipping cream**
2 Tbs	**butter,** melted
1 Tbs	**vanilla extract**
¼ tsp	**salt**
¼ tsp	**cinnamon**
⅛ tsp	**nutmeg**
1 cup	**pecan halves**

1. Preheat the oven to 350° F. Set the sweet potatoes in the oven and bake until soft — about 50 minutes. Remove from the oven and allow to cool. Then scoop out the flesh and set aside ¾ cup. Turn the oven down to 325° F.

2. Make the pastry, following the recipe on page 218 proceed to the point where you have an 8" pie pan lined with pastry, chilling in the fridge.

3. Make the syrup: Combine the sugar and corn syrup in a small saucepan. Set over medium heat until the sugar has melted, then remove and set aside to cool.

4. In a bowl, combine the ¾ cup sweet potato, the two sugars, the egg yolk, whipping cream, melted butter, vanilla, salt, cinnamon, and nutmeg; mix well together. Remove the chilled pie shell from the fridge and fill it with the sweet-potato mixture, smoothing out the top. Arrange the pecan halves in concentric circles on top of the filling.

5. Whisk the eggs and salt into the cooled syrup; pour it carefully over the pie filling. Bake in the preheated oven for 1 hour, until the top is golden and slightly puffed. Remove from the oven and allow to cool. It is best served warm with whipped cream.

PECAN TART

A simple but good pecan pie — perhaps not strictly a pie, since there is no top crust (that is where we draw the line between the two) but good all the same.

Serves 8.

1 recipe	**Sweet Pastry** (see page 218)
4 large	**eggs**
1 cup	**granulated sugar**
pinch of	**salt**
½ cup	**melted butter**
1½ cups	**light corn syrup**
2 cups	**pecans,** whole
2 tsp	**vanilla extract**

1. Make the pastry, following the recipe on page 218. Proceed to the point where you have a 9" pie pan lined with pastry, chilling in the fridge.

2. Preheat the oven to 350° F. In a medium bowl, beat together the eggs, sugar, and salt. Beat in the melted butter, corn syrup, and vanilla, then stir in the pecans. Remove the pie shell from the fridge and pour in the filling.

3. Bake in the preheated oven for 45 to 55 minutes. Serve warm with lightly whipped cream.

MARC'S CHOCOLATE BOURBON PECAN PIE

We thought there were enough pecan-pie recipes in the book until we tried this one: it is great. Marc is the assistant pastry chef at the new store on north Yonge Street.

Makes one 9" or 10" pie, serving 6 to 8 people.

1 recipe	**Sweet Pastry** (page 218)
3	**eggs**
¼ cup	**bourbon** or **brandy**
½ cup	**brown sugar**
½ tsp	**salt**
1 cup	**corn syrup**
1 cup	**molasses**
3 Tbs	**unsalted butter**, melted
2½ cups	**pecan halves**
1 cup	**chopped semi-sweet chocolate**

1. Make the sweet pastry, following the recipe on page 218, to the point where you have a pie tin lined with a fully baked pie shell (end of Step 5).
2. Preheat the oven to 325° F.
3. Whisk the eggs, bourbon, sugar, salt, corn syrup, molasses, and melted butter together until smooth.
4. Spread the pecans and chocolate pieces over the tart shell, then pour in the bourbon mix.
5. Bake in the preheated oven for 25 minutes, until the centre is bubbling. Then remove from the oven and allow to cool. Serve warm so that the chocolate is still soft.

APPLE WALNUT CREAM TART

A simple and delicious apple tart.

Makes one 9" pie, enough for 6 people.

1 recipe	**Sweet Pastry** (see page 218)
¾ cup	**whipping cream** (35%)
¾ cup	**granulated sugar**
1 large	**egg**
3 Tbs	**all-purpose flour**
1 tsp	**ground cinnamon**
1 tsp	**vanilla extract**
4 or 5	**apples**, peeled, cored, and quartered
1 cup	**chopped walnuts**

1. Make the sweet pastry, following the recipe on page 218; proceed to the point where you have a pie or tart pan lined with pastry, chilling in the refrigerator.
2. Preheat the oven to 350° F. In a bowl, combine the cream, sugar, egg, flour, cinnamon, and vanilla. Stir the mixture until thoroughly combined.
3. Cut the apple quarters into more or less even slices. Arrange the slices on the bottom of the unbaked sweet-pastry pie shell. Pour the cream mixture over the apples. Sprinkle the chopped walnuts on top.
4. Bake in the preheated oven for 45 to 55 minutes. The apples should be tender and the walnuts golden brown.

APPLE AND RED CURRANT COBBLER

A cobbler with a very light topping.

Serves 4.

FOR THE FILLING

2	**tart apples**, peeled, cored, and quartered
2 cups	**red currants**, fresh, stemmed and picked over
1 tsp	**ground cinnamon**
¹/₄ tsp	**ground nutmeg**
3 Tbs	**granulated sugar**
1 Tbs	**lemon juice**
¹/₂ tsp	**vanilla extract**
1 Tbs	**lemon zest**, finely grated (see page 210)

FOR THE TOPPING

¹/₂ cup	**all-purpose flour**
6 Tbs	**granulated sugar**
¹/₂ tsp	**baking soda**
2 Tbs)	**unsalted butter**, well chilled
¹/₂ tsp	**vanilla extract**
3 Tbs	**whipping cream** (35%)
1	**egg yolk**
2	**egg whites**
1 Tbs	**lemon zest**, finely grated

1. Preheat the oven to 350° F; butter a 4-cup oval gratin dish.

2. Slice the apples into a medium-sized bowl and add the red currants. Sprinkle the cinnamon, nutmeg, sugar, lemon juice, vanilla, and grated lemon zest over them and toss to combine. Transfer to the prepared gratin dish.

3. Prepare the topping: In a separate bowl, combine the flour, sugar, and baking powder. Roll the chunk of butter in flour and cut it into cubes; with a pastry cutter (or 2 knives) cut the butter into the flour until the mixture resembles coarse meal. Mix together the vanilla, cream, and egg yolk. Add this to the dry ingredients, mixing just until blended.

4. In a clean dry bowl, beat the egg whites to soft peaks (see page 24). Gently fold the egg whites into the batter (see page 128). Spread the batter evenly over the apples. Bake in the preheated oven for 20 minutes.

5. Serve warm with lightly whipped cream or vanilla ice cream.

PEACH AND CHERRY COBBLER

1 recipe **Apple and Red Currant Cobbler** (see above)

SUBSTITUTE:

2 or 3	**peaches**, peeled and stoned, for the apples
2 cups	**fresh cherries**, stoned, for the red currants

1. Follow the master recipe, replacing the apples with the peaches, and the red currants with stoned sweet black cherries.

CRANBERRY CRUMBLE

An easy fruit crumble for the wintertime. Served with your own Vanilla Ice Cream (page 132), or a bought honey-vanilla ice cream, it should lure Santa Claus down the chimney, even if it is not Christmas Eve.

Serves 3 or 4.

2 cups	**cranberries**, fresh or frozen (if frozen, do not thaw)
1 cup	**diced pear**

FOR THE CRUMBLE TOPPING

6 Tbs	**unsalted butter**, melted
1 cup	**rolled oats**
½ cup	**all-purpose flour**
½ cup	**light brown sugar**, well packed
¼ cup	**granulated sugar**

TO SPRINKLE ON TOP

2 Tbs	**ground cinnamon**
2 Tbs	**granulated sugar**

1. Preheat the oven to 375° F. Find a baking dish of 4- or 6-cup capacity; it does not need to be buttered.
2. Combine the cranberries and diced pear in a bowl, and toss to combine.
3. Melt the butter over medium heat. Combine the oats, flour, and two sugars in a bowl; pour in the butter, and stir until the topping is crumbly.
4. Transfer the fruit to the baking dish. With your hands, loosely mound the crumble topping over the fruit. Mix the cinnamon and sugar together and sprinkle over the top of the crumble.
5. Bake in the preheated oven for 30 to 40 minutes, until the topping is golden and the fruit bubbles up around the edges.
6. Serve warm, with honey-vanilla, or regular vanilla, ice cream, or with lightly whipped cream.

SOUFFLÉS

Soufflés and their exacting requirements are part of the standard repertoire of jokes about dinner parties, guests who arrive late, inquisitive friends who open the oven door at the wrong time, and people who refuse to sit down to dinner when asked. With such a reputation, it is hardly surprising that soufflés are not served more often.

Dessert soufflés at least have the advantage that your guests (or those of them who are coming at all) have arrived, are already sitting down at the table (so they cannot open the oven), and may even be in a somewhat more mellow and less critical mood. But, for the host or hostess they have the distinct disadvantage that the anxiety about success or failure is prolonged through the whole of dinner, turning the food, over which they have slaved for days, to ashes in their mouths.

There is, of course, no real cause for anxiety with soufflés; but I know that my telling you this will make no difference. The only way to know it for yourself is to make some soufflés, and to keep doing it until you gain the confidence that they really are not so mysterious after all.

In most cases (there are more dessert soufflé recipes in our first book), you can make the soufflé base ahead of time, then cover with plastic and refrigerate (or leave it at room temperature, but for no more than an hour). Whisk it and gently reheat, so that it is smooth and at room temperature; then beat the egg whites to stiff peaks (with a couple of tablespoons of sugar to guard against overbeating). It is a good idea first to stir about 1/4 of the whites into the base, to lighten it up; you will find it much easier to fold in the whites if the base is not thick and heavy (do not worry about deflating the whites at this point). Then, you can fold in the rest of the whites, in two or three batches, being careful not to knock the air out. Some soufflés (like the pecan) can sit like this for an hour, so that the actual work during dinner is very little — no more than putting it in the oven.

With soufflés, even more than with most other branches of cooking, confidence is the key to success; and the only way to get it is by practice. Your family really will not mind eating soufflés for dessert for a while. But, if you are still not convinced, you can always serve a frozen or chilled soufflé; they have many of the good points and none of the drawbacks of the real thing!

Frozen Bourbon Maple Soufflé

Serves 8.

2 large	**eggs**
2 large	**egg yolks**
½ cup	**granulated sugar**
¼ cup	**bourbon**
4 Tbs	**pure maple syrup**
2¼ cups	**whipping cream**

FOR DECORATION

crystallized maple sugar

1. Lightly oil a 6-cup soufflé dish. Cut a piece of parchment paper or aluminum foil, wrap it as a collar around the dish, and tie securely with string: it should extend 2" above the top.

2. Combine the eggs, yolks, sugar, and bourbon in a bowl that can go over hot water, or in the top of a double boiler. Set over simmering, but not boiling, water, and whisk to blend. Heat, whisking constantly, until the mixture begins to thicken and is warm to the touch (about 5 minutes). If you have an electric mixer, transfer the mixture to mixer bowl and beat until completely cool and tripled in volume, 8 to 10 minutes; or you may do the whisking by hand.

3. In a thin stream, pour in the maple syrup and beat until completely incorporated.

4. In a clean bowl, whip the cream to soft peaks (see page 31). Fold into the egg mixture (see page 128). Turn into the soufflé dish (the soufflé should come above the sides of the dish) and smooth the top. Refrigerate overnight or until firm.

5. To serve, gently remove the collar. Let stand at room temperature for 30 minutes. Press crystallized maple sugar onto the sides of the soufflé that extend above the edge of the dish, and serve at once.

CHILLED WHITE WINE SOUFFLÉ

Very light: a perfect ending to an elegant meal.

Serves 6 to 8.

7	**egg yolks**
²/₃ cup	**granulated sugar**
2 cups	**semi-dry white wine**
¼ cup	**water**
1 package	**unflavoured gelatine**
7	**egg whites**

FOR THE SAUCE

1 pint	**fresh strawberries**, hulled
1 Tbs	**granulated sugar**

FOR THE DECORATION

½ cup	**whipping cream** (35%)
10	**strawberries**, hulled and halved

1. Find a 2-quart soufflé dish: it does not need to be oiled.

2. Using an electric mixer (or by hand), beat the egg yolks with the sugar until pale yellow and quite thick. Transfer to a medium-sized saucepan and add the wine. Cook over medium-high heat, stirring, until it thickens up, but do not let it boil. Turn down the heat to low and keep warm.

3. Pour the water into a small bowl and sprinkle on the gelatine: allow it to soften. When soft, whisk it into the warm wine mixture and stir gently until completely dissolved. Remove from heat and set over an ice bath to cool, then set aside.

4. Using an electric mixer (or by hand), whip the egg whites to stiff, but not dry peaks (page 24). Carefully fold into the wine mixture (see page 128). Pour the mixture into the soufflé dish, cover, and cool overnight.

5. Not more than 2 hours before serving, make the sauce: Purée 1 pint of strawberries with the sugar in a food processor (or push through a sieve or food mill). Pour into a sauce boat and keep at room temperature.

6. Whip the cream to firm peaks (page 31). Transfer to a pastry bag fitted with a star tip, and pipe rosettes around the border. Place a half strawberry on top of each rosette. Serve with the strawberry sauce.

Hot Pecan Soufflé

Serves 4.

1⅓ cups	**pecan pieces**
1 cup	**milk**
3 large	**egg yolks**
⅓ cup	**granulated sugar**
1 Tbs	**all-purpose flour**
1½ Tbs	**corn starch**
4	**egg whites**
2 Tbs	**granulated sugar**
	icing sugar

FOLDING IN

A good folding technique is the key to light cakes, soufflés, and mousses. Practice makes perfect; but a few words of advice may not go amiss.
1. Fold with a spatula (or your bare hand — it is a very good tool).
2. Always fold the lighter ingredient into the heavier, not the other way round: egg whites into yolks; yolks into chocolate; chocolate into a batter; etc.
3. Scoop the lighter ingredient on top of the heavier one. Lay the flat side of your spatula down (or your palm down) on the surface in the middle, and press it gently down into the mixture. Now bring it towards you, twisting as you do so to bring as much of the mixture with it as you can, finally bringing it up towards the surface again. Turn the bowl as you do this so that on each stroke it rotates about ⅙ or ¼ or a turn, so that every part of the mixture gets its fair share of folding. Contine until the mixture is homogeneous.
4. Do not overfold; better there should be a few unincorporated bits than that you knock all the air out.

---

1. Preheat the oven to 375° F. Butter and sugar a 4-cup soufflé dish (or 4 individual soufflé ramekins).
2. Spread the pecans on a baking sheet and toast in the preheated oven for 8 to10 minutes. When cool, process in a food processor until finely chopped, then set aside.
3. Rinse out a small saucepan with water but do not dry. Pour in the milk and bring to a boil over medium heat. Set aside and keep warm.
4. Using an electric mixer (or by hand), beat together the egg yolks, sugar, flour, and corn starch until pale yellow and quite thick. Pour the hot milk into the egg mixture in a thin stream, whisking all the time. Return the custard to the saucepan (rinse out if there are mixed solids stuck to the bottom), and cook over a low heat, stirring constantly, until the mixture thickens (see page 133). Remove from the heat, stir in the pecans and set aside to cool slightly.
5. Using an electric mixer (or by hand), whip the egg whites to soft, but fully formed peaks (see page 24). Beat in the 2 Tbs sugar and beat to stiff but not dry peaks.
6. Stir ¼ of the egg whites into the pecan mixture, blending thoroughly. Carefully fold in the remaining egg whites in two batches. Turn the mixture into the prepared soufflé dish. They can be held at this point for 1 hour.

---

7. Bake in the preheated oven for 20 to 30 minutes, depending on the size of the mould. Be careful about opening the oven door; if you must, do it gently. Remove from the oven, sieve a dusting of icing sugar over the top, and serve immediately.

HOT LEMON SOUFFLÉ

A very light soufflé made with flour; timing is even more important than usual — but worth the effort for such a pure taste.

Serves 4.

4	**egg yolks**
¼ cup	**granulated sugar**
¼ cup	**fresh lemon juice**
1 tsp	**lemon zest** (see page 210)
4	**egg whites**
2 Tbs	**granulated sugar**
½ cup	**whipping cream** (35%)

1. Preheat the oven to 400° F. Butter a 4-cup soufflé dish.

2. Using an electric mixer (or by hand), beat the egg yolks with the sugar until pale yellow and quite thick. Add the lemon juice and zest, and beat until smooth.

3. Beat the egg whites until white and frothy; then add the sugar and continue beating until quite firm peaks form (see page 24).

4. Stir ¼ of the whites into the yolks, then fold in the rest in two batches (see page 128). Pour gently into the prepared dish, and bake in the preheated oven for about 12 minutes, until golden brown on top.

5. Whisk the cream to soft peaks, then pour into a small serving bowl.

6. Remove the soufflé from the oven — it should be served immediately; pass the cold whipped cream separately.

ICE CREAMS

Many people feel that they have a better chance of being struck by lightning than of being caught making their own ice cream. It is certainly true, with the profusion of good-quality commercial ice creams in most cities, that there seems to be no need to make it in order to enjoy eating it. For most of us, ice cream is no longer much of a treat; we can hardly imagine the magical excitement of eating ice cream in the sweltering heat of high summer, in the days when the only way it could be made was with ice cut from the river in the winter and stored under hay in the ice house for six months. That particular excitement is gone (we have a lot of others to replace it with), but there is still something very special about ice cream that you have made yourself.

Only when you have actually done it will you realize that making ice cream at home is not difficult at all, and does not take long to do — the preparation, that is; the freezing can take 4 or 5 hours if you are doing it in a home freezer, but that does not require much supervision.

Home-made ice cream has a different texture than ice cream that you buy in the stores, because it is hard to whip in as much air as a commercial producer does. This added air is called "overrun"; most commercial ice creams tend to have a lot of overrun, simply because air is a less expensive ingredient than sugar and milk. However, it is wrong to assume that the best ice cream is the one with no overrun; some overrun is desirable, as it helps the flavour to come through, and the ice cream with a bit of overrun will not feel so heavy in your mouth.

FREEZING ICE CREAM AT HOME

A home electric ice-cream machine will develop some overrun; you can achieve the same result even if you are making ice cream in a tray in your freezer (which is a perfectly fine way to make it). Make the custard, following the recipe, then allow it to cool; add the flavouring, and whisk the mixture together thoroughly in a medium-sized bowl (a hand-held electric mixer is an asset; or you can do it in the bowl of your electric mixer). Put the bowl in the freezer for half an hour or so (it will not yet have started to freeze), then take it out and whisk some more. Repeat this process of freezing and whisking as often as is convenient (you do not want to become a slave to your ice cream) until you have a partially frozen, whipped-up custard. Once it reaches this stage, transfer it to a shallow tray that will fit in the freezer (a large aluminum-foil pan is good, as it is an excellent conductor) and let it freeze all the way. In a few ice-cream recipes (such as the Brown Bread and Honey ice cream and Chocolate Cluster) some or all of the cream is whipped to soft peaks before it goes in the freezer, so that the overrun is already present, and it does not need to be whipped during freezing.

One of the nice things about ice cream, apart from the pleasure of having made it yourself and the opportunity to make all kinds of flavours that you cannot buy anywhere, is that it provides an excellent way of using up fruit that is slightly over the hill; in fact, the fruit you use for ice cream should be very ripe (but not rotten, of course). Not only will you have a feeling of satisfaction that you are taking better care of the fruits of the earth, and not wasting; but you will make all kinds of friends, both young and old, who think there is nothing nicer in the world than real home-made ice cream.

French Vanilla Ice Cream

A rich egg custard (that is why French vanilla is yellow), flavoured with vanilla. Simple, rich and delicious.

Makes 1 quart.

1 Tbs	**vanilla extract**
or	
3" length	**vanilla bean** (try Tahitian vanilla for a change)
1 cup	**half-and-half cream** (10%)
2 cups	**whipping cream** (35%)
6	**egg yolks**
³/₄ cup	**granulated sugar**

1. Rinse out a medium saucepan with water, but do not dry it (this helps prevent the milk solids from sticking to the bottom of the pan); then pour in the half-and-half and the cream, and bring to a boil over medium heat. Set aside.
2. Whisk the yolks with the sugar until pale yellow and quite thick (about 3 minutes).
3. Pour the hot cream over the yolks in a thin stream, whisking all the time.
4. Wash out the pan if there is a film on the bottom; then pour in the custard, and set over medium heat. Cook, stirring constantly with a wooden spoon, until the custard thickens and coats the back of a spoon (see page 133).
5. Remove from the heat and strain into a clean bowl and chill thoroughly; then transfer to the ice-cream machine, or freeze, following the directions at the beginning of this section.

Fresh Pear Ice Cream

An ice cream, not a sorbet, with a very fine flavour.

Makes 1¹/₄ quarts; enough for 10 to 12 people.

1 cup	**water**
¹/₂ cup	**sugar**
1	**cinnamon stick**
1 Tbs	**lemon juice**
1¹/₂ lbs	**ripe pears** (see page 7)
³/₄ cup	**whipping cream**
2" strip of	**vanilla bean**
4	**egg yolks**
1 cup	**fine sugar**
³/₄ cup	**whipping cream**

1. Combine the water, sugar, cinnamon stick, and lemon juice in a fairly large non-corrodable pan (see page 5). Bring to a boil over medium heat, then reduce to a simmer.
2. Peel, quarter, and core the pears, then add them to the sugar syrup. The syrup should just cover the pears; if it does not, add more water. Partially cover the pan and simmer gently until the pears are soft. Remove the pears to the workbowl of your food processor and reduce to a purée. Measure out 1¹/₂ cups of purée and set aside.
3. Rinse out a small saucepan with cold water, but do not dry it. Pour in ³/₄ cup of cream, add the

vanilla bean, and bring almost to boiling point.

4. Beat the egg yolks with the sugar until they become pale yellow and quite thick — the stage called "forming a ribbon" (see page 43). Pour on the hot cream, whisking all the time. Make sure that the saucepan does not have a film on the bottom (if it does, wash it out) and pour the cream and eggs back in. Set over medium-low heat and cook, stirring constantly with a wooden spoon, until the mixture coats the back of a spoon (see box below). Immediately remove from the heat, pour in the $^3/_4$ cup of cold cream, and strain through a sieve into a clean bowl. Cover with plastic wrap and chill completely.

5. When cold, stir the pear purée and the cream mixture together; freeze either in an ice-cream machine; or following the instructions at the beginning of this section.

COATING THE BACK OF A SPOON

You will often come across this expression when making egg-thickened sauces. It describes the stage at which the thickening action of the eggs has taken place, and the sauce is ready. Continuing to cook beyond this will give you (very thin) scrambled eggs.

When eggs are cooked to 165° F, their protein combines with the protein in the milk to thicken the mixture. The best way to judge the temperature you have reached, particularly when you are not familiar with this technique, is to use a thermometer. If you don't have one, there are a couple of tell-tale signs to watch for: **(1)** The whisking together of the beaten eggs with the hot milk or cream will produce bubbles on the surface of the mixture. As the sauce is heated, there comes a point at which these bubbles will almost all go away; this happens at a temperature very close to the one you want. **(2)** As you heat the sauce, there also comes a point at which steam will start to rise from the surface; this also happens just before you reach the desired temperature.

Two tips for making good egg sauces: Beat the eggs and sugar well together before you pour over the hot milk. I have tried it both ways, and I always get a smoother sauce when the eggs and sugar are starting to "ribbon" before the milk is added. Second, use a heavy-bottom saucepan, and be very careful when heating the sauce to keep stirring all the time. Naturally the sauce in contact with the bottom of the pan will get hotter than the sauce on top. If you see that you are getting even the slightest film of thickened sauce on the bottom of the pan before the rest of the sauce is ready, remove the pan from the heat, and stir it until you have again a completely smooth sauce. Then you can return it to the stove and heat some more.

KAHLUA COFFEE ICE CREAM

A very sophisticated ice cream. Given a choice, few people will actually choose coffee ice cream; but this is so good they will be glad that you made the choice for them!

Makes 1 quart, enough for 8 people.

2 cups	**whipping cream** (35%)
1 cup	**half-and-half** (10%)
3 Tbs	**instant espresso powder** or **regular instant coffee**
8	**egg yolks**
²⁄₃ cup	**light brown sugar**, firmly packed
2 Tbs	**kahlua**
¹⁄₂ tsp	**vanilla extract**

1. Rinse a pan out with cold water, but do not dry it. Pour in the cream and half-and-half and bring almost to boiling. Stir in the coffee powder, then remove from heat and set aside.

2. Whisk together the egg yolks and sugar until it becomes thick and starts to form a ribbon (see page 43). Slowly pour in the hot cream, whisking as you do so. Check that there is no film on the bottom of the pan (if there is, wash it out) and return the mixture to the pan. Set over medium-low heat and cook, stiring constantly, until the custard thickens and coats the back of a spoon (see page 133). Remove from the heat, add the kahlua and vanilla extract and allow to cool a little, stirring occasionally; then cover with plastic wrap and chill completely.

3. Freeze, either in an ice-cream machine, or following the instructions at the beginning of this section.

PLUM SWIRL ICE CREAM

A liqueur-enhanced plum sorbet swirled into vanilla ice cream.

Makes about 2 quarts, enough for 12 to 15 people.

3 cups	**milk**
6	**egg yolks**
³⁄₄ cup	**granulated sugar**
³⁄₄ tsp	**vanilla extract**
6	**firm plums** (about 1 lb)
¹⁄₄ cup	**granulated sugar**
1 Tbs	**fresh lemon juice**
1 Tbs	**Mirabelle** or **Slivovice** (or any plum liqueur)
1 cup	**whipping cream**

1. Rinse out a saucepan with water but do not dry. Pour in the milk, and bring to a boil over medium heat. Set aside and keep warm.

2. Whisk together the egg yolks with the sugar until pale yellow and quite thick. Pour the hot milk into the egg mixture, whisking constantly.

3. Wash out the pan if there is a film on the bottom, then pour in the custard and cook over medium-low heat, stirring constantly until the mixture thickens and coats the back of a spoon (page 133). Strain into a clean bowl, cover with plastic wrap, allow to cool, and then chill thoroughly.

4. Halve, pit, and slice the plums, then place them in a saucepan with ¼ cup of sugar. Cover the pan and cook over low heat for about 10 minutes, until the plums have started to soften and render their juice. Uncover and cook for an additional 15 minutes, until the plums are very soft and the juice has evaporated. Stir in the lemon juice and plum liqueur. Remove from the heat and cool completely.

5. Freeze the custard only — not the plums — in an ice-cream machine or in the freezer compartment of your fridge, following the directions at the beginning of this section. When it is almost frozen, swirl in the plum mixture, then continue to freeze. Allow to temper in the fridge for ½ hour before serving

MANGO ICE CREAM

Mangoes are one of the best fruits in the world, and this is one of the best ice creams. Soft, slightly over-ripe fruit that are not good enough to eat raw are perfect for this recipe; but you can also used canned mango purée.

Makes 1½ quarts, enough for 12 people.

2 cups	**whipping cream** (35%)
3	**eggs**, at room temperature
1	**egg yolk**
½ cup	**sugar**
2 cups	**mango purée** (the riper the better, so long as it is this side of bad)
1 Tbs	**kirsch**
1 tsp	**lemon zest** (see page 210)
½ tsp	**vanilla extract**
pinch of	**salt**
½ cup	**sour cream**
½ cup	**coarsely chopped mango flesh**

1. Rinse out a saucepan with cold water; do not dry. Pour in the cream and bring to scalding point (just below boiling) over medium-high heat. Remove from the heat and set aside.

2. Whisk the eggs, egg yolk, and sugar together, until they become pale yellow and start to "ribbon" (see page 43). Now, pour on the hot cream in a thin stream, whisking all the time. Make sure that there is no film on the bottom of the pan (wash it out, if there is) and return the cream to the pan. Heat over medium heat, stirring *CONSTANTLY*, until the custard is thick enough to coat the back of a spoon (see page 133). Strain through a fine sieve into a clean bowl. Stir in the mango purée, kirsch, lemon zest, vanilla extract, and salt. Cover with plastic wrap and chill completely in the refrigerator.

3. Make the ice cream, following the directions on the ice-cream machine, or at the beginning of this section. When the ice cream is almost set, stir in sour cream and chopped mango. Continue to freeze until set. Allow the flavours to develop for several hours before removing from the freezer. Allow to temper in the fridge for ½ hour before serving.

BROWN BREAD AND HONEY ICE CREAM

Perfect for Pooh Bears of all ages; the bread crumbs are cooked with butter and sugar to sweet crunchy granules, which are then folded into the honey-flavoured base and lightened with whipped cream.

Makes 3 cups, enough for 6 people.

1 cup	**whipping cream** (35%)
2	**egg yolks**
2 Tbs	**granulated sugar**
3 Tbs	**honey**
½ cup	**whipping cream** (35%)
3 oz	**unsalted butter**
2 cups	**coarse brown bread crumbs**, not too fresh
⅓ cup	**brown sugar**

1. Turn your freezer to very cold and find a shallow dish to freeze in (see the introduction to this section), or get your ice-cream maker ready.

2. Rinse out a saucepan with water, but do not dry it (this helps prevent the milk solids sticking to the bottom of the pan); pour in the cream, and bring to a boil over medium heat. Set aside.

3. Using an electric mixer with whisk attachment (or by hand), beat the egg yolks and sugar together until pale yellow and thick enough to form a slowly dissolving ribbon (see page 43). Gradually pour in the hot cream, whisking all the time.

4. Wash out the pan if there is any film on the bottom, then pour in the custard. Cook over medium heat, stirring constantly, until your finger leaves a trail when drawn across a spoon (page 133). Do not allow it to boil.

5. Strain the custard through a fine sieve into a clean bowl, then cover with plastic wrap and chill thoroughly.

6. Combine the honey and cream in a medium bowl and whisk until soft peaks form (page 31); fold into the cooled custard (see page 128) and freeze in an ice-cream maker; or in the freezer compartment of the fridge, following the directions at the beginning of this section.

7. Melt the butter in a large frying pan over medium heat. Add the breadcrumbs and cook, stirring frequently, until they start to brown. Then add the brown sugar and cook until quite a deep, rich brown, still stirring frequently. You are actually caramelizing the sugar (page 11), but it is hard to see it turn brown because everything else is brown already. Remove from the heat and allow to cool (or turn onto a baking sheet to cool it faster).

8. When the cream starts to freeze, fold the golden crumbs into it; then return to the freezer until quite firm; you may stir it occasionally.

9. Allow the ice cream to spend 30 minutes in the fridge before serving; the flavours will be better if it is not too cold.

APRICOT AND STRAWBERRY ICE CREAM

A good combination of flavours; ripe fruit is best. The apricots need to macerate overnight, so start the day before.

Makes 5¹/₂ cups, enough for 10 to 12 people

1 cup	**apricots**
7 Tbs	**fresh lemon juice**
1 cup	**whipping cream** (35%)
4	**egg yolks**
²/₃ cup	**granulated sugar**
³/₄ lb	**strawberries**

1. Slice the apricots, and chop them finely. Put them in a small bowl and pour in the lemon juice; then let them macerate overnight in the fridge.

2. Rinse out a saucepan with water, but do not dry it (this helps prevent the milk solids sticking to the bottom of the pan); pour in the cream, and bring to a boil over medium heat. Set aside.

3. Using an electric mixer with whisk attachment (or by hand), beat the egg yolks and sugar together until pale yellow and thick enough to form a slowly dissolving ribbon (see page 43). Gradually pour in the hot cream, whisking all the time.

4. Wash out the pan if there is any film on the bottom, then pour in the custard. Cook over medium heat, stirring constantly, until your finger leaves a trail when drawn across a spoon (page 133). Do not allow it to boil.

5. Strain the custard through a fine sieve into a clean bowl, then cover with plastic wrap and chill thoroughly.

6. Hull, slice, and mash the strawberries (but do not purée: small chunks of berry add an interesting texture); stir them, along with the apricot pieces and any remaining lemon juice, into the chilled custard.

7. Transfer mixture to the freezer (see introduction to this section) or your ice-cream machine and freeze according to the manufacturer's instructions. The ice cream is best if allowed to mellow for an hour in the fridge before serving. If frozen too solid it will have no flavour.

CHOCOLATE CLUSTER ICE CREAM

Quite an elaborate ice cream, but well worth the effort.

Makes about 1¹/₂ quarts, enough for 12 to 15 people.

FOR THE CARAMEL SAUCE
1¹/₃ cups **granulated sugar**
¹/₂ cup **water**
¹/₃ cup **whipping cream** (35%)

FOR THE CUSTARD
2 cups **milk**
1 cup **whipping cream** (35%)
4 **egg yolks**
¹/₃ cup **granulated sugar**
1 cup **whipping cream** (35%)
6 oz **semi-sweet chocolate**, coarsely grated or chopped
²/₃ cup **unsalted peanuts**, chopped (lightly salted is fine too)

1. Make the caramel first: Combine the sugar with the water in a heavy-bottom medium saucepan. Heat over medium heat until the sugar has dissolved, then increase heat to high and cook until the sugar turns a deep amber colour (see page 11). Brush down the sides of the pan occasionally with a wet brush to prevent sugar crystals from forming.

2. Immediately remove from heat and pour in the ¹/₃ cup of whipping cream. Be careful to cover your hand with a cloth and avert your face, as the mixture will bubble and sputter. Whisk until all the cream is incorporated and smooth, then cool by setting the pot in a large bowl filled with cold water.

3. Rinse out a saucepan with water, but do not dry it (this helps prevent the milk solids from sticking to the bottom of the pan). Pour in the milk, and bring to a boil over medium heat; then set aside and keep warm.

4. Meanwhile, using an electric mixer fitted with the whisk (may be done by hand), beat the yolks with the sugar until pale yellow and quite thick (see page 43). Pour the hot milk into the eggs in a thin stream, whisking constantly.

5. Wash out the pan if there is a film on the bottom, then pour in the custard. Cook over medium-low heat, stirring all the time, until the mixture is thick enough to coat the back of a spoon (page 133). Strain through a fine sieve into a clean bowl. Cover with plastic wrap, cool, and then chill thoroughly.

6. Whip 1 cup of whipping cream to soft peaks (page 31); then fold it (see page 128) into the chilled custard. Fold in the caramel sauce. Freeze in an ice-cream machine until almost set, or follow the instructions at the beginning of this section for freezing in the freezer.

7. When partially frozen, stir in the grated chocolate and chopped peanuts and continue freezing until set.

8. Allow the ice cream to soften in the refrigerator before serving.

GINGER ICE CREAM

A very sophisticated ice cream; and an answer to the old conundrum about what to serve for dessert after Chinese food. Ginger ice cream, on its own or with fresh lichees in syrup (canned, even), would be inspired.

Makes 1 quart, enough for 8 people.

¼ cup	**Szechuan peppercorns**
1¾ cups	**half-and-half cream** (10%)
2" length	**vanilla bean**, split lengthwise
8 oz	**fresh ginger**, peeled, and coarsely chopped
¾ cup	**granulated sugar**
¼ cup	**water**
9	**egg yolks**
1 cup	**whipping cream** (35%)

1. Cook the peppercorns in a dry frying pan over low heat until they become aromatic — about 3 to 5 minutes, swirling occasionally. Set aside.

2. Rinse out a saucepan with cold water, but do not dry. Pour in the half-and-half, add the vanilla bean, and scald (bring to almost boiling) over medium heat. Add the cooked peppercorns, remove from the heat, and allow to cool.

3. Combine the chopped ginger, sugar, and water in a small saucepan. Cook over low heat until all the sugar has dissolved, then increase the heat to medium and boil gently until the ginger is tender — about 25 minutes.

4. Whisk the egg yolks together in a medium bowl, then strain in the cooled cream. Whisk until well combined, then slowly pour in the hot ginger syrup (do not strain; we need the lumps for now).

5. Clean the milk film off the bottom of the saucepan (if necessary), then pour the custard into the pan and cook over medium heat until it coats the back of a spoon (see page 133). Remove from heat and strain into a clean bowl. Whisk in the whipping cream (not whipped); cover with plastic wrap and chill completely.

6. Freeze in an ice-cream machine, according to manufacturer's directions, or in your freezer following the directions at the beginning of this section.

PRALINE ICE CREAM

Canada's favourite flavour comes home.

Makes 5¹/₂ cups, enough for 12 to 15 people.

FOR THE PRALINE

2 oz	**slivered** or **sliced almonds**
2 oz	**hazelnuts**
1 cup	**granulated sugar**
5 Tbs	**water**

FOR THE CUSTARD

3 cups	**milk**
1	**vanilla bean**, split
8	**egg yolks**
1 cup	**granulated sugar**
1 cup	**whipping cream** (35%)

1. Preheat the oven to 350° F; then toast the almonds and hazelnuts until golden (see page 153). Remove from the oven and cool. Transfer to a lightly oiled cookie sheet.

2. Combine the sugar and water in a medium-sized heavy saucepan. Cook over medium heat until the sugar has dissolved, then increase the heat and cook until the sugar turns a deep golden caramel (see page 11). Pour the caramel over the nuts, and let them cool. *(DO NOT HANDLE THE COOKIE SHEET; IT WILL BE VERY HOT.)* When cold, break the brittle into pieces and transfer ²/₃ of it to the workbowl of the food processor, and process to a fine paste (about 10 minutes). Crush the rest to a chunky powder (can also be done in the food processor) and set aside.

3. Rinse out a saucepan with water but do not dry it (this helps to prevent the milk solids from sticking to the bottom of the pan). Pour in the milk, add the vanilla bean, and bring to a boil over medium heat. Set aside and keep warm.

4. Whisk together the egg yolks with the sugar until pale yellow and quite thick. Pour the hot milk into the egg mixture, whisking constantly.

5. Wash out the pan if there is a film on the bottom, then pour in the custard and cook over medium-low heat, stirring constantly until the mixture thickens and coats the back of a spoon (page 133). Strain into a clean bowl, cover with plastic wrap, allow to cool and then chill thoroughly.

6. Stir the praline paste into the cold custard until completely absorbed.

7. Whip the cream to soft peaks (page 31) and fold it into the custard.

8. Freeze in an ice-cream machine, or in the freezer compartment of your freezer, following the directions at the beginning of this section.

9. Sprinkle the reserved praline on top before serving.

FROZEN CARAMEL MOUSSE

The same ingredients, but a little lighter than an ice cream because the cream is whipped before being added to the caramel.

3 Tbs	**water**
1 cup	**granulated sugar**
½ cup	**boiling water**
8 large	**eggs**
1⅔ cups	**whipping cream** (35%)
1 tsp	**vanilla extract**

1. Bring some water to a boil; you will need ½ cup in Step 2.

2. Combine the water and sugar in a heavy medium-sized saucepan. Heat over a medium heat until the sugar has dissolved, then increase the heat to high, and cook until the sugar turns a pale gold colour (see page 11); do not allow it to get too dark or your mousse will taste burnt. As soon as the sugar reaches a golden hue, remove it from the heat and carefully pour in the boiling water, covering your hand with a cloth and averting your face, as it will sputter. (This stops the cooking and prevents further browning.)

3. Return the pan to the heat and simmer until the caramel has dissolved, stirring constantly. Set aside.

4. Beat the egg yolks with an electric mixer until pale yellow and quite thick — about 3 minutes (it can be done by hand).

5. Pour the caramel into the beaten egg yolks in a thin stream, whisking all the time. Continue beating until the mixture is completely cool and holds a soft shape.

6. In a separate bowl, whip the cream with the vanilla to soft peaks (page 31). Fold the cream into the caramel (see page 128): both the cream and the caramel must be stiff enough so they don't separate while freezing.

7. Put the bowl into the freezer for 30 minutes, then take it out and whisk the mousse. Continue to whisk and freeze (as described in the introduction to this section) until you have a partly frozen, well-whipped mixture. Then, turn into individual goblets or a 1 quart soufflés dish, and freeze completely.

8. To serve: Allow to temper in the refrigerator for 10 minutes if in glasses; or 30 minutes if in a large dish. Garnish with fresh fruit and praline (see recipe for Praline Ice Cream, see page 140); or for a dramatic effect, with a caramel cage (page 11).

CHOCOLATE MOUSSE ICE CREAM

A wonderful combination of chocolate and raspberries.

Makes one quart, enough for 6 to 8 people.

½ cup	**granulated sugar**
½ cup	**water**
4	**egg yolks**, room temperature
9 oz	**semi-sweet chocolate**
¾ cup	**raspberries**
1 cup	**whipping cream** (35%)

1. Combine the sugar and water in a heavy saucepan. Cook over low heat until the sugar is dissolved, then increase the heat and bring to a boil. Set aside.

2. Using an electric mixer fitted with the whisk attachment (or by hand), beat the egg yolks until pale yellow and quite thick. Then pour the hot syrup into the eggs in a gradual stream, whisking all the time. Return the mixture to the saucepan and cook over medium-low heat, stirring constantly, until the mixture thickens and coats the back of a spoon (see page 133). Strain through a fine sieve into a clean bowl and set aside to cool completely.

3. Place the chocolate in a small bowl that can go over hot water (or in the top of a double boiler); set it over simmering water and heat until melted. Remove from the heat and allow to cool completely.

4. When both the chocolate and the custard are cool, whisk them together.

5. Whip the cream to soft peaks (page 31), then fold into the custard (see page 128). Freeze in an ice-cream machine, or follow the directions at the beginning of this section for using your home freezer. When partially frozen, coarsely chop the raspberries and stir them into the ice cream. Then freeze completely.

6. Let the ice cream sit in the fridge for half an hour before serving, to soften and let the flavour develop.

Opposite: *Tiramisu, looking its best in a glass bowl (see recipe on page 28).*

PRUNE ICE CREAM

I know that this sounds doubtful but it is truly delicious.

Makes 1¼ quarts; enough for 10 to 12 people.

4 cups	**boiling water**
2	**Earl Grey tea bags**
¾ lb	**large pitted prunes**
½ tsp	**grated lemon zest** (page 210)
¾ cup	**whipping cream**
2" strip of	**vanilla bean**
4	**egg yolks**
1 cup	**fine sugar**
¾ cup	**whipping cream**

Optional:

¼ cup	**Armagnac** or **cognac**

1. Make the tea with the boiling water and the Earl Grey tea bags; then remove the bags and pour into a saucepan. Add the prunes, bring to a simmer, and poach gently until very tender (the time will depend on the freshness of the prunes)

2. When the prunes are soft, transfer them to the workbowl of your food processor and reduce to a purée. Measure out 1 cup of purée, stir in the grated lemon zest, and set it aside.

3. Rinse out a small saucepan with cold water, but do not dry it. Pour in ¾ cup of cream, add the vanilla bean, and bring almost to boiling point.

4. Beat the egg yolks with the sugar until they become pale yellow and quite thick — the stage called "forming a ribbon" (see page 43). Pour on the hot cream, whisking all the time. Make sure that the saucepan does not have a film on the bottom (if it does, wash it out) and pour the cream and eggs back in. Set over medium-low heat and cook, stirring constantly with a wooden spoon, until the mixture coats the back of a spoon (see page 133). Immediately remove from the heat, pour in the ¾ cup of cold cream, and strain through a sieve into a clean bowl. Cover with plastic wrap and chill completely.

5. When cold, stir the prune purée, the cream mixture, and the optional Armagnac together; freeze either in an ice-cream machine; or following the instructions at the beginning of this section.

BAKED ALASKA

A throwback for sure, but still a big hit. You will need a plank of wood about 15" by 8" (in fact, any size that will hold the Baked Alaska and fit in the oven). A wooden chopping board is fine; but baking it may not be good for the board. Bake it for 30 minutes at 500° F first, so that it can release any gases before you put your food on it.

Serves 10.

1 recipe	**sponge cake** (see page 224) or left-over sponge
2	**top-quality ice cream** (500 ml containers—not necessarily the same flavour; I like French vanilla with raspberry sorbet)

FOR THE MERINGUE

6	**egg whites**
1 cup	**granulated sugar**
¼ cup	**brandy** or other liqueur

or

1 recipe	**Italian Meringue** (see page 104)

1. Make the sponge following the recipe on page 224, but bake it in a rectangular cake pan; it need only be about ¾" thick. Cut the sponge so that you have a rectangle about 5" by 12" by ¾". This is the insulation on the bottom of the ice cream. Set it on the wooden board.

2. Allow the ice cream to soften at room temperature until malleable but still firm. Mound the ice cream on top of the cake, taking it right to the edges. Mould it in the shape of a brick, spreading one flavour on top of the other. Put the Alaska — still on the wood — into the coldest part of your freezer for several hours.

3. If you are making the Italian meringue, it too can be done now; it will store in the fridge for a week. This meringue gives a creamier and richer topping to the dish. *May be done a day ahead to this point.*

---

4. Preheat the oven to 500° F; it will take at least half an hour. Make sure there is nothing else in it!

5. When ready to serve: Remove the Alaska from the freezer to the fridge while you make the meringue. In a large bowl, beat the egg whites until broken up and foamy, then start to add the sugar, about ¼ cup at a time, while continuing to beat. Beat until all the sugar has been added and the meringue is smooth, glossy, and quite firm.

6. With a spatula or palette knife, spread a thick layer of meringue over the ice cream, making it as even and smooth as you can.

7. Bake in the preheated oven for about 5 minutes; it is hard to be precise because ovens vary enormously. It is OK to peek after 3 minutes (sooner if you smell burning!). All you need to do is brown the meringue: the ice cream does not need cooking!

8. While the Alaska is baking, warm the brandy in a small saucepan; it should just be warm. Set aside.
9. Remove the Alaska from the oven; get someone (who has a match) to help with the flaming part. Walk to the dining-room door and dim the lights. Ask your assistant to bring the brandy; light it in the pan and pour it over and along the Baked Alaska. Walk quickly into the dining-room, to thunderous applause.

PLUM CHAMPAGNE SORBET

A very elegant sorbet.

Makes one quart, serving 6 or 8 people.

8 firm	**plums**
1 cup	**water**
½ cup	**sugar**
½ cup	**dry champagne** (or facsimile thereof)

1. Cut the plums in half, remove the pits, then cut into quarters. Put them with the water and sugar in a medium-sized heavy saucepan. Bring to a boil over medium heat, then reduce the heat to a simmer and cook gently, covered, until the plums are very soft (about 20 minutes), stirring frequently.
2. In a food processor fitted with the steel blade, purée the plums, in batches if necessary, then strain the purée through a sieve. You should have 3⅓ cups. Stir in the ½ cup champagne. Chill thoroughly (or overnight) before proceeding.

4. Freeze in an ice-cream machine, or in the freezer compartment of your fridge, following the directions at the beginning of this section.
5. This is lovely presented in champange glasses with mint leaves as garnish.

COOKIES, BARS, AND CANDIES

The cookie kingdom is a large one, and includes a wide range of creations. In the middle are the sort of cookies—chocolate chip, oatmeal raisin, and peanut butter—that spring to mind when someone mentions the word. Their close cousins (on the cake-and-tart side of the family) are bars and squares—brownies, caramel pecan bars, and butter tarts too—which to many people are even better than a cookie. A little farther out towards the fringe are some things that are very close to being candy—Skor bar brittle, apple brandy bars—but have enough of a general resemblance to be included as part of the family (the ne'er-do-well side, in the opinion of more serious grown-ups). Recipes that are even more like candy than these—which are, in fact, candy, but thinly disguised—we have included in the Children's Desserts section.

On the other side of the family are cookies that have acquired airs, assumed French names, and now call themselves biscuits—Madeleines, almond tuiles, Baci di Dama. They are definitely the elegant side, and elevate in distinction and class anything they accompany. They are a wonderfully easy way of dressing up a simple dessert, such as fresh fruit or ice cream, and making it into something special. Quite close to these, although with more of the common touch, are shortbreads and brandy snaps, which are a personal favourite and one of the most vivid food memories I have from my childhood.

Cookies, particularly the regular ones and the bars, are among the easiest of sweet things to make, and definitely one of the most appreciated. However, even with these, care in handling the dough will repay you in lighter and more tender cookies. And, as always with baking, you must measure the ingredients accurately or the texture and consistency will not be what you hope.

The baking time for cookies is very important; cookies that are slightly underbaked will have a softer, chewier texture than cookies that are baked until crisp. The cookies we sell in the stores are deliberately underbaked to achieve this result; on the days that we accidentally overbake them (yes, it does happen) we get a lot of comments from disappointed customers. The timing for a particular cookie recipe when you make it at home will depend on the quirks of your oven; in general, if you have doubts about the accuracy of the oven temperature, set the dial on the cooler side; we find that cookies baked at a lower temperature will have the softer, chewy texture that you want. It is a good idea when you make cookies (or anything else for that matter), to make notes right in the cookbook about any adjustments you make to the recipe, and what the result was like—even if you made no changes. You will then have a much better chance of getting a good result the next time you come to make the recipe; I can guarantee that you will not remember what changes you made, particularly if any time has gone by.

Cooking the more elegant cookies is a bit more challenging, for two reasons: (1) their texture is generally more delicate, and this means a more delicate batter, which requires more careful handling, and (2) because of the way in which they are used—as accompaniments to dessert, or for more formal occasions—presentation and finish become important. However, they are, none of them, difficult, and all will repay the work that you put in.

HONEY BUTTER TARTS WITH WHOLE-WHEAT OATMEAL CRUST

An update on the old classic. The nutty crunch of the pastry goes well with the sweet honey filling.

Makes 16 tarts.

FOR THE PASTRY

1 cup	**stone-ground whole-wheat pastry (soft) flour**
1 cup	**oat flour**
	(both these flours are available in health food stores)
²/₃ cup	**cold butter**, cut into ¹/₄ " cubes
1 tsp	**salt**
¹/₃ - ¹/₂ cup	**very cold water**

FOR THE FILLING

1 cup	**butter**
1¹/₃ cup	**fragrant honey**
5	**egg yolks**
1 tsp	**vanilla extract**
¹/₄ tsp	**salt**
¹/₂ cup	**currants**
or	
¹/₄ cup	**currants** and ¹/₄ cup **chopped walnuts**

1. The easiest thing to make the tarts in is a muffin tin (or two). Combine the whole-wheat and oat flours and the salt in the workbowl of your food processor. Pulse once or twice to aerate. Roll the butter in flour (to make it easier to handle), then cut into slices. Roll these again in flour and cut them into sticks, then cut the sticks into cubes. Distribute these over the flour, then pulse briefly, just until the mixture has the texture of coarse meal. With the motor running, pour in ¹/₃ cup of cold water down the feed tube; process only until the water is incorporated. Turn the dough out onto your work surface and gather into a ball; wrap in plastic and refrigerate for 30 minutes or longer.

2. Prepare the filling: Melt the butter in a small saucepan then allow to cool a little. Beat in the honey, then the egg yolks one at a time. Stir in the vanilla and salt.

3. Preheat the oven to 400° F. Remove the dough from the fridge and cut into 12 pieces; carefully roll out each piece in turn on a well-floured surface to ¹/₈" thick. Line the muffin tins with the pastry, pressing it well onto the sides, and trim off the protruding edges. If there are any holes or gaps in the pastry, press scraps of pastry in to fill them. It is important that the tarts be water-tight or the filling will leak out. Carefully gather the trimmings together, then roll them out again for the last 4 tarts. Refrigerate the muffin tins for 30 minutes, or freeze for 10 minutes.

4. Transfer the pastry-lined muffin tins from the fridge to the centre of the preheated oven and bake for 12 minutes. Then remove and allow to cool slightly. Turn the oven down to 350° F.

5. Leave the baked tart shells in the muffin tin. Place 1 tsp of the currants in each of the shells, or a

NUTS AND HONEY
Middle-Eastern bakers, who use a lot of nuts, believe that the combination of nuts and honey is hard to digest. When making desserts with nuts they use a sugar syrup rather than honey as the sweetener. Follow your inclination—but don't say we didn't warn you!

mixture of currants and walnuts, or currants in some and walnuts in others; then carefully pour in the filling. Bake in the preheated oven for 12 to 15 minutes, until the filling has turned opaque and is almost set — the centres will still be jiggly. Remove from the oven and allow to cool completely.

6. When the tarts are completely cool, remove them from the tins: carefully slide a knife blade down the side of the tart and loosen it all around. Then gently lift up one side; it should come out without breaking.

CHOCOLATE CHIP COOKIES

(see photograph opposite page 158).

Makes about 15 good-size cookies.

1¼ cups	**all-purpose flour**
½ tsp	**baking soda**
½ tsp	**salt**
4 oz	**unsalted butter**
½ cup	**brown sugar**
¼ cup	**granulated sugar**
1 tsp	**vanilla extract**
1	**egg**
1 cup	**semi-sweet chocolate chips**
½ cup	**chopped walnuts**

1. Preheat the oven to 375° F. Butter and flour a baking sheet (or line with parchment paper). Sift together the flour, baking soda, and salt; then set aside.

2. Using an electric mixer (if you have one, or by hand), cream the butter with the two sugars and the vanilla until light and fluffy. Add the egg, and beat again until smooth.

3. By hand, stir in the sifted dry ingredients, then the chocolate chips and the walnuts.

4. Scoop up tablespoonfuls of the batter and scrape them off the spoon onto the baking sheet with a second spoon. They should be set 1" or 1½" apart.

5. Bake in the preheated oven for about 10 minutes, until golden brown; they are better if slightly undercooked. Remove from the oven and allow to cool for a few minutes on the baking sheets to firm up before transferring to a rack.

CHOCOLATE REVERSAL COOKIES

A dense dark chocolate batter with white chocolate chunks (See photograph opposite page 158).

Makes about 16 good-size cookies.

1 cup	**all-purpose flour**
1 tsp	**baking soda**
⅓ cup	**unsweetened cocoa powder**
6 oz	**unsalted butter**
½ cup	**brown sugar**, well packed
½ cup	**granulated sugar**
1½ tsp	**vanilla extract**
¼ tsp	**salt**
1	**egg**
1½ cups	**good-quality white chocolate**, coarsely chopped

1. Preheat the oven to 400° F. Lightly butter a cookie sheet (or line it with parchment paper). Sift together the flour, baking soda, and cocoa powder; then set aside.

2. Using an electric mixer (if you have one), or by hand, cream the butter with the two sugars until light and fluffy. Add the egg and the vanilla, and beat again until smooth.

3. By hand, stir in the sifted flour and cocoa mixture until completely incorporated; then stir in the white chocolate chunks.

4. Scoop up tablespoonfuls of the batter, then scrape off with another spoon onto the baking sheet. Flatten the mounds slightly with the heel of your hand.

5. Bake in the preheated oven for 12 to 14 minutes; the cookies are done when the top springs back when lightly touched. Do not over-bake. Remove from the oven and allow to cool on the baking sheet for a few minutes before transferring to a rack.

TULIPES AND LANGUES-DE-CHAT

Fine wafer biscuits to serve with ice cream; the tulipes can be used as an edible serving dish. The recipe is similar to the one for Almond Tuiles (page 152), but these wafers have less flour and no almonds.

Makes 14 medium tuiles.

4	**egg whites**
1 cup	**granulated sugar**
⅓ cup	**all-purpose flour**
¼ cup	**unsalted butter**, melted
1½ tsp	**water**
½ tsp	**vanilla extract**

1. Preheat the oven to 400° F. Butter a baking sheet or line it with parchment, and butter the paper (see page 152). To make *Tulipes*: Draw a 6" diameter circle on a square piece of stiff card, then cut out along the line (so that you have a hole in a square card): this is your template for shaping the Tuiles. The outer border should not be much more than 1" wide — if it is, your Tulipes will be too far apart. For *Langues-de-Chat*: A template with a hole in the shape that you want the finished cookies would be a help, usually an elongated oval; again the border should not be too wide.

2. Place the egg whites in a large bowl and whisk by hand just enough to break them up; they should be frothy and starting to turn white (stage 2 — see page 24).

3. Add the sugar, flour, melted butter (which should not be really warm), water, and vanilla, and beat well. Set the batter aside at room temperature for 5 minutes before proceeding.

4. Set your template in one corner of the baking sheet; drop 2 tablespoons of batter (for Tulipes; 1 tablespoon for Langues-de-Chat) into the circle and spread it out to fill the hole with a palette knife. Move the template and make another circle of batter; continue until the baking sheet is full.

5. Bake in the preheated oven for 8 to 10 minutes, until golden.

6. Open the oven door and set the baking sheet on the open door, so that the Tulipes are kept hot, but do not cook any more. The Tuiles are easy to mould when hot, but become hard as soon as they cool. You can make wafers by laying them on a rolling pin; tubes by wrapping them around the handle of a wooden spoon ; Tulipes by gently moulding them into muffin cups; or cornucopia by rolling them into a cone shape. It is helpful to have a glass of cold water at hand, to cool your hot fingers in; the baked cookies are hot and sometimes hard to handle.

7. Unbaked batter will keep in the fridge for 5 days.

ALMOND TUILES

These are very elegant wafers to serve with ice cream or poached fruit. A bit fiddly, but worth it for their very classy feeling.

Makes 18 medium Tuiles.

¹/₂ cup softened **butter**
1 cup **white sugar**
4 large **egg whites**
1 tsp **almond extract**
1 cup **all-purpose flour**
1 cup **sliced almonds**

PARCHMENT PAPER

For most baking, parchment paper (also called silicone paper) is a wonderful asset but not indispensable. Buttering and flouring a baking sheet works very well for cookies and shortbreads, even for meringues. But, for Tuiles, parchment paper is almost an essential, if you are to preserve your sanity; because, when making Tuiles, the ability to lift the circles off the baking sheet quickly and easily is vital. Buy some now.— and you will find that you use it for all your baking (it is reusable).

---

1. Preheat the oven to 375° F. Line a baking sheet with parchment (see box below). Draw a 6" diameter circle on a square of stiff card, then cut out around the circle (so that you have a hole in a square card): this is your template for shaping the Tuiles. The outer border should not be much more than 1" wide — if it is, your Tuiles will be too far apart.

2. Using an electric mixer (but may be done by hand), cream together the butter, sugar, egg whites, almond extract, and flour.

3. Set your template in one corner of the baking sheet; drop a tablespoon of batter into the circle and spread it out to fill the circle with a palette knife. Move the template and make another circle of batter; continue until the baking sheet is full. Sprinkle them with the sliced almonds.

4. Bake in the preheated oven for 6 to 8 minutes, until the edges turn golden brown.

5. Open the oven door and set the baking sheet on the open door, so that the Tuiles are kept hot, but do not cook any more. The Tuiles are easy to mould when hot, but become hard as soon as they cool. You can make wafers by laying them on a rolling pin; tubes by wrapping them around the handle of a wooden spoon ; cups (called Tulipes) by gently moulding them into muffin cups; or cornucopia by rolling them into a cone shape.

6. Serve with fresh berries, ice cream, sorbet, or simply lightly whipped cream.

VARIATION:
CHOCOLATE TUILES

Dip either the ends or the outside surface of the Tuiles in warm melted chocolate, then allow to cool.

Hazelnut Cookie Cones

Terrific ice-cream cones for the kids. For the grown-ups they make a very sophisticated dessert, served with sorbet and fresh berries; they go well with just about any sorbet.

Makes 30 small cones.

1¹/₃ cup	**hazelnuts**, toasted and peeled (see box below)
³/₄ cup	**granulated sugar**
¹/₄ cup	**all-purpose flour**
3 Tbs	**granulated sugar**
4	**egg whites**
¹/₄ cup	**hazelnut oil**

TOASTING AND PEELING HAZELNUTS

Preheat the oven to 350° F. Spread the hazelnuts on a baking sheet and roast for about 6 minutes, until well browned. They burn quite easily so watch them carefully after 5 minutes. Wrap the warm roasted nuts in a clean tea towel; roll them in the towel on your work surface so that the nuts rub against each other; this takes the skins off. Not all the skin will come off, but it doesn't matter.

---

1. Combine the hazelnuts and sugar in the work-bowl of a food processor fitted with the steel blade. Process to a fine meal, using the pulse action; do not process to the point where it becomes a paste. Add 3 Tbs sugar and the flour; blend them in using quick pulses.

2. In a medium-sized bowl, whisk the egg whites until just broken up, but not frothy. Stir in the nut mixture. Gently fold in the oil. Let batter rest at room temperature for 15 minutes.

3. Preheat the oven to 350° F. Butter a cookie sheet or line it with parchment paper. *Optional,* but makes life easier: Make a template for spreading the batter on to the baking sheet; draw a 3" circle on a 5" square of heavy cardboard, then cut it out so that you have a hole in the card. If you want larger cones, just use a larger piece of card. Also *optional:* Form a piece of card into a cone-shape and tape it so it stays; then cover with aluminum foil — this is your mould for shaping the cones.

4. Place your template in one corner of the baking sheet. Spoon 1 Tbs of batter into the hole (or if using the free-form method, just drop the batter onto the sheet). Using the back of a spoon dipped in water, spread the batter to fill the cirlce (or spread the batter freehand to a 3" round). Form 3 more rounds, spacing them 2" apart. If you want to make bigger cones, simply use more batter and spread your circle larger.

5. Bake in the preheated oven for 5 to 8 minutes, until golden brown. Open the oven door (leave the oven on) and let the baked cones sit on the open door for 1 minute to firm up a little. Remove the circles from the cookie sheet with a spatula, one at a time, and form them into a cone, using your foil cone as a mould. Repeat until all the batter is used up.

6. Store the cones in an airtight container.

MacDavid's Shortbreads

The MacDavid clan's family recipe for Scottish shortbread.

Makes about 60.

1 cup	**light brown sugar**, well packed
1 lb	**unsalted butter**
1 tsp	**vanilla extract** (optional)
3-4 cups	**all-purpose flour**

1. Preheat the oven to 350° F. Butter and flour a baking sheet, or line with parchment paper (see page 152). Sift the flour into a bowl.

2. Using an electric mixer (may be done the traditional Scottish way!), cream the butter, sugar, and vanilla together until light and fluffy.

3. Stir in — the traditional way only: no electric mixer here — 3 cups of flour; add more flour until the dough is just firm enough to roll out. Turn the dough out onto your work surface and roll out to $1/2$" thick. With a sharp knife, cut into fingers or roll out to $1/4$" thick and cut into fan shapes (Pettycoat tails).

4. Place on the prepared baking sheet and bake in the preheated oven for 15 to 20 minutes, until pale golden brown.

Oatmeal Health Cookies

A great, nutty and crunchy cookie.

Makes about 24.

$3/4$ cup	**flour**
$1/2$ tsp	**baking soda**
$1/2$ tsp	**salt**
$1/2$ cup	**butter** or **magarine**
$1/2$ cup	**white sugar**
$1/2$ cup	**brown sugar**
1 large	**egg**
1 Tbs	**water**
1 tsp	**vanilla extract**
$1\frac{1}{2}$ cups	**rolled oats**
$1/4$ cup	**chopped pecans**
$1/4$ cup	**chopped walnuts**
3 Tbs	**sunflower seeds**
$1/2$ cup	**chocolate chips** or **carob chips**
1 Tbs	**sesame seeds**

1. Preheat the oven to 350° F. Butter and flour a baking sheet; or line with parchment paper (see page 152). Sift together the flour, baking soda, and salt into a bowl and set aside.

2. Cream together the butter and the two sugars until light and fluffy; then beat in the egg, water, and vanilla.

3. Stir the sifted flour into the batter, then the rolled oats and the nuts, sunflower seeds, and chocolate chips.

4. Spoon the batter onto the prepared baking sheet and bake in the preheated oven for 10 to 12 minutes.

MACADAMIA BROWNIES

An excellent brownie on their own; but they also make a wonderful full-scale dessert when served with coffee ice cream and Kahlua Sauce (see photograph opposite page 158).

Makes twelve 3" square brownies, or 6 dessert-size helpings.

1 cup	**unsalted butter**
8 oz	**unsweetened chocolate**
5 large	**eggs**
3 cups	**white sugar**
1½ Tbs	**vanilla extract** or **favourite liqueur**
1½ cups	**all-purpose flour**, sifted
2½ cups	**macadamia nuts**, roughly chopped (if you can't get macadamia nuts, pecans make a good substitute)

1. Preheat the oven to 375° F. Butter a 9" x 13" cake pan. Sift the flour into a bowl.
2. Combine the butter and chocolate in a bowl that can go over hot water (or in a double boiler); set it over simmering water and heat, stirring occasionally, until melted. Remove from the heat and allow to cool.
3. Using an electric mixer (may be done by hand), beat the sugar, eggs, and vanilla (or other flavouring) on high speed for 8 minutes.
4. Pour in the melted chocolate and mix well; then stir in the sifted flour and the nuts.
5. Pour into the prepared cake pan and bake in the preheated oven for approximately 40 minutes. Remove from the oven and allow to cool completely in the pan. Cut into squares.
6. To serve with Kahlua sauce (see below): Cut the brownies into larger squares than normal; scoop coffee ice cream over the top, pour on the Kahlua sauce and garnish with toasted macadamia nuts: it will look good enough to eat!

KAHLUA SAUCE

1 cup	**whipping cream** (35%)
½ cup	**unsalted butter**
1¾ cups	**brown sugar**
pinch of	**salt**
1 cup	**cocoa**
½ cup	**Kahlua** or **Tia Maria**

1. Combine the butter and the cream in a small saucepan. Set over medium-low heat until the butter is melted, then whisk in the brown sugar.
2. Sift the cocoa into a bowl, then whisk it into the sauce a bit at a time until combined. Remove from the heat, stir in the Kaluha and serve.

PEANUT BUTTER COOKIES

A rich crumbly cookie that melts in your mouth, leaving the pure taste of peanut butter.

Makes 35 cookies.

1 cup	**all-purpose flour**
$\frac{1}{2}$ tsp	**baking soda**
$\frac{1}{2}$ tsp	**baking powder**
$\frac{1}{2}$ cup	**cornstarch**
$\frac{3}{4}$ cup	**butter**
1 cup	**brown sugar**, well packed
$\frac{1}{2}$ cup	**granulated sugar**
$1\frac{1}{2}$ cup	**homogenized peanut butter**, plain or crunchy
1	**egg**

1. Preheat the oven to 250° F (yes, that's right: we have found that you get the best texture by baking them slowly). Place the oven rack in the lower part of the oven. Lightly butter a cookie sheet (two, if you have them). Sift the flour, cornstarch, baking powder, and baking soda together into a bowl.
2. In an electric mixer (or may be done by hand) cream the butter, then add the sugars and beat until light and fluffy. Beat in the egg until well combined, and then the peanut butter.
3. By hand stir the sifted flour into the peanut-butter mixture, mixing only until the mixture is just blended. Cover the dough with plastic wrap and put in the fridge for $\frac{1}{2}$ hour (or longer) — the dough should be firm.
4. Scoop up tablespoons of the dough, roll into balls in your hand, and place 2" apart on the prepared cookie sheets. Press the balls down with the back of a fork, flattening them to about $\frac{1}{4}$" thick. Bake in the preheated oven for 12 to 14 minutes, until golden on the bottom (it may be wise to turn the sheets half way to ensure even browning). Remove the pan from the oven and let the cookies cool on it until they are firm enough to be removed from the pan.

JAVA STICKS

A delicious combination of chocolate and coffee; a good accompaniment to a fruit dessert.

Makes about 6 dozen.

1 cup	**unsalted butter**, soft
$\frac{1}{2}$ cup	**icing sugar**
$3\frac{1}{2}$ tsp	**instant coffee powder**
$1\frac{1}{2}$ cups	**all-purpose flour**
$\frac{1}{4}$ cup	**finely ground walnuts**
4 oz	**semi-sweet chocolate**

1. Preheat the oven to 350° F. Lightly butter a cookie sheet (two, if you have them) or line with parchment paper (see page 152).
2. Using an electric mixer fitted with paddle attachment (or by hand), cream the butter with the icing sugar until light and fluffy. Beat in the coffee powder, and scrape down the sides of the bowl.
3. With the mixer on low speed, add in the flour and the ground walnuts. Mix well, until the dough

gathers together: it should be quite stiff.

4. Scoop the dough into a pastry bag fitted with a star or ½" round tip, whichever you prefer (or have!). Pipe onto the prepared cookie sheet in 2" lengths. Bake in the preheated oven until golden brown, about 12 to 15 minutes. Remove from the oven and transfer to a rack to cool.

5. Place the chocolate in a bowl that can go over hot water (or in the top of a double boiler); set it over simmering, but not boiling, water and melt, stirring occasionally. Dip about ½" at each end of the cookies into the chocolate and then set on waxed (or parchment) paper to cool. Store in an airtight container.

WHOLE-WHEAT GRANOLA COOKIES

A great tasting cookie that's full of good ingredients; whether it's actually good for you is another question — on which we offer no guarantees.

Makes about 5 dozen.

2 cups	**granola**, plain or honeyed
1¼ cups	**whole-wheat flour**
⅓ cup	**toasted wheat germ** (available in health-food stores)
1 tsp	**baking soda**
¾ tsp	**ground cinnamon**
¼ tsp	**ground nutmeg**
¼ tsp	**salt**
1 cup	**butter**, soft
½ cup	**light brown sugar**, well packed
⅓ cup	**water**
zest of 1	**orange** (medium)
1 cup	**raisins**
1 cup	**almonds**, chopped (or chocolate chips, or shredded coconut, or walnuts)

1. Preheat the oven to 350° F. Lightly butter a cookie sheet (two if you have them) or line with parchment paper (see page 152). Combine the granola, whole-wheat flour, wheat germ, baking soda, cinnamon, nutmeg, and salt in a large bowl and mix well; set aside.

2. Using an electric mixer fitted with the paddle (may be done by hand), beat together butter, brown sugar, orange zest, and vanilla, until fluffy. Scrape down the sides, then stir in granola and flour mixture by hand, ½ cup at a time, adding a little water between additions until it is all incorporated. Stir in the raisins and nuts.

3. Drop heaping tablespoons of the dough 2" apart on the prepared cookie sheets. Bake in the preheated oven until brown around the edges (6 to 10 minutes). For a soft cookie, bake 6 minutes only; for a crisper cookie, bake the full 10 minutes. Cool briefly on the baking sheets and then transfer to racks to cool completely.

4. Store in an airtight container, should there be any left.

LEMON SABLES

A lemon cookie with a light grainy texture — a great way to dress up a dessert. The dough may be made the day before; it should chill for at least 3 hours before baking.

Makes about 24.

²/₃ cup	**ground almonds**
²/₃ cup	**icing sugar**
6 oz	**unsalted butter**, soft
1 large	**egg**
1 Tbs	**lemon zest**, finely chopped (page 210)
¼ tsp	**salt**
1½ cups	**all-purpose** or **cake flour** (page 225)

FOR THE GLAZE

2 Tbs	**icing sugar**
1	**egg yolk**
1 Tbs	**fresh lemon juice**

1. Combine the almonds and icing sugar in the workbowl of your food processor; process to a fine powder.

2. Transfer the almond mixture to the bowl of an electric mixer (or other bowl if working by hand); add the butter and cream until light and fluffy. Add the egg, lemon zest, and salt, and blend thoroughly.

3. By hand, mix in the flour, adding it all at once. This is a fragile cookie and it will become tough if you overmix, so be gentle. Gather the dough into a ball, wrap in plastic, and refrigerate for 3 hours (or longer).

4. Preheat the oven to 350° F. Butter and flour a cookie sheet (two, if you have them).

5. Divide the dough in half, and put one half back in the fridge. On a lightly floured surface, roll out the other half to a thickness of about ³/₁₆". Cut out cookies with a cookie cutter (or a glass). Reroll the scraps gently and cut more cookies from them (they will not be quite so tender, because of the extra rolling). Transfer to the prepared cookie sheet and refrigerate for 30 minutes, while you roll and cut out the other half.

6. Make the glaze: Mix the icing sugar, egg yolk, and lemon juice together. Brush this over the tops of the cookies.

7. Bake in the preheated oven for 15 to 18 minutes, until just starting to brown around the edges — they should still be quite pale on top.

8. Remove from the oven and cool on the baking sheet until firm; then transfer to a rack and cool completely. Store in an airtight container.

Opposite: *Chocolate Chip Cookies (see recipe on page 149). Chocolate Reversal Cookies*

GINGER AND CINNAMON CHOCOLATE CHIP COOKIES

The batter should be refrigerated for several hours or overnight before being baked.

Makes about 6 dozen.

2 cups	**all-purpose flour**
1 tsp	**baking soda**
1 tsp	**ground cinnamon**
1 tsp	**ground ginger**
1½ cups	**unsalted butter**, softened
1½ cups	**light brown sugar**, firmly packed
1 large	**egg**
1 tsp	**vanilla extract**
12 oz	**semi-sweet chocolate chips**
Optional:	
¾ cup	**chopped walnuts**

1. Sift together the flour, baking soda, cinnamon, and ginger into a bowl.
2. Using an electric mixer with the paddle attachment (may be done by hand), cream the butter; add in the brown sugar and beat until light and fluffy (2 to 3 minutes).
3. Beat in the egg and vanilla. With machine on low, blend in the flour mixture, mixing just until incorporated. With a spatula, fold in the chocolate chips and walnuts, if you are using them. Refrigerate until firm, or overnight.

4. Preheat the oven to 375° F. Lightly butter a cookie sheet (or two), or line with parchment paper (see page 152).
5. Break of a piece of dough (a small handful), roll into a ball, place it on the prepared cookie sheet, and flatten with the palm of your hand. Cookies should be spaced 2" apart.
6. Bake in the preheated oven for 10 minutes. Cool for 5 minutes on the sheets and then transfer to a rack to cool completely.
7. Store in an airtight container, in the unlikely event that they are not eaten straightaway.

RAISIN OAT DROPS

Makes about 5 dozen cookies.

1¼ cups	**quick-cooking rolled oats**
1¼ cups	**all-purpose flour**
1 tsp	**baking soda**
½ tsp	**baking powder**
½ tsp	**ground ginger**
½ tsp	**ground nutmeg**
½ tsp	**ground cinnamon**
pinch of	**salt**
½ cup	**unsalted butter**, room temperature
½ cup	**light brown sugar**, well packed
1 large	**egg**
1½ tsp	**vanilla extract**
1½ Tbs	**orange zest**, finely grated (see page 210)
¼ cup	**maple syrup**
1 cup	**raisins**

1. Preheat the oven to 375° F. Butter a cookie sheet (two if you have them) or line with parchment paper (see page 152).
2. Combine the rolled oats, flour, baking soda and baking powder, ginger, cinnamon, nutmeg, and salt in a large bowl. Mix well to combine.
3. Using an electric mixer fitted with the paddle (may be done by hand), cream together the butter and brown sugar until light and fluffy. Add the egg, vanilla, and orange zest, and beat well. Stir in flour, ¾ cup at a time, adding a little maple syrup between additions until both are completely incorporated. Fold in the raisins.
4. Drop tablespoonfuls of batter onto the prepared cookie sheets, about 2" apart. Bake for 6 to 10 minutes. For a soft cookie, bake 6 minutes only; for a crisper cookie, bake the full 10 minutes. Transfer to a rack to cool. Store in an airtight container.

DOUBLE FUDGE COOKIES

A very rich and chocolatey cookie — all made in a food processor. The unbaked dough keeps well in the refrigerator. My wife Nancy's favourites.

Makes about 20 large cookies.

1¾ cup	**all-purpose flour**, sifted
1 tsp	**baking soda**
10 oz	**semi-sweet chocolate**, finely chopped
1 cup	**granulated sugar**
1 cup	**light brown sugar**, well packed
1 cup	**unsalted butter**, room temperature
2 large	**eggs**, room temperature
1 tsp	**vanilla extract**
1 cup	**semi-sweet chocolate chips**

1. Sift together the flour and baking soda into a bowl.
2. In a food processor fitted with the steel blade, combine the semi-sweet chocolate and white and brown sugar; pulse 6 times to chop and combine. (If your chocolate is in larger chunks, you can do all the chopping in the food processor; the sugar will help prevent it becoming sticky.) Then process continuously for 1 minute until the mixture is powder fine. If some chocolate has gathered into a clump around the edge of the workbowl, scrape it down.
3. Cut the butter in 2 or 3 pieces, add to the workbowl, and process for 30 seconds. Add the eggs and vanilla, and process for another 30 seconds. Scrape down the sides of the bowl and

pulse 2 times. Add the sifted flour and chocolate chips. Pulse 8 or 10 times, then scrape down the sides of the workbowl and pulse 2 more times, until everything is completely blended.

4. Turn the cookie dough into bowl, cover with plasic wrap and refrigerate until firm, or overnight.

5. Preheat the oven to 350° F. Lightly butter a cookie sheet (two if you have them) or line with parchment paper (see page 152). Scoop out pieces of dough; the size will depend on how big you like your cookies. Roll into a ball with your hands and place on the prepared cookie sheets, leaving 2" or so between. Do not flatten as the cookies will flatten and spread by themselves in the oven.

6. Bake in the preheated oven for about 15 minutes, just until the edges have set; the centre will look underdone. Cool on cookie sheets, then transfer to an airtight tin to store.

7. Unused dough will keep in the fridge for 5 days.

MADELEINES

The cookie of the literary world; it was the taste of a madeleine dipped in a cup of tea that brought back to Marcel Proust a flood of memories that went on for twelve volumes. They are best eaten the day they are baked — but have your word processor ready before you taste!

Makes 12 to 18, depending on the size of the mould.

³/₄ cup	**unsalted butter**
¹/₂ cup	**all-purpose flour**
¹/₂ cup	**soft cake flour**
¹/₄ tsp	**salt**
¹/₂ tsp	**baking powder**
3 large	**eggs**
²/₃ cup	**granulated sugar**
1 tsp	**vanilla extract**
2 tsp	**grated lemon zest** (see page 210)
2 Tbs	**lemon juice**

FOR DECORATION
icing sugar

MADELEINES
The origin of madeleines being baked in a shell-shaped mould goes back to an ancient Provençal legend. According to this, Mary Magdalene ("La Madeleine" in French) lived with Mary, the mother of Jesus, for thirteen years following the Crucifixion. She was then expelled from the country, and cast adrift, in a open boat without sails or oars, with her sister Martha, Lazarus her brother, and two Marys, one the mother of James and John, the other the mother of James Minor. This boat eventually reached land safely where the town of Les Saintes Maries de-la-Mer now stands, at the mouth of the Rhone in the Camargue. This safe arrival is commemorated by the shell shape. La Madeleine did not stay there, but journeyed inland to the forest of Sainte-Baume, where she lived in a cave, leading the life of a hermit until her death.

1. Preheat the oven to 350° F. Butter and flour 2 madeleine moulds. Melt the butter in a small saucepan and allow to cool. Sift together the two flours, salt, and baking powder into a bowl.

2. Place the eggs, sugar, and vanilla in a good-sized bowl that can go over hot water. Set over simmering, but not boiling, water and beat until doubled in volume. Remove from the heat, and scoop into the bowl of an electric mixer, if you have one: if not just contine in the same bowl. Whisk until completely cool and almost doubled again in volume; the batter should be light and creamy with no large air bubbles.

3. Be as gentle as possible at this stage: Sift some (about ¹/₄) of the already-sifted flour over the batter; fold gently (see page 128) until the flour has disappeared from the top of the batter (it does not have to be completely folded in). Drizzle on some of the cooled butter, then sift in some more flour and gently fold both of them in. Add the lemon zest and juice, then repeat with the flour and butter until everything is folded in. The less you can deflate the eggs while folding the flour and butter in the lighter your madeleines will be; it is the butter that is the real balloon-popper.

4. Spoon the batter into the moulds until ³/₄ full; bake in the preheated oven for 15 to 20 minutes, until golden brown. Remove from the oven and take them out of the pan immediately, by rapping the upside-down pan sharply on the counter: the madeleines will come tumbling out. Dust them with icing sugar while they are still warm, then again when cool.

BACI DI DAMA (LADIES' KISSES)

Daphna learned how to make these cookies while living in Italy. They are originally from the Piedmont area, and there are many theories about how they got their fanciful name — the most popular one, that they in some way resemble the lips of a beautiful lady. This recipe can be made in either an electric mixer or a food processor. (The instructions for a food processor are in parentheses).

Makes 4 dozen cookies.

1 cup	**finely groud almonds**
1 cup	**granulated sugar**
4 oz	**unsalted butter**, soft
1 tsp	**vanilla extract**
1 tsp	**lemon zest**, finely grated (see page 210)
¼ tsp	**salt**
1 cup	**all-purpose flour**
4 oz	**semi-sweet chocolate**

1. Combine the almonds and sugar in the mixer bowl (or the workbowl of the food processor; pulse briefly). Add the butter, vanilla, lemon zest, and salt, and beat with the paddle (or process) until very light and fluffy. Stop once to scrape down the sides of the bowl. Scrape the dough into a bowl and stir in the flour by hand. Cover with plastic wrap and refrigerate for 30 minutes — longer if you wish.

2. Preheat the oven to 350° F. Do not butter the cookie sheet, although you can line it with parchment paper (see page 152) if you have it.
3. Using a ½ tsp measure (it is small — but it's right), scoop out pieces of dough. Roll each one into a ball and place 1½" apart on the cookie sheet.
4. Bake in the preheated oven for 15 minutes, until a delicate golden brown (if they seem to melt, your oven temperature is too high). Remove from the oven and transfer to racks with a spatula; allow to cool completely.
5. Melt the chocolate in the top of a double boiler or stainless-steel bowl set over simmering, but not boiling, water. Remove from the heat and stir until smooth. With a small spatula, spread some chocolate on the underside of a cookie. Take another cookie more or less the same size, and make a sandwich by joining its underside to the chocolate. Repeat until all the cookies are joined.
6. Place all the cookies on a rack, dip a fork in chocolate and rapidly shake it back and forth over the cookies, drizzling them with stripes of chocolate.
7. These cookies are best served the same day.

CHOCOLATE CARAMEL CHEWIES

Very decadent, almost like candy. The method is a candy-making one and a sugar thermometer will be helpful.

Makes about 18 chewies.

FOR THE COOKIE BASE

4 oz	**unsweetened chocolate**
1 cup	**unsalted butter**
1¾ cups	**light brown sugar**, packed
¼ tsp	**salt**
1½ tsp	**vanilla extract**
2 large	**eggs**
1½ cups	**all-purpose flour**

FOR THE CARAMEL TOPPING

1⅓ cups	**light brown sugar**, well packed
¾ cup	**whipping cream (35%)**
¾ cup	**light corn syrup**
⅓ cup	**butter**
1½ tsp	**vanilla extract**
1½ cups	**toasted chopped pecans**

FOR THE CHOCOLATE GLAZE

2 oz	**semi-sweet chocolate**, coarsely chopped
1 Tbs	**whipping cream (35%)**
½ tsp	**vanilla extract**

1. Preheat oven to 350° F. Butter a 9" by 13" baking pan.

2. Make the cookie base: Combine the unsweetened chocolate and butter together in a bowl that can go over hot water (or the top of a double boiler), and melt over simmering, but not boiling, water. Stir until smooth, but do not beat any more than necessary.

3. Remove from the heat and beat in the brown sugar and salt, mixing until smooth. Beat in the vanilla and the eggs. Blend in the flour, ½ cup at a time, beating well after each addition. Spoon into the prepared pan and smooth the top. Bake in the preheated oven for 25 minutes, until a tester just comes out clean. Set aside to cool.

4. Make the caramel topping: Combine the sugar, cream, corn syrup, and butter in a heavy medium-sized saucepan. Cook over medium heat, stirring occasionally, until the mixture reaches 230° F on a candy thermometer (the thread stage — see page 11). Immediately remove from the heat and stir in the vanilla and pecans. Pour the hot caramel over the cookie base, and spread it out evenly. Let stand at room temperature until cool.

5. Make the glaze: Combine the chocolate, cream, and vanilla in the top of a double boiler set over simmering, but not boiling, water, and stir until smooth. With a fork, drizzle the chocolate in a lacy pattern over the caramel. Allow to cool, then cut into bars with a sharp knife.

6. The chewies will keep for 1 week in an airtight container at room temperature.

CHOCOLATE-GLAZED CARAMEL PECAN BARS

Even better than the caramel chewies — with extra chocolate on top and a shortbread base. A candy thermometer will make your life easier.

Makes about 60 small bars or 25 larger ones (each 2" by 3").

FOR THE BASE

³⁄₄ cup	**unsalted butter**, soft
1 cup	**light brown sugar**, well packed
1 tsp	**vanilla extract**
pinch of	**salt**
2 cups	**all-purpose flour**
2¹⁄₂ cups	**pecan halves**

FOR THE CARAMEL FILLING

1¹⁄₃ cups	**brown sugar**, well packed
³⁄₄ cup	**whipping cream**
³⁄₄ cup	**light corn syrup**
¹⁄₃ cup	**unsalted butter**
¹⁄₈ tsp	**salt**
1¹⁄₂ tsp	**vanilla extract**

FOR THE CHOCOLATE TOPPING

10 oz	**semi-sweet chocolate**, coarsely chopped
¹⁄₄ cup	**unsalted butter**
3 Tbs	**half-and-half** or **milk**
³⁄₄ tsp	**vanilla extract**

1. Preheat the oven to 250° F. Lightly butter a 10" by 15" jellyroll pan.

2. Make the cookie base: Using an electric mixer fitted with the paddle (may be done by hand), cream together the butter, brown sugar, vanilla, and salt, until light and fluffy. Stir in the flour, ¹⁄₂ cup at a time, blending well after each addition. With floured hands, turn the dough into the prepared pan and pat out to an even thickness. Cover with tight rows of pecan halves, pressed lightly into the dough. Bake in the preheated oven until golden brown, 18 to 22 minutes. Remove from the oven and cool completely.

3. Make the caramel: Combine the brown sugar, cream, corn syrup, butter, and salt in a medium heavy-bottom saucepan. Cook over medium-high heat, stirring occasionally, until mixture reaches 230° F on a candy thermometer (the thread stage — see page 11). Immediately remove from the heat and add the vanilla. Pour the hot caramel over the shortbread base and spread it out evenly. Allow to cool at room temperature.

4. Make the topping: Combine the chocolate, butter, and cream in a small saucepan. Cook over low heat, stirring constantly until the mixture is melted and smooth. Remove from the heat and add vanilla. Pour the topping over the cooled caramel and spread it evenly with a spatula. Allow to cool; then cut with a sharp knife into 60 small bars.

5. The bars will keep for a week in an airtight container at room temperature.

APPLE BRANDY BARS

A rich, sweet bar that needs no icing.

Makes 18 large bars (each 2" by 3") or up to 40 small ones.

2 cups	**all-purpose flour**
1 tsp	**salt**
1 tsp	**cinnamon**
1 tsp	**baking soda**
2 cups	**apple slices**
2	**eggs**
2 cups	**granulated sugar**
1¼ cups	**oil**

Optional:

⅓ cup	**brandy**
1 cup	**chopped walnuts** or **pecans**
1 tsp	**vanilla extract**

1. Preheat the oven to 350° F. Butter and flour a 9" by 13" cake pan. Sift the flour, salt, cinnamon, and baking soda together into a bowl. Peel, quarter, core, and slice the apples; you will need 2 cups of slices.

2. Using an electric mixer (or by hand), whisk the eggs and sugar until light and quite thick, then gradually beat in the oil and brandy (if you are using it). Stir the sifted flour into the eggs, then fold in the apples and nuts (see page 128 on folding technique).

3. Scoop the batter into the prepared pan and spread it evenly. Bake in the preheated oven for 35 to 40 minutes, until the top is light brown and dry.

4. Allow to cool on a rack completely before cutting into squares with a sharp knife.

SKOR BAR COOKIE BRITTLE

Easy and quick to make; and very good to eat.
The brittle is quite irregular in size, so quantity is hard to estimate — but 50 smallish pieces would be a good guess.

4	**Skor Bars**
1 cup	**butter**
1 cup	**sugar**
1 tsp	**vanilla extract**
½ tsp	**salt**
2 cups	**all-purpose flour**
¾ cup	**finely chopped pecans** or **walnuts**
1 cup	**chocolate chips**

1. Preheat the oven to 325° F. Find a 10" by 15" cake pan. Coarsely chop the Skor Bars and set aside.

2. Using an electric mixer, cream the butter, then slowly beat in the sugar until it is light and fluffy. Beat in the vanilla and salt, then stir in the flour (if you have young helpers, they can use their hands — and so may you), until well combined. Stir in the nuts, Skor Bars, and chocolate chips.

3. Press the dough evenly into an ungreased 10" by 15" pan. Bake in the preheated oven for 15 to 20 minutes until golden brown. Remove from the oven and place on a rack to cool.

4. When completely cool, break into pieces and eat.

Almond Pecan Buttercrunch Corn

A candy thermometer is helpful for this recipe.

Makes 6 to 8 cups.

1 cup	**popcorn**, unpopped
1 tsp	**salt**
1 lb	**unsalted butter**
1 cup	**white sugar**
1 cup	**brown sugar**
¹/₂ cup	**corn syrup**
¹/₃ cup	**water**
2 cups	**unblanched almonds**
2 cups	**pecans**

1. Pop the corn; then place the popped corn in a large heat-proof bowl. Sprinkle with the salt and toss.

2. Melt the butter in a heavy-bottom deep saucepan. Add the two sugars, corn syrup, and water. Bring to a boil over medium-high heat, stirring constantly. Keep stirring until the mixture reaches 295° F on a candy thermometer. Remove from the heat and pour immediately over the popcorn. Add the nuts, stir, and toss using 2 large wooden spoons, until the popcorn is well coated. Spread out on 2 large cookie sheets to harden.

3. Store in an airtight container.

Maple Almond Granola

Not exactly a cookie — but a delicious snack. Very simple to make.

Makes about 3¹/₂ cups.

2 cups	**rolled oats** (not the quick-cooking kind)
1 cup	**whole almonds**, coarsely chopped, skin on
¹/₃ cup	**sunflower oil**
¹/₄ cup	**maple syrup**
¹/₂ tsp	**vanilla extract**
¹/₄ tsp	**salt**

1. Preheat the oven to 350° F. Find an 11" by 15" baking sheet.

2. Mix the oats, almonds, oil, maple syrup, vanilla, and salt together in a large bowl. Spread it out thinly on the baking sheet. Bake in the preheated oven for 20 to 25 minutes, until golden brown. Store in an airtight container at room temperature.

CHILDREN'S DESSERTS

Cooking with children can be a real pleasure, or an exercise in frustration: it all depends on what your expectations are. It is futile to expect a young child to assist seriously in the preparations for a dinner party, particularly if you are pressed for time. A child cannot set his or her mind on such a distant goal, and will quickly get bored with the seemingly meaningless series of preparations. To enjoy cooking with children, you must devote yourself to, and involve the child in, each step in the process. As your child gains more experience, he or she will learn that the process and the product are both part of the thing called "cooking", and that one cannot have one without the other. When your child reaches the point of understanding this connection, he or she will, indeed, be able to help you with the preparations for dinner.

The absence of goal orientation is very frustrating for us grown-ups, who are conditioned to value this attitude above most others. We think that, in cooking with children, we are teaching them; but in fact, the really important learning that takes place is ours. If we can fully experience the enjoyment of mixing a cake batter — and how much better the batter tastes eaten off the mixing spoon than the finished cake ever will! — we will have learned something much more valuable than how to make a perfect-looking cake. It is part of a child's nature to find the pleasure in things; if we can curb our inclination to feel frustrated with the apparent lack of progress when a child stops to taste everything at each step, and follow his or her lead, we may not only discover that we find cooking a lot more enjoyable, but we may rediscover what good cooks have been telling us for years: to make really good food you have to taste, taste, taste all the time!

A child can help with almost any of the recipes in the book, not just those in this section. In fact some of the recipes in this section — the caramel and taffy ones — are not ideal for children to make because they involve very hot sugar syrups, which can be dangerous. The recipes here are chosen because they are things that, as grown-ups, we don't eat any longer, but that, for me at any rate, were an essential part of parties when I was young. They were treat food (a good idea still, with the amount of sugar in most them); but I can remember to this day the taste and crunch of a brandy snap full of whipped cream, even though it is more than thirty years ago. I, too, may learn from my children that a little bit of what you fancy will do you no harm.

AMBROSIA

This is a little bit of nostalgia. Karen recommends making it as a cure for food dogma, a preciousness about purity of style and ingredients, which is an occupational hazard of the food business, and to which we succumb every now and again. If you want to go all out, dye some shredded coconut with different colours of food dye and decorate the top with it just before serving.

Makes 16 servings.

3 cups	**sour cream**
1 can	**mandarin oranges**, (10 oz) well drained
1 can	**pineapple chunks**, (19 oz) drained
²/₃ cup	**maraschino cherries**, cut in half
4 tbs	**maraschino cherry juice**
6 cups	**miniature marshmallows**

1. Mix the sour cream, mandarin oranges, pineapple, and cherry juice together. Fold in the marshmallows. Place it in a serving bowl and smooth the top. Cover with plastic wrap and chill overnight.

2. Eat with good friends.

CARAMELIZED APPLES

A sweet, sticky, and very delicious snack. (See photograph opposite page 174.)

4	**firm apples**, peeled and cut into 1" wedges
4 Tbs	**butter**
²/₃ cup	**sugar**
¹/₃ cup	**lemon juice**

1. Peel, quarter, and core the apples. Cut each quarter lengthwise into 2 or 3 wedges, then set aside.

2. Combine the butter, sugar, and lemon juice in a wide heavy-bottom pan. Bring to a boil over high heat, stirring occasionally. Reduce the heat to medium and cook without stirring until a caramel is formed (see page 11 — the process is much the same as that used in cooking a sugar syrup to a caramel).

3. Add the apple wedges (carefully, as they may spit at you), and reduce the heat to low. Sauté the apples for 3 to 4 minutes. Remove from the heat and pour onto a plate to cool. Do not refrigerate. Serve warm, or at room temperature.

ALICE'S TAFFY APPLES

The classic red apple with a clear, hard coating. Really hard work for your teeth, but, strangely, children do not seem to mind. (See photograph opposite page 174.)

Makes 10 apples.

³/₄ cup	**granulated sugar**
¹/₂ cup	**corn syrup**
¹/₄ cup	**warm water**
10	**red apples**
10	**wooden sticks** or **skewers**
Optional:	**red food colouring**

1. Oil a baking sheet, or line it with parchment. Stick a skewer into the stem area of each apple.
2. Combine the sugar, corn syrup, and water in a heavy-bottom saucepan. Cook over medium-low heat, until the sugar has dissolved, then turn up the heat to medium-high. See page 11 for instructions on cooking a sugar syrup: continue cooking until all the water has evaporated (a lot of bubbles on the surface at this point), and then cook further to the hard-crack stage (295° F to 300° F on a candy thermometer); this is about 50° F before the caramel stage. In case you go a bit too far, have ready a pan or sink of cold water; if you are judging your progress by eye and you begin to see the slightest trace of caramelization, immediately remove the pan from the heat and plunge its bottom in the cold water, just until the sizzling stops.
3. Add the food colouring if you wish.
4. Dip each apple in turn into the sugar syrup, rolling it around to coat it well. Set on the prepared baking sheet to cool and harden.

TOFFEE APPLES

These apples have a soft, brown toffee coating. A candy thermometer is useful when making them.

Makes 8 apples.

2 cups	**dark brown sugar**, well packed
²/₃ cup	**molasses**
¹/₂ cup	**unsalted butter**
1 Tbs	**vinegar**
8	**crisp apples**
8	**wooden sticks**

1. Oil a baking sheet or line it with parchment. Push the sticks into the stem end of the apples. Fill a roasting pan or sink with cold water, to cool the sugar when it is ready.
2. Combine the sugar, molasses, butter and vinegar in a heavy-bottom saucepan. Cook over medium heat, until the sugar has dissolved, then increase the heat to medium high and cook to the hard-crack stage (300° F on the thermometer: see page 11 on

cooking sugar syrups). You can test by dropping a little of the syrup into cold water — it should become very hard and brittle. Remove the pan from the heat, and immerse its bottom in the pan of cold water, just until the sizzling stops.

3. Dip each apple into the toffee, rolling it around so that it is well coated. Stand on the prepared baking sheet to cool and harden.

VANILLA CARAMELS

Very popular with children; but not really suitable for them to make by themselves as it involves a very hot sugar syrup. A candy thermometer is helpful.

Makes 40 to 50 candies.

2 cups	**granulated sugar**
½ cup	**corn syrup**
½ cup	**milk**
4 Tbs	**unsalted butter**
1 cup	**whipping cream** (35%) or **condensed milk**
1 tsp	**vanilla extract**

1. Lightly butter an 8" by 8" jellyroll pan.
2. Combine the sugar, corn syrup, milk, butter, and cream (or condensed milk) in a heavy-bottom saucepan; bring to a boil over medium-low heat, stirring occasionally until the sugar has dissolved. Increase the heat to high, and cook to the hard-ball stage (about 245° F — see page 11). Remove from the heat, pour in the vanilla, and swirl to mix it in. Pour into the prepared pan, and set aside to cool.
3. When cold, turn the caramel out of the pan and cut into squares.

WHITE PULL TAFFY

This is the classic pull taffy; fun to make, and simple enough once you have cooked the syrup to the right point — a candy thermometer is a good idea for this.

Makes about 24.

2 cups	**granulated sugar**
½ cup	**water**
1 tsp	**glycerine** (from the drug store)
2½ Tbs	**white vinegar**
1 tsp	**vanilla extract** or **lemon extract**

1. Oil a baking sheet with sides (low is fine).
2. Combine the sugar, water, glycerine, and vinegar in a saucepan; bring to a boil over medium heat, swirling frequently until the sugar is melted. Then turn up the heat to high and cook to the hard-ball stage (260° F — see page 11). When it reaches this point, remove from the heat and add the flavouring, then, turn out onto the greased baking sheet.
3. When the taffy is cool enough to handle, oil your hands lightly and pick it up. Stretch it out, then double it over and pull out again. Keep doing this until the taffy has become quite white. At this point, stretch it into a long rope, then cut it with scissors into short pieces. Store at room temperature in a tightly closed tin.

MOLASSES TAFFY

Another pull taffy, with the distinctive molasses flavour.

Makes about 24.

2 cups	**molasses**
1 cup	**granulated sugar**
¾ cup	**water**
⅛ tsp	**baking soda**
4 Tbs	**unsalted butter**
½ tsp	**vanilla extract**

1. Oil a baking sheet with sides.
2. Combine the molasses, sugar, and water in a saucepan. Bring to a boil over medium heat, then increase the heat slightly and cook to the hard-ball stage (260° F — see page 11). It is a good idea to stir during the latter stages, as molasses has a tendency to burn.
3. Remove from the heat and add the soda, butter, and vanilla. Stir enough to mix, then turn onto the oiled sheet.
4. When the taffy is cool enough to handle, oil your hands lightly and pick it up. Stretch it out, then double it over and pull out again. Keep doing this until the taffy has become quite light in colour. At this point, stretch it into a long rope, then cut it with scissors into short pieces. Store at room temperature in a tightly closed tin.

ALICE'S BUTTERSCOTCH TAFFY

A crisp butterscotch brittle. A candy thermometer is a good idea.

Makes about 24.

2 cups	**brown sugar**, well packed
¼ cup	**corn syrup**
½ cup	**water**
¼ tsp	**salt**
⅓ cup	**unsalted butter**
½ tsp	**vanilla extract**

1. Oil a jellyroll pan (baking sheet with sides).
2. Combine the sugar, corn syrup, water, and salt in a heavy-bottom saucepan. Cook over medium low heat, stirring frequently, until the sugar is dissolved; then increase the heat to high and cook to the hard-ball stage (245 ° F on a candy thermometer — see page 11 on cooking sugar syrup).
3. Add the butter carefully — it may spit at you; then continue to cook over medium high heat to 300° F (hard-crack stage). Remove from the heat and swirl in the vanilla.
4. Pour into the prepared pan and allow to cool. When cold break into pieces.

VARIATION:
PECAN BUTTERSCOTCH
BRITTLE

1 recipe	**Butterscotch Taffy** (see above)
1 cup	**pecans** or **pecan pieces**

1. Make the butterscotch taffy following the recipe above to the end of Step 3.
2. Add the pecans to the hot taffy, and stir in with a wooden spoon.
3. Pour and scoop the taffy onto the prepared jellyroll pan; allow to cool, then break into pieces.

GINGERBREAD MEN AND WOMEN

Easy to make — and a lot of fun to decorate. (See photograph opposite page 206.)

Makes about 30 small, or 12 large.

5 cups	**all-purpose flour**
2 tsp	**baking soda**
¹/₂ tsp	**salt**
3 tbs	**powdered ginger**
2 tsp	**ground cinnamon**
2 tsp	**nutmeg**
1 tsp	**allspice**
8 oz	**unsalted butter**
1 cup	**light brown sugar**, firmly packed
³/₄ cup	**molasses**
2 large	**eggs**

TO DECORATE

1 recipe **White Icing** (see page 213)

1. Preheat the oven to 350° F. Lightly butter a cookie sheet (two, if you have them) or line with parchment paper. Sift together the flour, baking soda, salt, ginger, cinnamon, nutmeg, and allspice.
2. Using an electric mixer fitted with the paddle (may be done by hand), cream the butter with the sugar until light and fluffy. With the machine running, pour in the molasses in a thin stream; then beat in the eggs, one at a time.
3. Add the sifted flour to the batter and beat until completely incorporated. Remove the dough from the machine; cover with plastic wrap and chill for 1 hour (longer if you wish).
4. On a floured work surface, roll out the dough to a ¹/₄" thickness. Cut out figures with cookie or gingerbread cutters, or by hand. With a long palette knife or spatula, carefully transfer the cookies to the prepared baking sheets. Bake in the preheated oven for 8 to 10 minutes, until crisp around the edges.
5. Remove from the oven and transfer to a rack to cool.
6. Make the icing following the recipe on page 213; use food colouring to get the colours you want. Make paper icing bags (see page 63), then decorate.

Opposite: *Caramelized Apple (see recipe on page 169), Taffy Apple (see recipe on page 170), and Chocolate Cupcakes with White and Chocolate Icing (see recipe on page 176).*

MERINGUES

We always had these for birthday parties when I was a child, and children still love them. They are also good served with whipped cream and raspberries for dessert. There are two secrets to these meringues; fold the sugar in gently — do not beat it in; and cook them slowly — the process is as much one of drying out as cooking. My mother used to leave them overnight in the warming oven of the Aga (with a red ribbon tied to the door to remind her!); at the store we make them last thing at night, and leave them in the turned-off but still warm ovens. The meringues should be baked as soon as the final sugar has been folded in.

For 12 large meringue halves or 24 small ones (which will make 12 whole ones when filled).

4	**egg whites**
1 cup	**granulated sugar**
½ tsp	**white vinegar** or **lemon juice**
½ cup	**whipping cream**

1. Preheat the oven to 275° F. Line a baking sheet with parchment (or butter and flour it generously — meringues are inveterate stickers).

2. In a large bowl, beat the egg whites till white and frothy (see page 24). Add about 2 Tbs of the sugar and continue beating to firm peaks.

3. Add the lemon juice, then gently fold in (see page 128) the rest of the sugar in 3 batches. The meringue will be quite granular, but this is all right (it is correct, in fact!).

4. Scoop the meringue into a piping bag fitted with a large plain tip (or into a heavy plastic bag with the corner cut off), and pipe egg shapes on to the prepared sheet — about 3" long by 2" wide. Bake in the preheated oven for 1 to 1½ hours, until lightly browned and crisp on top. Remove from the oven and allow to cool.

5. Shortly before serving, whip the cream to firm peaks (not too firm, but more than you usually would). Spread a spoonful of cream onto the base of one meringue, then gently press another meringue base against it, so that you have a sandwich. You have to separate the halves to eat it, but it looks good presented like this.

CHOCOLATE CUPCAKES

Very easy to make. (See photograph opposite page 174).

Makes 24 cupcakes.

1¼ cups	**all-purpose flour**
5 Tbs	**unsweetened cocoa powder**
1½ tsp	**baking soda**
¼ tsp	**salt**
1 cup	**granulated sugar**
1 cup	**water**
6 Tbs	**vegetable oil**
2 tsp	**vanilla extract**
1 Tbs	**white vinegar**

FOR THE OPTIONAL DECORATION

1 recipe	**White Icing** (see page 213)
	food colouring

1. Preheat the oven to 325° F. Line 24 muffin cups with paper cups (may be done in 2 batches if you only have a 12-cup tin).
2. Sift together the flour, cocoa, baking soda, and salt into a bowl; then mix in the sugar.
3. Combine the water, oil, vanilla, and vinegar in a large bowl; whisk to mix. Pour in the dry ingredients, then mix just enough to combine: the batter will be quite thin.
4. Pour the batter into the prepared muffin cups, then bake in the preheated oven for 13 to 15 minutes, until the top springs back to the touch, and a cake tester comes out almost clean.
5. Decorate the tops with icing if you wish (see page 63 on how to make a paper icing cone).

LEMON SNOW

A very popular dessert with children; a simpler version of Snow Eggs (page 22), which is also a big hit.

FOR THE LEMON SNOW

1 Tbs	**gelatine**
¼ cup	**cold water**
1 cup	**boiling water**
½ cup	**granulated sugar**
pinch of	**salt**
2 Tbs	**lemon zest**, finely chopped (page 210)
¼ cup	**lemon juice**
2	**egg whites**
¼ cup	**granulated sugar**

FOR THE CUSTARD

2 cups	**milk**
3	**egg yolks**
¼ cup	**granulated sugar**
2 tsp	**vanilla extract**

1. Make the Lemon Snow first; it needs to set. Lightly oil a mould for the Snow; you can use individual ramekins, an angel-cake pan, soufflé dish, or any other mould.
2. Pour the cold water into a small bowl, spinkle the gelatine over, and allow it to dissolve. Then, pour on the hot water and add the sugar and the pinch of salt, and stir well until everything is melted. Stir in the lemon zest and juice, and set aside in the fridge to chill until almost set. (Check it from time to time, and stir. It should be starting to set around the edges when it is folded in to the egg whites, in Step 3.)
3. When the lemon is beginning to set, beat the egg whites to soft peaks, then add ¼ cup of sugar and beat to quite stiff peaks. Stir ⅓ of the whites into the lemon (to lighten up the lemon), then fold in the rest (see page 128 on folding technique). Pour into

the prepared mould and refrigerate until set. *(May be done up to 1 day ahead.)*

---

4. Make the sauce: Rinse out a pan with water but do not dry; pour in the milk and bring almost to boiling point over medium heat. Set aside while you beat the eggs.

5. Using an electric mixer (may be done by hand), beat the eggs with the sugar until pale yellow and quite thick. Pour in the hot milk in a thin stream, whisking all the time, then return the custard to the pan (wash it out first if there are milk solids sticking to the bottom), and cook over medium-low heat, stirring constantly, until the it thickens and coats the back of a spoon (see page 133). Remove from the heat, stir in the vanilla, cover with plastic wrap, and refrigerate until ready to serve. *(May be done 1 day ahead to this point.)*

---

6. To serve: Dip the mould quickll1y in hot water or wrap it in a hot cloth. Invert the mould onto the serving platter (or onto plates if using the individual moulds); pour a little of the custard around and pass the rest in a sauceboat.

BRANDY SNAPS

One of the real treats of children's parties in the days when I used to play musical chairs. Not difficult; just requires a little patience at the rolling up stage. This recipe makes a nice thin brandy snap.

Makes about 8 large brandy snaps.

⅓ cup	**all-purpose flour**
½ tsp	**ground ginger**
3 oz	**unsalted butter**
½ cup	**granulated sugar**
2 Tbs	**corn syrup** or **golden syrup**

1. Sift together the flour and ginger into a bowl; set aside.

2. Using an electric mixer (or may be done by hand), cream the butter and sugar until light and fluffy, then add the syrup and cream some more. Pour in the sifted flour and blend it in thoroughly. Cover the bowl and refrigerate for 1 hour or longer (so that the glutens in the flour can relax).

3. Preheat the oven to 375° F. Line a baking sheet with parchment; if you have no parchment, you can butter and flour it generously, but parchment is much more reliable for this purpose. Have ready two wooden handles to form the brandy snaps around; wooden spoons are a bit small but will do in a pinch. I use a carving knife that has a round wooden handle.

4. Place small dessert-spoons of dough on the prepared baking sheet, about 6" apart (they will spread a bit during baking). Press them down with the palm of your hand, then into quite flat circles with the back of a fork. Do not crowd the sheet. Bake in the preheated oven for 10 minutes, until deep golden brown and bubbling.

5. Remove from the oven and allow to cool and firm up: it will take a couple of minutes. Then slide a knife underneath to release them, and roll up around the handle to form a tube about 1" in diameter: you will get the hang of it after one or two. Allow to firm up completely, then remove from the spoon.

6. Store in an airtight container at room temperature; they will keep for a week.

7. Just before serving: Whip the cream to firm peaks, flavour with the vanilla or brandy if you wish, and pipe or spoon the cream into each end of the brandy snaps.

CHRISTMAS DESSERTS

Christmas is the time of year when even those who never bake will find themselves making some cookies for friends, or stirring a Christmas pudding. It is as good a way as any to discover the pleasure of cooking, and how much people appreciate the things that we take the trouble to make.

We often say about gifts at Christmas that it is the thought that counts (and most of the time we mean it!); it is just as true of the food. Not that we should not make it as well as we can; but much more important is the spirit in which we do it, and the Christmas spirit of giving (and receiving, which can be even harder) is the perfect one to encourage in our cooking.

If you are one of those who cook only at this time of year, enjoy it to the full; may it be the beginning of something more. And those of us who already cook can enjoy making things that never seem quite right at any other time of year, but which are the tastes and smells that, years from now, will bring back memories of these Christmases more truly than any home video will ever be able to. Whichever group you belong to, I hope that among our recipes you will find a few that you like well enough to try, and perhaps will repeat down the years, until they have become a part of your own family's Christmas tradition.

CHRISTMAS PIE

This pie is so named because the kumquats and marzipan give it a flavour that is reminiscent of fruitcake. Don't save it for Christmas though: it is excellent during any of the cold weather months.

Serves 8 to 10.

1 recipe	**Sweet Flaky Pastry** (see page 219)
1 cup	**pitted prunes**
1½ cups	**boiling water**
⅔ cup	**Candied Kumquats** (see page 3)
3 or 4	**apples**, peeled, cored, and sliced (3 cups of slices)
10 oz	**marzipan**
¼ cup	**butter**
2	**eggs**
1 Tbs	**flour**
2 Tbs	**syrup from the kumquats** **eggyolk glaze**

1. Make the pastry, following the recipe on page 219. Proceed to the point where the dough is resting in the fridge, but has not yet been rolled out.
2. Preheat the oven to 425° F. Choose a 10" pie pan.
3. Place the prunes in a bowl and pour 1½ cups boiling water over them. Cover the bowl and let the prunes steep for 10 minutes; then drain completely. Coarsely chop the prunes and kumquats and mix with the sliced apples. Set aside.
4. Crumble the marzipan into the workbowl of your food processor. Pulse a few times to loosen up the marzipan. Add the butter and blend until smooth. With the motor running, add the eggs one at a time. Set aside.
5. Roll out the pastry into a 15" round. Place the pastry in the pan, but do not trim off the excess. Pour the marzipan mixture into the pan, spreading it evenly. Toss the fruit mixture with the kumquat syrup, then with the flour; pile it on top of the marzipan. Fold the excess pastry over the filling, letting it fall where it may (it will have a casual, draped appearance). Brush the pastry with the egg-yolk glaze.
6. Bake in the centre of the preheated oven for 15 minutes, then reduce the heat to 350° F and bake for 30 to 40 minutes longer, until the crust is golden brown. Remove from the oven to cool.
7. Serve warm, or at room temperature.

CHRISTMAS CRANBERRY TARTS

See photograph opposite page 206.

Makes 12 small tarts.

FOR THE CREAM CHEESE PASTRY

½ cup	**unsalted butter**, soft
3 oz	**cream cheese**, soft
1 cup	**all-purpose flour**

FOR THE CRANBERRY FILLING

2½ cups	**cranberries**, fresh or frozen
1 cup	**granulated sugar**
1 Tbs	**water**
2 Tbs	**cornstarch**
2 Tbs	**Grand Marnier** or **Cointreau**

FOR THE DECORATION

| 1 Tbs | **candied orange zest** (see page 32) |

1. First make the pastry: Using an electric mixture fitted with the paddle, cream the butter and cream cheese together, until light and fluffy. Turn the mixer to low, add the flour, and beat until thoroughly combined.

2. This pastry does not get rolled out: you press the dough with your fingertips into miniature muffin cups or into barquette shells, until they are fairly evenly lined with dough. Trim off any excess dough around the top of the cups, then refigerate for 30 minutes.

3. Preheat the oven to 350° F.

4. While the pastry shells are chilling, make the filling: Combine the cranberries, sugar, and water in a heavy-bottom saucepan. Bring to a boil over medium-high heat, stirring frequently; the berries should just begin to pop and burst.

5. Dissolve the cornstarch in the Grand Marnier and add to the cranberry mixture. Continue cooking over high heat until the mixture has thickened and boiled for 2 minutes. Make sure that it comes to a full boil or the raw taste of the cornstarch will remain. Remove from heat, and cool to room temperature.

6. Prick the bottom of each pastry shell with a fork. Bake in the preheated oven for 25 to 30 minutes, until golden brown. Remove and allow to cool completely.

7. Remove the pastries from the moulds. Spoon the filling into shells, mounding it up a bit. The tarts should be assembled as close to serving time as possible as the filling will soften the pastry if allowed to sit for too long.

8. Decorate the tops of the tartlets with candied orange zest (see page 32).

UNCLE LEO'S STEAMED CRANBERRY PUDDING WITH EGGNOG SAUCE

This pudding has been a Christmas tradition in Karen's family for years. Even when you're stuffed with turkey, it is irresistible. You'll be flattered by how many people ask you for your recipe!

Enough for 8.

6 Tbs	**unsalted butter**, softened
³/₄ cup	**granulated sugar**
2	**eggs**
2¹/₄ cups	**flour**
2¹/₂ tsp	**baking powder**
¹/₄ tsp	**salt**
¹/₂ cup	**milk**
2 cups	**fresh cranberries**
¹/₂ cup	**pecans**, coarsely chopped

FOR THE EGGNOG SAUCE

1 cup	**unsalted butter**
¹/₂ cup	**sugar**
2 cups	**egg nog**
¹/₂ cup	**rum** or **brandy**

HOW TO MAKE YOUR OWN EGG NOG

To make 1 quart: Beat together 4 egg yolks and ¹/₂ cup of sugar, until pale yellow and quite thick. Heat 2 cups of whipping cream (35%) until quite hot to your finger, then pour into the eggs. Stir until the sugar is completely dissolved (warm over medium-low heat, if necessary). Pour in 1 cup of coffee cream (18%), and 1 cup of rum or brandy, add 1 tsp of ground nutmeg, and ¹/₂ tsp of ground cinnamon, and whisk until well combined. Refrigerate until required.

1. Using an electric mixer (or by hand if you wish), cream the butter and the sugar until light and fluffy. Beat in the eggs one at a time. Sift together the flour, baking powder, and salt. Add them to the butter mixture alternately with the milk, stirring well after everything has been added. Now fold in the cranberries and pecans (see page 128).

2. Generously butter a 6-cup pudding mould, and spoon in the batter, packing it down well. If your mould has no lid, generously butter a double thickness of tin foil and secure it, buttered-side down, with a heavy elastic band or with string. Place in a large pot and pour in boiling water until it reaches half-way up the mould. Set the pot on the stove and bring to boiling point over medium heat, then turn down the heat and regulate it so the water is just above a simmer. Cover the pot (with a lid, or aluminum foil) and steam gently for 2 hours, replenishing with more boiling water when necessary. Remove the pudding from the pot and uncover. Let cool for 10 to 15 minutes before turning it out of the mould. (This pudding may be cooled to room temperature, wrapped securely, and frozen for up to 1 month. Thaw and reheat [by steaming again] before serving.)

3. To make the sauce: Combine the butter, sugar, and eggnog in a heavy saucepan, bring to a boil, and cook over high heat for 5 minutes, stirring constantly. Remove from the heat, and add the rum or brandy. (The sauce may be made in advance and reheated gently over low heat: but do not refrigerate the sauce or it will separate when reheated.)

4. Cut the pudding into slices (as you would a

cake), and pass the sauce around in a sauce boat. *NOTE:* If you want to flambé the pudding, warm ½ cup rum or brandy in a small saucepan. Carry the pudding on its platter and the warm rum in the saucepan to the door of the dining room. Ignite the rum, still in the pan, with a match and quickly pour it over the pudding. Rush it proudly to the table before the flames die out.

EGGNOG CAKE

A seriously rich cake with a rather alchoholic glaze. Serve with lightly whipped cream.

Serves 12.

3 cups	**all-purpose flour**
1 Tbs	**baking powder**
1½ tsp	**ground nutmeg**
½ tsp	**ground cinnamon**
1 cup	**eggnog** (see page 182)
2 tsp	**brandy**
1 cup	**unsalted butter**, soft
1⅓ cups	**granulated sugar**
4	**egg yolks**
4	**egg whites**

FOR THE GLAZE

1 cup	**granulated sugar**
½ cup	**unsalted butter**
¼ cup	**water**
½ tsp	**ground nutmeg**
¼ cup	**dark rum**
¼ cup	**brandy**

1. Preheat the oven to 325° F. Butter and lightly flour a 12-cup bundt pan. Sift together the flour, baking powder, nutmeg, and cinnamon. Combine the eggnog and the brandy in a measuring jug or bowl.
2. Using an electric mixer (may be done by hand), cream together the butter and sugar until light and fluffy. Add the egg yolks, one at a time, beating well after each addition. Stop once or twice to scrape down the sides of the bowl.
3. With the mixer on low speed, add ⅓ of the sifted flour, then ½ of the eggnog; repeat, then add the last of the flour.
4. In a clean bowl, whip the egg whites to soft peaks (see page 24). Gently fold the whites into the batter (see page 128). Turn the batter into the prepared pan, and smooth the top with a spatula. Bake in the preheated oven for 50 to 55 minutes, until a cake tester comes out clean. Remove from the oven and allow to cool in the pan.
5. Make the glaze: Combine the sugar, butter, water, and nutmeg in a small saucepan. Bring to a boil over medium-high heat, and continue to boil for 5 minutes, stirring continuously. Remove from heat and mix in the rum and the brandy.
6. Turn the cake out of the pan; prick it all over with a skewer. Brush the hot glaze over the top and sides of the cake, letting the excess run underneath and be soaked up at the bottom. Use all of the glaze. *Let the cake rest at room temperature for 2 hours before serving.* Serve with lightly whipped cream.

CHRISTMAS CURRANT COOKIES

Daphna created this cross between two traditional cookies: one a Moravian Christmas cookie, the other a Scottish shortbread. For those who are wondering, a Moravian Christmas cookie is a soft chewy cookie made from puréed currants.

Makes about 48 cookies.

1 tsp	**Grated Lemon Zest** (see page 210)
1½ tsp	**brandy**
3	**egg yolks**
1½ cups	**cake flour** (see page 225)
1½ cups	**all-purpose flour**
¾ cup	**granulated sugar**
¼ tsp.	**grated nutmeg**
½ tsp	**ground cinnamon**
⅛ tsp	**ground cloves**
1 cup	**unsalted butter,** very cold
1½ cups	**dried currants**

1. Preheat the oven to 350° F. Line two or three cookie sheets with parchment paper (see page 152), or butter and flour them. In a small bowl, combine the lemon zest, brandy, and egg yolks, and mix well.

2. Combine the two flours, the sugar, the nutmeg, cinnamon and cloves in the workbowl of your food processor, or in a large bowl, if working by hand.

3. Roll the butter in flour (to make it easier to handle), then cut it into slices, roll again in flour, then cut the slices into sticks, and the sticks into cubes. Distribute the cubes over the flour in the workbowl, and process briefly, until the mixture looks like coarse meal; be careful not to over process, as it will make your cookies tough. If working by hand, rub or cut the butter into the flour to the same stage.

4. Pour the egg yolk and brandy mixture down the feed tube, and process again, but only until the dough just starts to come together. Better to under process, and knead it together by hand than to process too much. Again, the liquids can be stirred in by hand if you wish.

5. Turn the dough out onto a lightly-floured work surface, add the currants to the pile and knead gently until you have a cohesive dough. Then roll it out to a thickness of ¼", and cut it into shapes with cookie cutters, or an upside down glass. Transfer to the prepared cookie sheets, and bake in the preheated oven for 10 to 15 minutes, until pale golden brown. Remove from the oven, slide onto racks, and allow to cool. Store in an airtight container.

CHRISTMAS COFFEE CAKE

A moist and light coffee cake, not just for Christmas. At other times you can let your imagination loose and alter the filling to suit your mood. It is very quick and easy to make as it relies on baking powder for leavening, not on yeast — not, of course, that yeast is difficult; but it does take more time.

Serves 8 to 10.

FOR THE TOPPING

1½ tsp	**ground cinnamon**
¾ cup	**light brown sugar**, lightly packed
2½ Tbs	**instant coffee powder**

FOR THE FILLING

½ cup	**walnut pieces**
1 cup	**cranberries**
6 Tbs	**shredded unsweetened coconut**

FOR THE BATTER

1 cup	**soft cake flour** (see page 225)
½ cup	**all-purpose flour**
1½ tsp	**baking powder**
1 tsp	**baking soda**
¼ tsp	**salt**
½ cup	**unsalted butter**, soft
1 cup	**granulated sugar**
2 large	**eggs**
½ tsp	**vanilla extract**
1 cup	**sour cream**

1. Make the topping: In a small bowl, combine the cinnamon, brown sugar, and instant coffee and toss together. In a second small bowl, make the filling: Toss together the walnut pieces, cranberries, and coconut. Set them both aside.

2. Preheat the oven to 350° F. Lightly butter and flour an 8½" springform cake pan. Sift together the cake flour, the all-purpose flour, baking powder, baking soda, and salt into a bowl.

3. Using an electric mixer (may be done by hand), cream together the butter and sugar until light and fluffy. Add the eggs, one at a time, beating well after each addition. Then beat in the vanilla.

4. The mixing from now on is best done by hand as it gives a much finer crumb ("crumb" refers to how coarse or fine the final texture is). Blend the sifted flour into the batter. Then, blend in the sour cream, making sure there are no pockets of unincorporated flour.

5. Spread half of the batter into the prepared springform. Sprinkle half of the brown sugar and cinnamon mixture over the batter; then sprinkle all of the cranberry filling over. Top with remaining batter. The rest of the brown-sugar mixture goes over the top.

6. Bake in the preheated oven for 40 to 45 minutes, until a cake tester comes out clean.

7. Allow to cool in the springform pan. It is best served still warm.

CHRISTMAS CHERRY COOKIES

Makes about 2 dozen cookies.

⅛ tsp	**salt**
1 cup	**all-purpose flour**
½ tsp	**baking powder**
½ cup	**unsalted butter**, soft
¼ cup	**granulated sugar**
1 large	**egg**
½ tsp	**vanilla extract**
½ cup	**finely chopped almonds**
24	**glacée cherries** (one per cookie)

1. Preheat the oven to 350° F. Lightly butter 2 cookie sheets or line them with parchment paper . Sift together the salt, flour, and baking powder into a bowl.

2. Using an electric mixer fitted with the paddle (or by hand), cream the butter with the sugar until light and fluffy. Add the egg and vanilla, and blend well.

3. Add the sifted flour to the batter, and blend thoroughly; add the almonds and mix again — the dough will be quite stiff.

4. Spoon the dough into a pastry bag fitted with a large rosette tip. Pipe out cookies, about 1½" apart. (Or they can be shaped by hand if a you can't find a pastry bag.)

5. Place a cherry in the centre of each cookie. Bake in the preheated oven for 15 to 20 minutes, until pale golden brown. Remove from the oven and allow to cool.

SUGAR COOKIES

Great for Christmas-time, and making cookie cutouts. They can be used as decorations, if you pierce a hole in the cookie for stringing a ribbon through and hanging on the tree.

Makes about 24.

2¼ cup	**all-purpose flour** (sifted)
¼ tsp	**salt**
2 tsp	**baking powder**
½ cup	**unsalted butter**
1 cup	**granulated sugar**
2 large	**eggs**
1 tsp	**vanilla extract**
1 Tbs	**milk**

1. Preheat the oven to 350° F. Butter and flour a baking sheet. Sift together the flour, salt, and baking powder into a bowl and set aside.

2. Using an electric mixer (may be done by hand) cream the butter and sugar together until light and fluffy. Add the eggs, one at a time, beating well between each.

3. Add the vanilla and the milk, then stir in the sifted flour. Turn the dough out onto your work surface and knead gently just enough to bring it together.

4. Roll the dough to a ¼" thick; cut out shapes or circles and set them on the prepared baking sheet. Bake in the preheated oven for 12 minutes. Remove from the oven and allow to cool.

5. Decorate as desired. You can sprinkle them with sugar, sprinkles, or other cake decorations; or they may be iced with White Icing (see page 219) — which does not of course have to be white; use food colouring to mix the colour you want.

Christmas Fruitcake

This is fruitcake for people who (think they) don't like fruitcake; they will be converted for sure.

Makes 2 cakes, each the size of a standard loaf.

1 cup	**unsalted butter**
1 cup	**brown sugar**, well packed
¹/₂ cup	**honey**
5	**eggs**
2 cups	**all-purpose flour**
1 tsp	**baking powder**
1 tsp	**cinnamon**
¹/₂ tsp	**allspice**
¹/₃ tsp	**salt**
1³/₄ lbs	**dried apricots**, sliced
1 lb	**pecan halves**
¹/₂ lb	**sultanas**
³/₄ lb	**pitted dates**
2 oz	**dried apples**
¹/₂ cup	**walnuts**
¹/₂ cup	**orange juice**
¹/₄ cup	**whipping cream** (35%)
¹/₂ cup	**brandy**
¹/₄ cup	**orange liqueur**

1. Preheat the oven to 350° F. Butter 2 standard loaf pans. Sift together the flour, baking powder, cinnamon, allspice, and salt into a bowl.

2. Using an electric mixer (may be done by hand), cream together the butter and sugar until light and fluffy. Add the honey, then beat in the eggs one at a time, mixing well between each. Stir ¹/₂ the flour into the batter, and mix lightly.

3. To the rest of the flour, add the sliced apricots, pecans, sultanas, dates, apples, and walnuts; stir until they are well coated. By hand, mix them into the batter.

4. Pour into the two prepared pans; bake in the preheated oven for 2¹/₂ to 3 hours, until a tester comes out clean. Remove from the oven and allow to cool for 15 minutes, then turn the cakes out onto a rack and sprinkle the brandy and orange liqueur over them. When cool wrap tightly in plastic wrap and store in an airtight container.

YULE LOG (BUCHE DE NOEL)

A traditional Christmas dessert in France, but it tastes good in Canada, too.
Make the meringue toadstools the day before. (See photograph opposite page 206.)

Serves 8.

FOR THE TOADSTOOLS
1 recipe **Swiss Meringue** (page 213)

FOR THE LOG
1 recipe **Chocolate Sponge** (page 224)
1 recipe **Chocolate Buttercream** (page 206)
2 oz **semi-sweet chocolate**

FOR DECORATION
real holly leaves
icing sugar

1. Preheat the oven to 250° F. Butter and flour a baking sheet (or , preferably, line it with parchment paper — see page 152). Make the Swiss meringue following the recipe on page 213. Scoop it into a piping bag fitted with a ¼" plain tip, and pipe out little mounds for the mushroom caps, and thin strips for the stems (you will assemble them later, when they are baked). Bake in the preheated oven for 1 hour, until crisp; but they should hardly be browned at all (although don't worry if they are; the icing sugar will cover it up).

2. For the chocolate sponge: Preheat the oven to 350° F; butter an 11" x 17" x 1" (approximately) jellyroll pan and line it with parchment (or you can use wax paper in a pinch).

3. Make the chocolate sponge, following the recipe on page 224, except that (a) you'll be using a different pan; (b) the oven temperature is now 350° F; and (c) the baking time is 35 to 40 minutes. The cake should be slightly springy on top when you press it with your finger. Remove the cake from the oven.

4. Spread out a damp kitchen towel on your work surface. Run a knife around the edge of the cake pan to loosen the edges, then invert the pan and turn out the cake onto the towel. Remove the baking sheet, peel off the parchment, and, starting from one of the long sides, roll up the cake and towel quite tightly, jellyroll fashion. Allow the cake to cool completely.

5. Make the chocolate buttercream, following the recipe on page 206, then set it aside at room temperature.

6. Unroll the cake and towel on a clean work surface, and spread a thin layer of buttercream over the entire surface. With the help of the towel, roll up the cake again quite tightly with the buttercream inside (try not to get the towel in there too!). The outside may develop cracks, but they will be covered up later. You should have a long thin log.

7. Cut off a piece of one end about 3" or 4" long, making the cut on the diagonal; this acts as the stump of a branch. Set it aside.

8. Ice the log and the stump (separately) with the buttercream, until they are completely covered on all sides. Do not worry about the surface finish at this point.

9. Place the stump on top of the log (or on the side), using extra buttercream as the glue, so that it looks real.

10. Place the chocolate in a small bowl that can go over hot water (or in the top of a double boiler); set it over simmering water until melted and smooth.

11. Create the decorations: Draw the tines of a fork (or a pastry comb) along the top and sides of the log and the stump to create the look of bark. Smooth off the ends.

12. Make a paper cone (see page 63), and spoon in the melted chocolate. Draw concentric chocolate circles on the ends of the log and of the stump, to look like growth rings.

13. With the point of a sharp knife, dig out a small hole in the underside of each mushroom cap, for the stem to fit in. Dip one end of the stems in chocolate, and apply them to the caps. Stick them onto the log in appropriate places. Dot the caps with little dabs of chocolate if you like the effect. Garnish with holly leaves, then sift icing sugar to make fresh snow.

SWEET BREADS AND COFFEE CAKES

Sweet breads fall into two main categories: those that are leavened with yeast, and those that rely on chemicals, such as baking powder or soda, for the rising action. Of the two, the chemically leavened are much the easier to make; although really the difference is one of speed rather than of difficulty.

Yeast, although intimidating to many would-be bakers, is not hard to use, and can be a source of tremendous satisfaction. Few activities in cooking can so effectively give you a taste of the elemental as working with a yeast dough. The use of yeast to leaven bread is as old as civilization, and kneading and working with gives the feel of participating in one of the foundations of our culture, a tradition that goes back to the very beginnings of the human race. Waverley Root (in *Food*, page 587) quotes biochemist George Wald's statement that "as living creatures, we are more like yeast than unlike it. Yeast and man had a common ancestor. Some of the ancestor's progeny became yeasts and some went the other way and became men, and these two journeys resulted in a change of only 53 nucleotides out of 312." The Zen ideal of "no separation" (between the baker and the bread, me and you, being and non-being) is within our grasp when working with yeast.

The days of wondering whether your yeast is still active, or of having to fit your life around the risings and punching downs, have all but gone. Commercial yeasts are now so reliable, and so easy to use, and refrigeration allows us to slow down the leavening process if we need to, that anyone able to fit an hour of work into a morning around the house can make excellent breads and coffee cakes.

There is a lightness and spring in the texture of yeast doughs that quick breads, for all their convenience, can never match. Where yeast doughs require you to be active and vigorous, quick breads need just the opposite treatment. The secret of these batters is to keep the wet ingredients separate from the dry until just before you are ready to bake, and then to mix them as lightly and as little as you can, while still getting the powder or soda thoroughly moistened. You want as much as possible of the carbon-dioxide gas (which is produced when the baking soda [or powder] comes in contact with an acidic liquid, like fruit juice or buttermilk) to be released after the bread is in the oven. If it is released before it goes in, the gas will escape too soon and the bread will be tough and heavy. Over-mixing, or mixing too early, will both produce this result. (Baking powder is called "double action";

it releases gas twice — once on contact with an acid ingredient; and again on contact with heat. Although you effectively get a second chance when using it as a leavening agent, it is still a good idea to be as quick and light in your mixing as you would be otherwise.)

I have found that mixing quick breads is one area where children need to be watched closely; their enthusiasm tends to get the better of them, with disappointing results for the bread (muffins require the same gentle treatment). The discipline in making quick breads is to stop yourself mixing almost as soon as you have started, and quite a while before you think that you have mixed enough. There will still be clumps of unincorporated flour, very wet patches and quite dry patches. Have faith — you will be amazed at how much better the end product will be. (Use this technique wherever there is a chemical leavening in the recipe — pancakes, for example — and you will see a great improvement in the result.)

STICKY BUNS

Just what the name says.

Makes 12.

¹/₄ cup	**warm water**
1 package	**dry yeast**
1 cup	**milk**
3 Tbs	**granulated sugar**
¹/₂ tsp	**salt**
1 large	**egg**
3¹/₂ cups	**all-purpose flour**

FOR THE GLAZE

4 oz	**unsalted butter**
1¹/₂ cups	**light brown sugar**, well packed
¹/₂ cup	**light corn syrup**
1 cup	**chopped walnuts**

FOR THE FILLING

¹/₂ cup	**raisins**

1. Pour the warm water (just warmer than body temperature) into a bowl, then sprinkle the yeast over the surface. Stir and let stand at room temperature for 5 minutes to dissolve. (It should bubble and foam, and smell like yeast; if it doesn't your yeast is inactive.)

2. Warm the milk to body temperature, then pour into a large mixing bowl; add the soft butter, salt, and egg, and beat to blend.

3. Add the yeast to the milk, then add half of the flour, and mix thoroughly. Keep adding the flour, a bit at a time, until you have a soft, pliable dough. Do not add all the flour at once — factors like the air temperature and humidity and the condition of the flour will influence how much you need. Knead the dough for 2 minutes and then let it rest for 8 to 10 minutes. Knead the dough again until smooth and elastic, about 6 to 8 minutes.

4. Lightly oil a bowl — preferably one with high, straight sides as this makes the dough stretch more as it rises. Roll the dough around the bowl so that it is lightly oiled all over. Cover with plastic wrap and place in a warm draft-free area for about 1 hour, or until doubled in bulk.

5. Make the glaze: Combine the butter, brown sugar, and corn syrup in a saucepan. Cook over low heat until the sugar has dissolved and the butter is melted. Stir to blend thoroughly. Pour 1 cup (approximately) of the glaze over the bottom of a 10" cake pan, then sprinkle the chopped nuts on top. Set aside the rest of the glaze in the pan for Step 6.

6. Punch the dough down. Turn it out onto a lightly floured surface, and roll out to a large rectangle about 20" by 14". Spread the reserved glaze over the surface, but leave an unglazed ¹/₂" border all around. Sprinkle the raisins over the glaze.

7. Loosely roll up (like a jellyroll), starting with one of the long sides. Cut into 1¹/₂" thick slices. Place the slices, flat-side down, into the cake pan with the glaze. Cover loosely with plastic wrap and let rise in the warm place for 30 to 45 minutes.

8. Preheat the oven to 375 ° F.

9. Bake the buns in the preheated oven for 35 to 45 minutes, until a tester comes out with no dough clinging to it. Turn out onto your work surface, pull the buns apart, and serve warm.

CRANBERRY TEA BREAD

Simple to make; but best made the day before. (The directions for making it in a food processor are in parentheses.)

Makes one standard loaf.

2 cups	**all-purpose flour**
2 tsp	**baking powder**
pinch of	**salt**
2 oz	**unsalted butter**, chilled
³/₄ cup	**granulated sugar**
1 cup	**unsalted pistachios**, shelled
²/₃ cup	**fresh orange juice**
1 Tbs	**orange zest**, finely chopped (page 210)
1 large	**egg**
2 cups	**fresh cranberries** (or thawed if previously frozen)
1 Tbs	**whipping cream** (coffee cream will do)

1. Preheat the oven to 350 ° F. Lightly butter a 9" by 5" loaf pan. Sift together the flour, baking powder, and salt into a bowl (or combine them in the workbowl of your food processor and pulse once or twice to aerate).

2. Roll the butter in flour to make it easier to handle, then cut it into slices. Roll in flour again, then cut into sticks, and the sticks into cubes. If making it by hand, use a pastry cutter to cut the butter into the flour until the mixture resembles fine meal. (Or distribute the butter over the flour in the food processor and process briefly to a fine-meal texture; then turn into a bowl.) Add the sugar, pistachios, and orange zest, and toss to blend well.

3. Beat the egg and the orange juice together, then pour over the dry ingredients; stir only until the batter begins to cling together — there will still be lumps, but this does not matter. Add the cranberries, and stir just enough that they are evenly distributed.

4. Turn the batter into the prepared pan and smooth the top with a spatula. Brush the cream over the surface.

5. Bake in the preheated oven for about 1 hour and 15 minutes, until golden brown and crusty on top, and a cake tester inserted in the centre comes out clean.

6. Cool in pan for 20 minutes; then invert onto a rack; turn right side up and cool completely. It is easier to cut if refrigerated overnight.

BUTTERMILK CURRANT SCONES

A very good, plain scone; the secret to a light texture is to mix and knead as little and as gently as possible once the liquid has been added. (The cutting in of the butter can be done in a food processor; directions for this are in parentheses.)

Makes about 20 small scones, or 12 wedges.

3 cups	**all-purpose flour**
¹/₃ cup	**granulated sugar**
2¹/₂ tsp	**baking powder**
¹/₂ tsp	**baking soda**
¹/₂ tsp	**salt**
6 oz	**unsalted butter**, chilled
1 cup	**buttermilk**
³/₄ cup	**currants**
2 tsp	**orange zest**, finely grated (see page 210)
2 Tbs	**whipping cream** (coffee cream is *OK*)

1. Preheat the oven to 425° F. Lightly butter a baking sheet. Sift the flour, sugar, baking powder, soda, and salt into a large mixing bowl (or combine them in the workbowl of your food processor and pulse once or twice to aerate).

2. Roll the cold butter in flour to make it easier to handle, then cut it into slices. Roll in flour again, then cut into sticks, and the sticks into cubes. If making it by hand, use a pastry cutter to cut the butter into the flour until the mixture has a breadcrumb texture. (Or distribute the butter over the flour in the food processor and process briefly to the breadcrumb texture; then turn into a bowl.)

3. Add the buttermilk, currants, and orange zest. Mix lightly with a fork — just enough that the mixture is moistened and forms a soft dough.

4. Turn the dough out onto a lightly floured surface. Knead very gently for 8 to 10 turns, then pat the dough out into a large circle ¹/₂" thick. Using a cookie cutter (or an upside-down glass), cut out round circles of dough, or cut them into pie-shaped wedges. Place them 1" apart on the prepared cookie sheet. Brush the tops lightly with the cream.

5. Bake in the preheated oven for 12 to 15 minutes, until golden brown. Serve warm, with fresh butter and home-made jam (Devon cream, whipped till it holds its shape — available in specialty stores — is a wonderful addition).

CRANBERRY SCONES

A rich scone with a holiday spirit; mix and knead the dough as little as possible for the best result. (Cutting in the butter may be done in a food processor; directions for this are in parentheses.)

Makes 4 large wedges, each a generous serving for one.

1¾ cups	**all-purpose flour**
½ cup	**cake flour**, sifted
½ cup	**sugar**
2 tsp	**baking powder**
¼ tsp	**salt**
½ tsp	**ground cinnamon**
2 oz	**unsalted butter**, chilled
1 cup	**whipping cream** (35%)
¾ cup	**fresh cranberries**, (or thawed if previously frozen)

1. Preheat the oven to 425° F. Lightly butter a baking sheet. Sift the cake flour, sugar, baking powder, salt, and cinnamon into a large bowl, then add the all-purpose flour; do not sift it — you will get a more scone-like, and less cake-like, texture, if you do not sift. (Or combine these ingredients in the work bowl of your food processor.)

2. Roll the cold butter in flour to make it easier to handle, then cut it into slices. Roll in flour again, then cut into sticks, and the sticks into cubes. If making it by hand, use a pastry cutter to cut the butter into the flour until the mixture resembles coarse meal. (Or distribute the butter over the flour in the food processor and process briefly to a coarse meal texture; then turn into a bowl.)

3. Set aside 2 Tbs of the cream for Step 5. Add the rest of the cream and the cranberries to the flour mixture. Mix gently with a fork — only enough that the batter starts to cling together and form a soft dough.

4. Turn the dough out onto a lightly floured surface and knead gently for 4 to 5 turns — just enough to bring it together. Roll out the dough to a 7" circle, and cut into 4 wedges.

5. Place the wedges on the prepared cookie sheet about 1" apart. Pierce the tops with fork tines, then brush them with the reserved 2 Tbs cream.

6. Bake in the preheated oven for 15 to 20 minutes, until golden brown. Serve warm.

Blueberry Scones

A light and fresh-tasting scone. It is important to mix the dough as little as possible; the blueberries are only added at the last moment, as their natural dye quickly stains the batter a very unprofessional purple colour. (Directions for cutting in the butter with a food processor are in parentheses.)

Makes 8 good-size wedges, each serving one person generously.

4 cups	**all-purpose flour**
2 Tbs	**granulated sugar**
4 tsp	**baking powder**
¼ tsp	**salt**
½ tsp	**cream of tartar** (see page 67)
6 oz	**unsalted butter**, chilled
1	**egg yolk**
1½ cups	**half-and-half cream** (10%)
1½ cups	**fresh blueberries** (or thawed if previously frozen)
1	**egg white**
1 Tbs	**granulated sugar**

1. Preheat the oven to 425° F. Lightly butter a large cookie sheet. Sift the sugar, baking powder, salt, and cream of tartar into a large bowl, then add the all-purpose flour; do not sift it — you will get a more scone-like, and less cake-like, texture, if you do not sift. (Or combine these ingredients in the work bowl of your food processor.)

2. Roll the cold butter in flour to make it easier to handle, then cut it into slices. Roll in flour again, then cut into sticks, and the sticks into cubes. If making it by hand, use a pastry cutter to cut the butter into the flour until the mixture resembles coarse meal. (Or distribute the butter over the flour in the food processor and process briefly to a coarse-meal texture; then turn into a bowl.)

3. Whisk the egg yolk together with the half-and-half. Add this mixture to the dry ingredients, and mix lightly with a fork — just until the batter begins to cling together and form a soft dough.

4. Turn the dough out onto a lightly floured surface and knead gently for about 6 turns. Add the blueberries and knead enough to distribute them (if they were added earlier, they would stain the dough purple). Divide the dough in two. On a lightly floured surface, roll out one half to a 7" circle, and cut into 4 wedges. Repeat with the other half.

5. Place the wedges, 1" apart, on the prepared baking sheets. Pierce the tops with fork tines, then brush them with the egg white and sprinkle with the sugar.

6. Bake in the preheated oven for 15 to 18 minutes, until golden brown. Serve warm.

Pistachio Sour Cream Coffee Cake

A simple, quick, and very good coffee cake.

Enough for 10 to 12 people.

2¼ cups	**all-purpose flour**
1 tsp	**baking powder**
1½ tsp	**baking soda**
6 oz	**unsalted butter**
1½ cups	**granulated sugar**
3	**eggs**
1½ cups	**sour cream**

FOR THE FILLING AND TOPPING

½ cup	**brown sugar**
2½ tsp	**cinnamon**
1 cup	**pistachios** or **pecans** or **walnuts**, chopped

1. Preheat the oven to 325° F. Butter and flour an angel-cake pan, or a 9" by 13" cake pan. Sift together the flour, baking powder, and baking soda into a bowl. Set aside.

2. Make the filling: Mix together the sugar, cinnamon, and chopped nuts in a small bowl and set aside.

3. Using an electric mixer (or by hand), cream the butter and sugar until light and fluffy. Add the eggs one at a time, beating after each, then mix in the sour cream.

4. By hand, stir the sifted flour into the batter, mixing just until incorporated.

5. Pour half the batter into the prepared pan. Sprinkle half the filling over it, then pour in the rest of the batter. Sprinkle the rest of the topping over the top.

6. Bake in the preheated oven for about 50 minutes, or until a tester comes out clean.

7. Allow to cool for 15 minutes in the pan, then turn out. This is at its best served warm.

DANISH PECAN ROLL

An excellent sweet roll for brunch; or any time you are serving coffee.

1 cup	**milk**
½ cup	**unsalted butter**
⅓ cup	**sugar**
¼ tsp	**salt**
¼ cup	**warm water**
2 pkgs	**dried yeast**
1 Tbs	**light rum**
1 large	**egg**
4 cups	**all-purpose flour**
⅓ cup	**granulated sugar**
3 Tbs	**unsalted butter**
½ tsp	**cinnamon**
¼ tsp	**nutmeg**
1 cup	**raisins**
½ cup	**pecan pieces**
1	**egg**
1 Tbs	**water**

1. Heat the milk in a saucepan until it feels warm to your finger. Add the butter, sugar, and salt to the milk. Remove from the heat and stir until the butter has melted. Set aside to cool until the mixture is lukewarm. (If the milk is too hot, it will kill your yeast and your dough will not rise.)

2. Pour the warm water into a large mixing bowl and sprinkle the yeast on top; set aside for 5 minutes to dissolve.

3. Pour the lukewarm milk into the yeast and stir well to blend. Stir in the rum and egg. With a wooden spoon, blend in 2 cups of the flour, stirring until you have a smooth batter. Gradually add more flour, a bit at a time, until you have a soft dough that can be formed into a ball. (Do not add the last 2 cups of flour all at once — how much you will need depends on the air temperature and humidity, as well as on the flour itself.)

4. Turn the dough out onto a lightly floured work surface and knead gently until smooth and elastic, about 5 to 8 minutes.

5. Transfer the dough to a lightly oiled bowl — preferably one with high, straight sides as this makes the dough stretch more as it rises. Cover with a damp towel or plastic wrap and let rise in a warm, draft-free place until doubled in bulk, 45 minutes to 1 hour.

6. Punch down the dough and turn out onto a lightly floured surface. Knead the dough gently for a few seconds, then roll it out to a rectangle about 20" by 12".

7. Make the filling: Mix the sugar, butter, cinnamon, nutmeg, raisins, and pecans together in a small bowl, then sprinkle it over the dough, leaving a 1" border without filling all around.

8. Beat the egg and water together to form a glaze, then brush it over the border.

9. Roll it up (like a jellyroll), starting with one of the long sides, and place seam-side down on a buttered cookie sheet. Shape into a large crescent or horseshoe shape. Cover lightly, and let rise again in

a warm place for about 1 hour.
10. Preheat the oven to 375° F.
11. Brush the outside of the roll with the rest of the egg glaze. Bake in the preheated oven for 20 to 25 minutes, until golden. Serve warm.

LEMON LOAF

A simple loaf with a nice lemony icing. Make it the day before you plan to serve it.

FOR THE CAKE

1½ cups	**all-purpose flour**
1 tsp	**baking powder**
½ tsp	**salt**
4 oz	**unsalted butter**
1 cup	**granulated sugar**
2	**eggs**
½ cup	**milk**
zest of 1	**lemon** (see page 210)

FOR THE TOPPING

juice of 1	**lemon**
¼ cup	**icing sugar**

1. Preheat the oven to 350° F. Butter and flour a regular loaf pan. Sift together the flour, baking powder, and salt into a bowl.
2. Make the cake first: Using an electric mixer (or by hand), cream together the butter and sugar until light and fluffy. Then add the eggs, one at a time, beating well between each.
3. Add ½ the sifted flour and mix it in by hand, then ½ the milk and mix again; then the rest of the flour and finally the last of the milk, mixing each time.
4. Pour the batter into the prepared loaf pan, and bake in the preheated oven for 1 hour.
5. Make the topping while the loaf is baking: Whisk together the sugar and lemon juice until combined.
6. Remove the loaf from the oven and poke holes in the top with a skewer (to allow the icing to sink in). Leaving the loaf in the pan, pour the icing over the top.
7. Allow to set one day before turning out and serving.

BRIOCHE

There is nothing better with a cafe au lait than a good brioche, rich, buttery, and with a nice, fine texture; it doesn't even need butter and jam. The initial preparation will take about 40 minutes (half that if you use an electric mixer), and the rising 6 hours (two the first rise, then four the second); but it can take as long as 24 hours, if you want to make it a day ahead. Brioche are normally baked in special brioche moulds; but you can also use a standard loaf pan, a saucepan, or even a tin can; if you use any of these moulds, they are best lined with parchment paper to facilitate removal. The recipe may be made either by hand or in an electric mixer. (The instructions for an electric mixer are in parentheses).

Makes about 24 small brioche.

6 cups	**all-purpose flour**
1 cup	**granulated sugar**
10	**eggs**
1 tsp	**salt**
2 oz	**fresh yeast** (or 2 Tbs **instant dry yeast**)
³/₄ lb	**unsalted butter**, very soft, at room temperature

FOR THE GLAZE

1	**egg**

1. Combine the flour, sugar, eggs, salt, and yeast in a large bowl. Mix together with a wooden spoon to bring the dough together, then roll up your sleeves and knead it with your hands until it is smooth and elastic — it will take about 20 minutes of kneading. (Combine the flour, sugar, eggs, salt, and yeast in the bowl of the mixer, fitted with the dough hook; mix for about 10 minutes, until it is smooth and elastic.)

2. Add the soft butter ¹/₄ at a time, kneading very well between additions, so that the butter is completely amalgamated before the next piece is added. Continue to knead until the dough is perfectly smooth, glossy, and quite elastic. You may need to add a little more flour as the heat of your hands will tend to make the dough very sticky. (Add the soft butter ¹/₄ lb at a time, mixing one in completely before adding the next. Mix for 5 to 10 minutes, until the dough is glossy, and comes away from the sides of the bowl, and from the hook.)

3. Cover the bowl with a cloth, and allow to rise in a warm place for 2 hours.

4. Punch the dough down with your fingers. (The dough may be wrapped in plastic and frozen at this point. To thaw, place in the refrigerator for 5 or 6 hours, then proceed with the recipe.) Cover it again with the cloth, and refrigerate for at least 4 hours, up to 24 hours. *(May be prepared up to 24 hours ahead to this point.)*

5. To mould the brioche: Turn the dough out onto a lightly floured work surface. Divide the dough into balls that will almost fill the brioche moulds; place the balls in the moulds, then form smaller balls, and place these on top of the dough already in the moulds.

6. Beat the egg well to form an egg glaze. Brush the surface of the brioche lightly with the glaze, working from the outside inwards, being careful not to let it run onto the mould (if it does, it will adhere the dough to the mould and prevent the brioche from rising properly). Allow to rise in a warm place until doubled in volume — about 20 minutes for individual brioches, 1½ hours for a large one.

7. Preheat the oven to 400° F.

8. Lighly glaze the brioche again, using the same technique. Bake in the preheated oven for 8 to 10 minutes for individual moulds, 35 to 40 minutes for large. Remove from the oven and unmould immediately, then cool on a rack.

SAVARIN WITH RUM SYRUP

*These are called Rum Babas when made in individual moulds; they are delicious
served with fresh fruit salad and lightly whipped cream. Almost all of the work can be
done a day ahead.*

Makes one large savarin, serving about 8 people.

FOR THE DOUGH

1½ cups	**all-purpose flour**
1 Tbs	**sugar**
0.6 oz	**fresh yeast** or
1 pkg`	**instant dry yeast**
¼ tsp	**salt**
¼ cup	**milk**
2	**eggs**
½ cup	**unsalted butter**, soft

FOR THE RUM SYRUP

1 cup	**water**
½ cup	**granulated sugar**
½ cup	**rum**

1. Using an electric mixer, fitted with the paddle attachment, mix together the flour, sugar, yeast, and salt (or you can mix by hand with a wooden spoon in a large bowl). Add the milk and eggs and mix on a low speed until a smooth dough is formed.

2. With the machine running, add the butter, a bit at a time, working each piece thoroughly into the dough before adding the next. Continue mixing the dough until it is smooth. It is quite a sticky dough and so it must be mixed completely. Transfer the dough to a lightly oiled bowl (or dish with straight sides; this makes the dough stretch more as it rises). Cover with plastic wrap and place in a warm, draft-free place for about 1 hour, until doubled in volume.

3. Punch down the dough, return it to the mixer, and beat until elastic — about 10 minutes. Scoop spoonfuls of the dough into the savarin mould until ⅓ full. Then return to the warm spot and let rise until doubled in bulk.

4. Preheat the oven to 450° F.

5. Bake the savarin in the preheated oven for 25 to 30 minutes, until golden brown. Remove from the oven and allow to cool in the pans for 5 or 10 minutes. Then, while still warm, turn out onto wire racks to cool.

6. Make the rum syrup: Combine the water and sugar in a small saucepan and bring to a boil over medium heat, stirring until the sugar has dissolved. Remove from the heat, add the rum and allow to cool.

7. Set the savarin on a plate and brush the rum syrup over it until completely soaked.

8. Serve with fresh fruit salad and lightly whipped cream.

BASICS

The recipes in this section are the building blocks of dessert making — pastries, icings, buttercreams, custards, and many more. They appear frequently through the book. It is worth learning to make them well, because they determine the quality of so much of what you bake.

BUTTERCREAMS

BASIC MERINGUE BUTTERCREAM

The basic recipe for the classic icing; very rich — to the point where children often do not like it, so probably not a good choice for a birthday cake; but a treat for adult taste buds. Remember that buttercream behaves a lot like butter. When it is cold it will be hard and difficult to cut; at room temperature it is soft and its full flavour comes out. To bring out the best flavour and texture, a cake finished with buttercream should be served at room temperature. Buttercream will keep in the fridge for 2 weeks if well covered; but bring it to room temperature and beat it well before icing the cake.

3 large	**egg whites**
²/₃ cup	**granulated sugar**
10 oz	**unsalted butter**, soft

1. Combine the egg whites and sugar in a large bowl that can go over hot water; whisk until white and frothy. Set the bowl over a pan of simmering water, and keep whisking until the whites are too hot for you to keep your finger in for more than a moment. Quickly scrape the meringue into the bowl of an electric mixer (only, of course, if you have one; if you don't, it can be done by hand), and mix on medium-high speed, until very thick and quite cool.

2. When the meringue is cool (if it is not the butter will simply melt), add the softened butter ¹/₃ at a time, mixing very well between additions.

3. The buttercream is now ready for the flavouring. Make sure that it (the flavouring) is cool (again, if it is not, it will melt the butter and spoil the buttercream). Add and mix on low speed, scraping down the sides once or twice, until completely blended.

CARAMEL BRANDY BUTTERCREAM

A little bit tricky, so use a candy thermometer. An electric mixer is very helpful as well.

1 cup	**water**
¹⁄₃ cup	**granulated sugar**
1 Tbs	**light corn syrup**
2 Tbs	**water**
¹⁄₃ cup	**granulated sugar**
2 large	**egg yolks**
1 large	**egg**
¹⁄₂ tsp	**salt**
1 tsp	**vanilla extract**
4-6 Tbs	**brandy**, to taste
1 cup	**unsalted butter**, softened

1. Bring a small pan of water to a boil; then turn the heat down and keep at a simmer; you will use ¹⁄₃ cup of this water in Step 2.

2. In a heavy-bottom saucepan, combine the sugar and corn syrup with the water. Cook over medium-low heat until the sugar has completely dissolved, stirring occasionally. Increase the heat to high and boil without stirring, until the sugar has caramelized (see page 11). As soon as the sugar has reached a mahogany brown, add ¹⁄₃ cup of the boiling water to prevent the sugar from caramelizing further: be careful to avert your face and cover your hand with a cloth as it will spit up at you. Add the second ¹⁄₃ cup sugar to the pan and continue cooking over high heat to the soft-ball stage (see page 11), 244° F on a candy thermometer.

3. Meanwhile, combine the egg yolks, whole egg, salt, vanilla, and brandy in the bowl of an electric mixer (may be done by hand), and start to beat, using the whisk attachment.

4. As soon as the sugar syrup has reached the soft-ball stage, pour the syrup over the eggs in a thin stream, whisking constantly. Continue to whisk until the mixture has cooled to room temperature (about 15 minutes): it must not be warm enough to melt the butter in Step 5.

5. Make sure the butter is soft but not liquid. Add the butter ¹⁄₃ at a time, and beat until smooth and fluffy.

6. Buttercream will keep in a closed container in the fridge for 5 days.

CHOCOLATE BUTTERCREAM

2 oz	**unsweetened chocolate**, in chunks
4 oz	**semi-sweet chocolate**, in chunks
1 recipe	**Meringue Buttercream** (see page 204)

1. Combine the two chocolates in a small bowl that can go over hot water; set it over a pan of simmering water and melt the chocolate, stirring occasionally. Remove the bowl from the heat and set aside to cool.

2. Prepare the buttercream, following the recipe on page 204; when cool, add the cooled chocolate, and mix until completely blended.

MAPLE BUTTERCREAM

1 cup	**maple syrup**
1 recipe	**Meringue Buttercream** (see page 204)

1. Pour maple syrup into a small saucepan; bring to a boil over medium heat, then set aside to cool.

2. Make the buttercream, following the recipe on page 204. When both the buttercream and maple syrup are cool, whisk them together until they are completely blended. Store, well covered, in the refrigerator; bring to room temperature and whisk well before using.

ORANGE COINTREAU BUTTERCREAM

Expensive, but worth it.

zest of 1	**orange** (large) (see page 210)
1 cup	**Cointreau** or **Grand Marnier**
1 recipe	**Meringue Buttercream** (see page 204)

1. Combine the orange zest and the orange liqueur in a small saucepan; bring to a boil over medium heat, then remove and set aside to cool.

2. Prepare the buttercream, following the recipe on page 204.

3. When both the orange liqueur and the buttercream are cool, strain the liqueur into the buttercream and mix until completely blended.

Opposite: *Yule Log (see recipe on page 188), Gingerbread Shapes (see recipe on page 174), and Cranberry Tartlets (see recipe on page 181).*

CREAMS

CREME FRAICHE

One of the easiest ways to make Crème Fraîche, which doesn't involve heating, straining pots, or a thermometer. Crème Fraîche will keep for two weeks in the refrigerator.

Makes 2¹/₂ cups.

2 cups	**whipping cream** (35%), room temperature
¹/₂ cup	**sour cream**, room temperature

1. The important thing is that both ingredients must be at room temperature, or it simply won't work. Whisk together the whipping and sour cream in a large bowl. Cover with plastic wrap. Place in a warm, draft-free spot for 12 hours or overnight. (A gas stove with the pilot light on is ideal.)

2. Chill completely; then transfer to smaller containers.

CURDS

LEMON CURD

Really delicious; little shortcrust pastry tartlets filled with this would go down very well at tea time.

Makes about 2¹/₂ cups.

¹/₂ cup	**unsalted butter**
³/₄ cup	**fresh lemon juice**
¹/₄ tsp	**salt**
1¹/₂ cups	**granulated sugar**
3 large	**eggs**
3	**egg yolks**

1. Combine the butter, lemon juice, salt, and sugar in a bowl that can go over hot water. Set it over a pot of simmering water, and heat, stirring occasionally, until the butter is completely melted and the sugar dissolved.
2. Whisk together the yolks and eggs in a separate bowl. Slowly pour in ¹/₄ of the hot lemon-juice mixture, whisking constantly, then pour the rest in, in a thin stream. Place back over the hot water and cook, stirring occasionally, until thick; but do not try to boil it. Remove from the heat and strain into a clean bowl or jar, cover tightly, and refrigerate for at least 12 hours.

RASPBERRY CURD

1½ cups	**Raspberry Purée** (see page 211)
½ cup	**granulated sugar**
2 oz	**unsalted butter**
2 tsp	**lemon juice**
2	**large eggs**
2	**large egg yolks**

1. Heat the raspberry purée in a non-corrodable saucepan. Add the sugar and the butter, and stir until the sugar is dissolved; then stir in the lemon juice.

2. Whisk the eggs and egg yolks together. Whisk ¼ cup of the hot raspberry mixture into the eggs to temper them (to accustom them to the heat so they will not separate on contact with the hot mixture). Then, whisk the eggs into the raspberry mixture in the pan, and cook over low heat, stirring constantly until the mixture thickens; be careful not to bring it close to boiling. Transfer to a clean bowl or container, cover tightly and refrigerate.

3. Raspberry curd will keep in the refrigerator for a week.

CUSTARDS

CREME ANGLAISE — METHOD 1

This is the classic method; make sure to cook it over a medium-low heat, and to stir constantly. If you notice the sauce thickening on the bottom of the pan, immediately remove it from the heat and stir, off the heat, until the thicker sauce has been reincorporated. Then, return to the heat and continue stirring — the thickening must occur throughout the sauce.

Makes approximately 3 cups.

2 cups	**homogenized milk**
1	**vanilla bean**
6	**egg yolks**
½ cup	**granulated sugar**

1. Rinse out medium-sized, heavy-bottom saucepan with water, but do not dry it (this helps prevent the milk solids sticking to the bottom of the pan). Pour in the milk, add the vanilla bean, and bring to a boil over medium heat. Remove from the heat and set aside to infuse.

2. In a medium bowl, beat the egg yolks with the sugar until pale yellow and quite thick.

3. Strain the hot milk directly into the yolks, whisking all the time (the vanilla bean can be washed, wrapped in a plastic bag, and used again).

4. Make sure the bottom of the pan is clean, then pour in the custard. Cook over low heat, stirring constantly with a wooden spoon, until a finger drawn across the back of a spoon leaves a clean

path (see page 133). Do not boil or you will be serving scrambled eggs.
5. Strain into a clean bowl, cover with plastic wrap and allow to cool. Refrigerate until ready to serve.

CREME ANGLAISE — METHOD 2 (QUICK)

A foolproof method, if you are worried about cooking the custard to just the right point; but a bit richer than the classic version as it uses whipping cream as well as milk. Best made the day before.

Makes about 3 cups.

1 cup	**homogenized milk**
1 cup	**whipping cream** (35%)
½ cup	**granulated sugar**
1	**vanilla bean**
5	**egg yolks**

1. Rinse out medium-sized, heavy-bottom saucepan with water, but do not dry it (this helps prevent the milk solids sticking to the bottom of the pan). Pour in the milk, the cream, and the sugar, add the vanilla bean, and bring to a boil over medium heat, stirring carefully until the sugar has dissolved. Remove from the heat and set aside to infuse.
2. In a medium bowl, beat the egg yolks until pale yellow (see page 43).
3. Bring the cream to a boil again, then strain directly into the yolks, whisking all the time (the vanilla bean can be washed, wrapped in a plastic bag, and used again).
4. Strain the custard into a clean bowl, cover with plastic wrap and refrigerate overnight.

ORANGE CREME ANGLAISE

1 recipe	**Crème Anglaise** , either method (see pages 208-9)
3 Tbs	**Orange Zest** (see page 210)
1 Tbs	**Grand Marnier** or **orange liqueur**

1. It is not necessary to use the vanilla bean. Add the orange zest to the cold milk (or milk and cream); bring to the boil, then simmer for 5 minutes; this allows the liquid to pick up the full flavour of the orange.
2. Beat the eggs as directed in the recipe; then strain in the hot milk.
3. *If using the classic method,* return the custard to the pan and cook over low heat until thick enough to coat the back of a spoon (page 133). Then strain into a clean bowl, cover and allow to cool. Stir in the Grand Marnier before serving.
4. *If using the overnight method,* strain the custard into a clean bowl, cover tightly, and chill overnight. Stir in the Grand Marnier before serving.

FRUIT

GRATED LEMON, LIME, OR ORANGE ZEST

This method is easier on your fingers than using a cheese grater.

lemons or **limes** or **oranges**, as many as you need

1. Using a lemon zester (a very useful implement and well worth the investment) or (if you are not convinced) a vegetable peeler, remove the zest from the lemons (limes or oranges).
2. Place the zest on your chopping board; it doesn't really matter whether it is in thin zester strips or wider peeler ones. With a large cook's knife chop the zest as finely as you can: hold the handle of the knife in your dominant hand and, with the fingers of the other hand, lightly hold the upper edge of the blade close to the tip. Use a short, quick up-and-down chopping action with your main hand, while the other keeps the tip pressed lightly on the chopping board. Move the blade back and forth over the zest, until it is chopped the way you want.
3. This chopping method is the approved one for garlic and most fresh herbs.

MOROCCAN PRESERVED LEMONS

The peel of these lemons is a delightful addition to chicken or lamb dishes as well as desserts. The peel becomes soft and fragrant and can be used in its entirety because of this treatment.

12	**lemons**
½ cup	**salt**
large	**jar(s)** with leakproof lids
	lemon juice, freshly squeezed, if needed

1. Wash the lemons well, then make a cut from the top to ¾ of the way down (as if cutting the lemon in half, but do not cut all the way through). Make a second cut at right angles to the first (as if cutting the lemon in quarters), again not cutting all the way through. Open the lemons slightly and sprinkle the cut surfaces with salt.
2. Place 1 Tbs of salt on the bottom of the jar (of each jar, if using more than one). Push the lemons into the jar cut-side down; pressing down well to squeeze out the juice. Sprinkle with salt. Continue packing in the lemons tightly, pressing down and sprinkling each layer with more salt. If the juice

does not cover the lemons, pour some freshly squeezed lemon juice over them. Seal the jars tightly.

3. Let the lemons sit at room temperature for 30 days; turn the jar over every day. The lemons will keep indefinitely, refrigerated, and the pickling liquid may be used again to make more preserved lemons.

RASPBERRY PURÉE

3½ pints **fresh raspberries**
or
1 package **unsweetened frozen
          raspberries
          icing sugar
          Kirsch**

1. Place raspberries in the workbowl of a food processor fitted with the steel blade. Pulse a few times until the berries are liquified. Do not overprocess or the seeds will be ground up and be impossible to remove.

2. A bit at a time, press the purée through a fine sieve into a bowl, extracting all the juice. Discard the seeds.

3. Sweeten to taste with the icing sugar and a dash of Kirsch.

ICINGS

BASIC CHOCOLATE ICING

5 oz	**semi-sweet** or **bittersweet chocolate**
2 oz	**unsalted butter**
¾ cup	**icing sugar**
3 Tbs	**cold water**

1. Melt the chocolate in a double-boiler set over simmering water. When it is melted, add the butter, and then the icing sugar. Stir until completely incorporated. The mixture will become very firm and slightly grainy; but it will come back together when you add the water. Remove from the heat and allow to cool slightly: the icing will spread much more easily when it is warm; but not so warm that it runs all over the place.

2. Now add the cold water, 1 Tbs at a time, and stir until it is well mixed. The icing should have a thick pouring consistency.

3. Pour the icing over the top of the cake. If the icing is the right consistency, you can pour it around the perimeter in such a way that it runs down the sides and coats them with chocolate. If it is a bit too thick, you will have to use your palette knife to spread it over the sides as well as top. If it is too thin, it will just run off onto the work surface; in this case, let the icing cool a bit more. Use your palette knife to spread the chocolate as smoothly as possible on the sides and top of the cake. Dipping it in hot water will help to stop the chocolate sticking to the blade.

FUDGE ICING

This is a very easy icing recipe; but a food processor is required.

Makes enough for one 8" or 9" cake.

8 oz	**unsalted butter**
2 cups	**icing sugar**
⅓ cup	**unsweetened cocoa powder**
1 tsp	**vanilla extract**
2 Tbs	**whipping cream** (35%)
6 Tbs	**strong coffee**, hot

1. Combine the butter, sugar, and cocoa in the workbowl of your food processor, and pulse a few times until well combined.

2. Add the vanilla, cream, and coffee to the workbowl, and process until completely smooth; scrape down the side of the bowl once to make sure everything is mixed in.

3. This icing should be used immediately, as it will set as it cools.

MOCHA FROSTING

Enough for one 8" or 9" cake.

1 cup	**icing sugar**
2/3 cup	**unsweetened cocoa powder**
1/2 cup	**unsalted butter**, softened
1 tsp	**vanilla extract**
1 Tbs	**milk**
3 Tbs	**strong coffee**, hot (instant is *OK*)

1. Sift together the icing sugar and cocoa powder, then scoop them into the workbowl of your food processor (you may do it by hand). Add the butter and process for 20 seconds.
2. Add the vanilla, milk, and coffee and process for another 30 seconds, until smooth.

WHITE ICING

A simple icing for decorating gingerbread people or cupcakes, or writing on a dark cake.

1	**egg white**
3/4 cup	**icing sugar** (approximately)
Optional :	
	food colouring

1. Whisk the egg white in a bowl until broken up, then start to add the icing sugar, mixing it in thoroughly. Keep adding sugar until the icing becomes quite stiff (the amount you need will depend on the size of the egg white).
2. Add a few drops of food colouring, to achieve the colour you want.
3. Make a paper icing bag (page 63), fill it with the icing and decorate the cookies.

MERINGUES

SWISS MERINGUE

The stuff of which decorations (for Yule logs) are made; but not for eating meringues.

3 **egg whites**
3/4 cup **granulated sugar**

1. In an electric mixer (may be done by hand) whisk the egg whites to soft peaks. Then gradually add the sugar, beating until you have stiff, glossy peaks.

PASTRY

CHOCOLATE PASTRY

1 cup	**all-purpose flour**
½ cup	**granulated sugar**
½ cup	**unsweetened cocoa powder**
6 oz	**unsalted butter**, chilled
1	**egg**

1. Combine the flour, sugar, and cocoa in the workbowl of a food processor fitted with the steel blade. Pulse 2 or 3 times to aerate. Roll the butter in flour to make it easier to handle, then cut into slices. Roll these in flour, then cut into sticks, and finally into small dice. Distribute them over the flour. Process just until the mixture resembles coarse meal — be careful not to overprocess.

2. With the motor running, drop the whole egg through the feed tube. Process very briefly — do not let the dough come together into a ball or your pastry will be tough. Remove the dough from the workbowl, work it gently into a ball, and set aside at room temperature for 30 minutes.

3. Pick up a small amount of pastry in your fingers, and press into the tart tin. Continue in this way until the bottom and sides of the tart tin are more or less evenly lined. Refrigerate until ready to use.

4. Preheat the oven to 375° F.

5. Bake the chilled tart in the preheated oven for 20 to 25 minutes, until completely set and cooked. Remove from the oven and allow to cool.

CLASSIC PUFF PASTRY

This is the classic method, and it still produces the best result — the highest puff and the crispest pastry. The trick is to have both the flour dough (the détrempe*) and the kneaded butter as close to the same consistency as possible, so that they roll out well together.*

2 cups	**all-purpose flour**
1 cup	**cake flour**
1 tsp	**salt**
1½ tsp	**fresh lemon juice**
¾ - 1 cup	**cold water**
1 Tbs	**unsalted butter**, chilled
½ cup	**all-purpose flour**
¾ pound	**unsalted butter**

1. Sift the all-purpose flour with the cake flour into a large mixing bowl. Make a well in the centre, and add the salt, lemon juice, ¾ cup of water, and 1 Tbs butter. Work the ingredients together with your fingertips until a rough dough is formed; if it is too dry, add a bit more water. Knead lightly until fairly smooth, but do not overknead or the dough will become too rubbery. It does not need to be very smooth at this point; it will become smooth as it is rolled out later. This dough is called the *détrempe*.

PREPARING PUFF PASTRY FOR BAKING

When the puff pastry has been rolled out to the size and thickness required in the recipe, there are 3 things that will help you achieve a perfect result:

1. Scallop the edges of the pastry: Set the pastry on the baking sheet and place the tip an ordinary knife (the dull edge is better than the sharp) against the edge of the pastry, so that the knife is vertical, and draw it in towards the centre of the pastry about $\frac{1}{8}$". This will make a vertical line on the edge, and the pastry will be pulled in a little. Make these lines about every $\frac{3}{4}$", all the way round the edge of the pastry: their purpose is to ensure that it will rise straight as it puffs in the oven.

2. Refrigerate the pastry on the baking sheet for about 20 minutes (or longer); this helps to relax the glutens that will have been developed in the final rolling out. And it chills the butter completely, which helps in the baking (see next point).

3. Preheat the oven to at least 425° F (some recipes may call for more): the oven should already be very hot when the pastry goes in. The idea is that the pastry must cook and set before it gets a chance to melt. Chilling the butter first (Step 2, above) means that it will take longer to melt; by the time it does, the hot oven will have set the dough and the pastry will be able to hold its shape and puff straight up. If the total cooking time is longer than 15 or 20 minutes, you should turn down the oven to 350° F after about 15 minutes, so that the pastry does not burn.

Wrap in plastic wrap and chill for 30 minutes.

2. Spread the $\frac{1}{2}$ cup of flour on your work surface. Place the butter on top and dust it with flour. With a rolling pin, flatten the butter — beating hard butter helps to soften it without warming it up. Keep working with the rolling pin until the butter has the same consistency as the *détrempe*. Shape the butter into a 5" square and flour lightly.

3. Remove the *détrempe* from the refrigerator. Roll it out to a 12" square. Set the butter in the centre on the diagonal (like a diamond in a square) and fold the flaps of dough up around it — so that it looks like the back of an envelope. Press the dough firmly together so that the butter is completely sealed. Roll gently into a rectangular shape. Wrap it in plastic and chill for 30 minutes; this ensures that the butter and dough are at the same temperature and makes rolling easier.

4. Return the pastry to a lightly floured work surface. Beat it a few times with your rolling pin to get the butter flowing. Gently roll the dough into a long rectangle about 16" long and 5 or 6" wide. Do not roll too vigorously on this first turn — the dough is still delicate and will become too resilient if over-rolled. Lift one end of the dough and fold it over onto itself, leaving the top $\frac{1}{3}$ of the dough still uncovered (just as you would fold a business letter). Now fold the top of the dough down over the first fold and press firmly all around to seal the edges . What you have just done is called a "turn". Roll out again to the same size and then fold in three. This makes 2 turns. Keep a note of the turns by pressing the appropriate number of fingertips gently into the dough. Wrap the dough in plastic and chill for 30 minutes (or longer).

---

5. Repeat the rolling and folding process twice more, giving the dough 6 turns altogether, chilling at least 30 minutes in between every 2 turns. Chill for another 30 minutes before using.

6. If you are not using it immediately, the dough should be stored at 4 turns. Puff pastry will keep, well wrapped, in the refrigerator for 5 days or for 3 months frozen.

QUICK PUFF PASTRY

Not, in fact, all that quick, as the dough has to rest between turns just as classic puff pastry does; but it is very simple, and no one need be intimidated by the prospect of making it — anyone with the desire to do it can make excellent puff pastry this way. Total time is about 4 hours; or you may spread it over a day or more. This pastry is flakier than the classic version, and does not puff as much, so it works very well for Napoleons (page 80), and Gâteau Saint-Honoré (page 92).

3 cups	**all-purpose flour**
½ tsp	**salt**
1 lb	**unsalted butter**, very cold
½ cup	**cold water**

1. Combine the flour and salt in the workbowl of your food processor; pulse a few times to aerate.
2. Roll the block of butter in flour (to make it easier to handle), then cut into slices about ¼" thick. Roll the slices in flour, then cut them into sticks; cut the sticks across into cubes. Distribute the cubes over the flour in the food processor.
3. Pulse very briefly about 6 times; it should not run for more than a second each time. This will mix the butter cubes into the flour; but it will not chop them much smaller than when they started: this is just fine.
4. Turn the dough onto your work surface, and spread it out. Sprinkle the water over the dough, then knead it gently to get the water into the dough. It will look like a real mess, but it doesn't matter.
5. Form the dough into an oblong, with one of the narrow ends nearest you. Take the rolling pin and roll it to a thickness of about ¾". Slide a thin-bladed knife under it to release it from the surface, then lift the end nearest you and fold it over so that it is lying on the other part of the dough, with the top ⅓ of the dough still uncovered (just as you would fold a business letter). If the dough is too soft to hold its shape, knead a little bit longer to bring it together and try again. Now fold the top of the dough down over the first fold and press firmly to seal the edges all around. What you have just done is called a "turn".
6. Rotate the dough clockwise ¼ turn so that the last flap is facing to your right, as if it was the cover of a book. Now, roll the dough out into another oblong, again with the short edge closest to you, and the long side going away. Roll it a bit thinner this time; then fold up the bottom leaving the top ⅓ exposed, and then fold the top down over the first fold, just

as you did before. Press to seal, then wrap in a plastic bag and refrigerate for at least 1 hour.

7. Remove the dough from the fridge and repeat Step 6 twice — i.e., give it two more turns. Then rewrap in the plastic bag and refrigerate for another hour (or more).

8. Again, take the dough out of the fridge and do the same again — two more turns. Then back to the fridge for another hour. The dough is now ready for use (see page 215).

WHOLE-WHEAT PUFF PASTRY

1⅓ cup	**whole-wheat pastry flour**
2 cups	**all-purpose flour**
1 tsp	**salt**
1½ tsp	**fresh lemon juice**
1 cup	**cold water**
2 Tbs	**unsalted butter**, very cold
½ cup	**all-purpose flour**
¾ lb	**unsalted butter**, very cold

1. Follow the recipe for Classic Puff Pastry (page 214), substituting the whole-wheat flour for the cake flour.

SWEET PASTRY

This is a very easy pastry to make in a food processor. Because it has so much sugar in it, it is very sticky and a bit harder to work with than some other pastries. However, it has two great advantages; it is very forgiving, in that, if it falls apart while you are lining your tart tin, you can simply press scraps in to fill up the holes; in fact, you can line your whole tart tin that way, pressing smaller pieces of pastry together until the whole thing is lined. Its second great asset is that it does not have to be baked "blind" (the old method of lining the pastry shell with foil or parchment paper, then filling with beans or rice to hold the pastry in shape while you bake it). If you chill it well before baking, and if your oven is hot (about 375° F), it will bake to a perfect tart shell just as it is. To me these advantages are worth practising a bit of patience while working with sticky pastry.

Makes one 9" tart shell.

1¼ cups	**flour**
¼ cup	**granulated sugar**
3½ oz	**unsalted butter**, well chilled
1 tsp	**lemon zest** (see page 210)
Optional	
1	**egg**

1. Put flour and sugar in the workbowl of your food processor and pulse once or twice to aerate.

2. Roll the butter in flour, then cut into slices. Roll the slices in flour, then cut into sticks, and then cubes. (***NOTE***: Rolling the butter in flour makes it much easier to handle; it will not stick as much.) Distribute the cubes over the flour and sugar, then process briefly, just until the mixture resembles a fine meal. Don't process so much that it becomes sticky and starts to form a ball.

3. Have the egg ready, then start the motor and drop the egg down the feed tube of the food processor. Again, process only very briefly, just until the egg is incorporated. Now, turn out the pastry onto your work surface and knead gently to bring it together into a ball. A little extra kneading will make it easier to roll out; but you pay the price in slightly tougher pastry. Refrigerate for at least an hour. It may be made up to 3 days ahead, and kept in the refrigerator.

4. Sprinkle your work surface generously with flour, and have an extra little pile at the side. Start to roll out the pastry, turning it over frequently to make sure that the side in contact with the work surface is well coated with flour. A knife with a long thin blade (or a palette knife) is very helpful to slide under the pastry and free it when it does stick (which it will). Roll out to a thickness of ⅛" to ³⁄₁₆", and a diameter about 3" larger than your tart tin. Roll the pastry up around your rolling pin, then unroll carefully over the tart tin. This is where you need to practise patience; the pastry is delicate and its own weight will tear it; but do not despair — just patch and press together until the bottom and sides of the tin are completely covered. Trim off the excess around the rim, and set the tin in the fridge for at least an hour, until very well chilled.

5. Preheat the oven to 375° F. Make sure that it is good and hot; then transfer the pastry-lined tin to the centre of the oven and bake for 15 minutes. If it is browning to much around the edges, turn the oven down to 325° F. The object of this pre-baking is to get the bottom of the tart cooked. Remove from the oven and allow to cool before adding your filling.

SWEET FLAKY PASTRY

Makes two 9" to 11" tarts; or 1 double-crust pie.

3⅓ cups	**all-purpose flour**
4 Tbs	**granulated sugar**
9 oz	**unsalted butter**, very cold
2	**egg yolks**
6 to 8 Tbs	**cold water**

1. Combine the flour and sugar in the workbowl of your food processor; pulse once or twice to aerate.

2. Roll the butter in flour (this makes it much easier to handle), then cut it into slices. Roll these slices in flour, then cut them into sticks, and the sticks into cubes, and scoop them into the workbowl on top of the flour.

3. Process very briefly, until the mixture resembles very coarse meal (i.e., the butter cubes have not been completely amalgamated).

4. Beat the egg yolks with 6 Tbs of water in a small bowl or measuring jug; with the motor running, pour them down the feed tube of the processor and process for just a few seconds — do not let the dough form a ball or the pastry will be tough.

5. Turn out the dough onto your work surface, and knead gently to get it to stick together. Then wrap in a plastic bag and refrigerate for 30 minutes, or longer.

CHOUX PASTE

The stuff of which great things are made, including many of the best recipes in the Pastry section. A little tricky to do at first; each egg must be completely incorporated before the next is added — but, once successful, always successful.

2½ cups	**all-purpose flour**
2 cups	**water**
8 oz	**unsalted butter**
1 tsp	**salt**
10 large	**eggs**

1. Sift the flour into a bowl.

2. Cut the butter into small pieces and place in a heavy-bottom pan with the water and salt. Bring to a boil over medium-high heat; then remove from the heat and immediately toss in the flour. Beat vigorously with a wooden spoon until the batter is smooth and comes away from the sides of the pan.

3. Return to a medium heat, and stir the pastry constantly for 5 to 10 minutes, scraping it off the bottom all the time to prevent sticking (the purpose is to evaporate some of the water and make the pastry better able to absorb the eggs in Step 4). Again remove from the heat.

4. Then, either by hand or using an electric mixer fitted with the paddle attachment (which is much easier), beat in the eggs two at a time, beating vigorously and completely incorporating one lot before adding the next. The batter should be sticky and heavy.

5. Choux paste is best used when still warm; but it will keep for two days in the fridge if necessary.

SWEET SHORTCRUST PASTRY

Makes one 9" to 11" tart.

1½ cups **all-purpose flour**
¼ cup **granulated sugar**
6 oz **unsalted butter**, well
chilled
1½ tsp **white vinegar**

1. Combine the flour and sugar in the workbowl of a food processor fitted with the steel blade. Pulse 2 or 3 times to aerate.

2. Roll the butter in flour (to make it easier to handle), then cut into slices; roll the slices in flour, then cut them into sticks, and the sticks into cubes. Distribute them over the flour in the workbowl, then process briefly, until the mixture resembles fine meal — be careful not to process too much.

3. With the machine running, pour the vinegar through the feed tube and process for 5 seconds. Do not overprocess — the dough should still resemble very fine meal and should not gather into a ball.

4. Remove the dough from the workbowl and allow to rest at room temperature for 30 minutes before using.

5. *To make a fully baked shortcrust pastry shell* : Gather up a small amount of pastry and knead it between your fingers until it comes together. Press this piece into the tart tin; continue until the bottom and sides of the tin are completely covered. Try to make the pastry as even as possible; it is melt-in-the-mouth pastry, but you still don't want it too thick. Refrigerate the pastry-lined tin for 30 minutes (or longer).

6. Preheat the oven to 375° F.

7. Place the chilled tart shell in the preheated oven and bake for 20 to 30 minutes, until pale golden brown and completely cooked. Remove from the oven and allow to cool. When cool, gently remove the pastry shell from the tin.

PASTRY CREAMS

BASIC PASTRY CREAM

The basis for most pastry fillings, and the pastry cook's most important ingredient.

Makes 1¹/₂ cups.

1 cup	**milk**
¹/₄ cup	**sugar**
1 Tbs	**all-purpose flour**
2 tsp	**cornstarch**
1 large	**egg**
2 Tbs	**unsalted butter**
¹/₂ tsp	**vanilla extract**

1. Rinse out a medium-sized heavy saucepan with water, but do not dry it — this prevents the milk solids from sticking to the bottom of the pan. Pour in the milk and bring to a boil over medium heat. Draw off the heat and set aside.

2. Sift togther the sugar, cornstarch, and flour into a medium bowl. Add the egg and whisk until light in colour and quite thick — about 2 minutes. Whisking continuously, pour the hot milk into the egg mixture in a thin stream (this tempers the eggs and prevents them from separating when cooked).

3. If the saucepan has a film on the bottom, wash it out; then return the pastry cream to the pan. Cook over high heat, stirring constantly with a whisk, until the mixture boils and thickens. It should boil for a full minute to cook off any raw taste of flour and cornstarch.

4. Remove from the heat, and stir in the butter and vanilla. Transfer to a bowl, cover with plastic wrap, and chill completely.

APRICOT PASTRY CREAM

Makes 2¹/₂ to 3 cups.

1 recipe	**Pastry Cream** (see above)
2 cups	**dried apricots**
¹/₂ cup	**water**

1. Make the pastry cream, following the recipe above. Cover with plastic wrap and set aside to cool.

2. Poach the apricots in the water until completely soft and tender. Then purée in a food processor or food mill. Fold the purée into the cooled pastry cream.

CARAMEL PASTRY CREAM

Makes 1¹/₂ cups.

1 recipe **Pastry Cream** (see page 222)
¹/₄ cup **granulated sugar**
3 Tbs **water**

1. Following Step 1 of the Pastry Cream recipe on page 222, scald the milk, then set aside to keep warm.
2. Sift together the sugar, cornstarch, and flour, whisk in the egg, and beat well (Step 2 of the Pastry Cream recipe; but do not pour in the hot milk yet).
3. Combine the sugar and water in a medium-sized saucepan. Cook over medium-low heat until the sugar dissolves, then increase the heat to high and cook to a deep amber colour (see page 11 on cooking sugar syrup). Immediately pour in the warm milk, averting your face as the mixture will sputter and spit at you. Stir over a medium heat until the caramel has melted completely and the mixture is smooth.
4. Pour the caramel milk into the egg in a thin stream, whisking all the time; then return to the pan (rinse out if necessary), and cook over high heat till the cream comes to a boil. Cook 1 minute longer, then remove from the heat and add the butter and vanilla.
5. Transfer to a bowl, cover with plastic wrap, and allow to cool completely.

SAUCES

CHOCOLATE COFFEE SAUCE

A quick and easy sauce to dress up desserts.

¹/₂ cup **milk**
¹/₂ cup **strong coffee**
3 Tbs **coffee beans**
8 oz **bittersweet chocolate**

1. Combine the milk, coffee, and beans in a medium-sized saucepan, and bring to a boil over medium heat.
2. Chop the chocolate into chunks, then place in a bowl. Strain the hot coffee-milk-beans mixture onto the chocolate, and whisk until melted and smooth.
3. Serve at room temperature.

SPONGES

SPONGE CAKE

A simple sponge that can be quickly transformed into a simple cake (Afternoon Tea Sponge, page 51); or used as the base for Trifle (page 20) or Lemon Carousel Cake (page 46).

5	**eggs**
1½ cups	**granulated sugar**
1 cup	**all-purpose flour**

1. Preheat the oven to 350° F. Lightly butter and flour a 9" springform pan.

2. Combine the eggs and sugar in a medium bowl that can go over hot water, and whisk to combine. Set the bowl over a pan of simmering water, and whisk steadily until the eggs are just warm to your finger.

3. Scoop the eggs into the bowl of your electric mixer (if you don't have one, all this can be done by hand, or with a hand mixer), and beat on medium-high speed until tripled in volume and quite cool. The eggs should be beaten to the point where the batter falling from the beaters back into the bowl is thick enough that you can draw your initial in it, and it is only slowly reincorporated.

4. Gently fold the flour into the batter (see page 128), then pour into the prepared pan. Bake in the preheated oven for 25 to 30 minutes, until the top springs back when pressed, and the sides have started to come away from the pan.

5. Remove from the oven and allow to cool for 5 minutes in the pan; then take it out of the pan and cool completely.

CHOCOLATE SPONGE

A very light sponge — actually a genoise (because it is enriched with butter).

½ cup	**cake flour**
3 Tbs	**unsweetened cocoa powder**
2 Tbs	**granulated sugar**
3 Tbs	**unsalted butter**
4 large	**egg yolks**
4 large	**eggs**
1 cup	**granulated sugar**

1. Preheat oven to 325° F. Lightly grease and flour a 8½" springform pan. Sift together the flour, cocoa, and 2 Tbs sugar; set aside.

2. Melt the butter in a small saucepan and set aside to cool; but it should not solidify.

3. Combine the egg yolks, whole eggs, and 1 cup sugar in a bowl that can go over hot water, and whisk to combine. Set the bowl over a pan of simmering water and whisk until the eggs are thoroughly warmed — they should be quite hot to your finger. Do not leave them unattended or allow them to stay too long or you will cook the eggs. Immediately transfer to the bowl of an electric mixer and beat at high speed until doubled in volume, or to the ribbon stage (or you may leave it in the bowl and beat by hand).

4. Sprinkle ½ the flour and cocoa mixture over the eggs and gently fold in, then fold in the rest (see page 128). Pour in the cooled butter in a thin stream and gently fold in. Pour the batter into the prepared springform pan and bake for 55 to 65 minutes or until the centre of the cake springs back when lightly pressed.

5. Remove from the oven and allow to cool in the pan for 10 minutes, then remove from the pan and cool completely.

WHY PASTRY SHOULD REST AND BE KEPT COLD

Wheat flour contains gluten, the substance that makes bread doughs springy and elastic as you knead them. Gluten is an essential part of making bread, because it allows the dough to expand as the bread rises. Without gluten the dough would break rather than expand, the gases from the yeast would escape and the bread would collapse. Rye flour, for example, contains very little gluten; rye breads almost always contain some wheat flour to provide this missing element.

In pastry making, the elastic properties of gluten are not required; in fact, gluten has the effect of making pastry hard and tough, so all your efforts must be directed to **NOT** developing the gluten. There are several things that can be done:

1. Use soft or cake flour for part of the total amount. There are different grades and types of flour; those with a high gluten content (about 12 to 14%) are called "hard flours", and are used for bread making. *Cake flour* has a lower gluten content (around 8 or 9%); it feels softer and finer between your fingers; it will give you a finer cake. *All-purpose flour* is designed to be just that — a good compromise; its gluten content is around 10 or 11%. When making pastry, all-purpose is a good choice; but for a softer pastry you may want to cut it with about ⅓ cake flour.

2. Don't work the dough too much. The more you work the dough, the more the glutens will develop; that is why we suggest just mixing the dough the minimum necessary to get it to stay together.

3. Keep it cold. Glutens develop more slowly when the flour is cold. Pastry chefs use marble work tables to keep the dough cool as they work; and they put the dough in the fridge whenever they are not working on it.

4. Let it rest and relax. The glutens will relax if you give the pastry time to rest. So, resting pastry in the fridge serves a double purpose.

LADYFINGERS

Ladyfingers are a central ingredient in tiramisu and in charlottes; they are also very good served with a fruit dessert. A good ladyfinger is light but not dry, and the only way to get it right is to make your own. They are not difficult; the trick is to beat both the egg yolks and the egg whites until very stiff indeed; and the secret is an electric mixer — or a very strong right arm.

Makes about 20.

1 cup	**cake (soft) flour** (all-purpose will do)
4	**egg yolks**
4 Tbs	**granulated sugar**
1 tsp	**vanilla extract**
4	**egg whites**
1/8 tsp	**cream of tartar** (see page 67)
1/2 cup	**granulated sugar**
1 cup	**icing sugar**

1. Preheat the oven to 400° F. Lightly butter and flour two cookie sheets, or line them with parchment paper (see page 152). Sift the flour into a bowl.

2. Using an electric mixer (may, as we said, be done by hand), whisk the egg yolks, sugar, and vanilla together until pale yellow and very thick (see page 43) — it will take 5 to 8 minutes.

3. In a clean bowl, whisk the egg whites to soft peaks (page 24). With the machine running, gradually add the sugar in a thin stream. Beat until the whites are very stiff, but not to the point where they are dry and lifeless.

4. Fold together the yolks, whites, and sifted cake flour: Add 1/3 of the whites to the yolks. Sift 1/3 of the flour over top and gently fold together. When almost incorporated, add another 1/3 of the whites, sift a second 1/3 of the flour over the top, and fold again. Repeat with the remaing whites and flour.

5. Gently scoop the mixture into a pastry bag fitted with a 3/4" nozzle. Pipe 2" or 3" long strips onto the prepared baking sheets, leaving 1 1/2" between. Sift the icing sugar over the top. Bake in the preheated oven for 12 to 15 minutes. The ladyfingers must be cooked enough so that they don't collapse as they cool — but not so cooked that they become dry and boring. They should look light to medium brown at the edges while still pale on the tops.

6. Ladyfingers will keep for 3 days in an airtight tin, stored at room temperature.

SUGAR SYRUPS

LIGHT SUGAR SYRUP

For fruit salads.

Makes 1¹/₂ cups.

1¹/₄ cups	**water**
¹/₂ cup	**granulated sugar**

1. Place water in a medium-sized saucepan. Add the sugar. Stir to blend well. Bring to a boil over medium heat. As soon as it comes to a boil, remove from heat. Cover tightly and refrigerate.
2. Will keep covered in the refrigerator up to 6 months.

REGULAR SUGAR SYRUP

For soaking cakes and poaching soft fruit.

Makes 2 cups.

2 cups	**water**
1¹/₂ cups	**granulated sugar**

1. Place water in a medium-sized saucepan. Add the sugar. Stir to blend well. Bring to a boil over medium heat. As soon as it comes to a boil, remove from the heat. Cover tightly and refrigerate.
2. Will keep covered in the refrigerator up to 6 months.

APPENDIX

METRIC CONVERSION CHART

WEIGHT CONVERSIONS

1 pound = 454 grams	1 kilo = 2.24 lbs
8 ounces = 227 grams	500 grams = 1.12 lbs
4 ounces = 113 grams	250 grams = 0.56 lbs
1 ounce = 28 grams	100 grams = 3.5 oz

LIQUID MEASURES

1 cup = 240 ml	1 litre = 4½ cups
½ cup = 120 ml	500 ml = 2¼ cups
1 Tbs = 15 ml	100 ml = 6½ Tbs

TEMPERATURE CONVERSIONS

200°F = 95°C	375°F = 190°C
225°F = 110°C	400°F = 200°C
250°F = 120°C	425°F = 220°C
275°F = 135°C	450°F = 230°C
300°F = 150°C	475°F = 250°C
325°F = 160°C	500°F = 260°C
350°F = 175°C	

COMMON INGREDIENTS – Approximate Equivalents

All-purpose flour	1 cup = 150 grams	100 grams = ⅔ cup
Granulated sugar	1 cup = 210 grams	100 grams = ½ cup
Icing sugar	1 cup = 135 grams	100 grams = ¾ cup
Light brown sugar	1 cup = 200 grams	100 grams = ½ cup
Rolled oats	1 cup = 95 grams	100 grams = 1 cup
Graham-cracker crumbs	1 cup = 120 grams	100 grams = ⅘ cup
Cocoa powder	1 cup = 125 grams	100 grams = ⅘ cup
Chocolate chips	1 cup = 175 grams	100 grams = generous ½ cup
Sultanas, raisins	1 cup = 165 grams	100 grams = generous ½ cup
Almonds – sliced	1 cup = 75 grams	100 grams = 1⅓ cups
Almonds – ground	1 cup = 120 grams	100 grams = ⅘ cup
Hazelnuts – whole	1 cup = 140 grams	100 grams = ¾ cup
Hazelnuts – ground	1 cup = 105 grams	100 grams = 1 cup
Walnut halves	1 cup = 110 grams	100 grams = 1 cup
Walnut pieces	1 cup = 120 grams	100 grams = ⅘ cup
Pecans (whole)	1 cup = 110 grams	100 grams = 1 cup
Peanut butter	1 cup = 225 grams	100 grams = scant ½ cup

INDEX

ACKNOWLEDGEMENTS

We wish to thank the following for the loan of props for the photography:

Cover shot: Table and chair — Designer Furniture Galleries
Cookies shot: Glass — Ming Wo Ltd.
Children's shot : Lego toys and Transformer robot — Kids at Work
        Jacks set — Granville Island Toy Company
Christmas shot: Plates — Gormann Emmerling and Associates Inc.
        Cake Server — Presents of Mind
        Christmas decorations — Robert J. Scott Prop Rentals, Vancouver
Pear/Orange shot: Surface — Manhattan Glass Bowl — Derik Murray
Figs in Phyllo shot: Black Lacquer Platter — David Wood
Tiramisu shot: Bowl — Presents of Mind
        Gothic Column — Chachkas